Scotland's Last Royal Wedding

To the memory of

ALAN CARRUTH STEVENSON, 1909-1995
and
ANNIE GORDON SHEILA STEVEN, 1913-1989

They gave more to me than I could ever express

Scotland's Last Royal Wedding

The Marriage of James VI and Anne of Denmark

DAVID STEVENSON

With a Danish Account of the Marriage
translated by Peter Graves

JOHN DONALD PUBLISHERS LTD
EDINBURGH

© David Stevenson 1997

All rights reserved.
No part of this publication may be reproduced
in any form or by any means without
the prior permission of the publishers
John Donald Publishers Limited,
138 St Stephen Street, Edinburgh, EH3 5AA.

ISBN 0 85976 451 6

British Library Cataloguing in Publication Data.
A catalogue record for this book is available
from the British Library.

Front cover: This portrait, by Adrain Vanson, was probably sent to Denmark by James in 1586 when he opened negotiations about a marriage. He looks younger than his twenty years. The portrait came to light in Germany a few years ago, and was purchased from the Weiss Gallery, London, by Historic Scotland in 1996, and now hangs in Edinburgh Castle.

PostScript Typesetting & Origination by Brinnoven, Livingston.
Printed & bound in Great Britain by Bell & Bain Ltd, Glasgow.

CONTENTS

List of Maps and Plates vi

Preface vii

Acknowledgements xi

Abbreviations and Conventions xii

  1. The Quest for a Bride 1

  2. Negotiations and Proxy Marriage 17

  3. Storm-tossed Lovers 24

  4. Marriage in Norway 34

  5. Winter Journey 40

  6. Danish Diversions 45

  7. Scottish Celebrations 57

  8. And they did not live happily ever after 63

THE DANISH ACCOUNT OF THE MARRIAGE

  I   The Making of the Treaty 79

  II Norway and Denmark 86

  III Scotland: The Coronation 100

  IV Scotland: The Entry into Edinburgh 107

  V   The Departure of the Danish Ambassadors 120

Notes 123

Select Bibliography 149

Index 155

MAPS

1. (a) Scotland, with South-east Scotland inset
   (b) South-east Scotland, enlarged   xv
2. Location Map: Denmark, Norway and Sweden   xvi
3. Queen Anne's entry into Edinburgh   xvii

PLATES
(between pages 62 and 63)

1. Prospective bride: Princess Anne
2. Father-in-law, deceased: King Frederick of Denmark
3. Mother-in-law: Queen Sophia
4. Brother-in-law: Christian IV of Denmark
5. Wooden tablet commemorating James VI's visit to Tonsberg
6. Sir John Maitland of Thirlestane
7. Kronborg Castle and Elsinore
8. Tyge Brahe's Empire
9. Views of Copenhagen
10. Signatures of James and Anne
11. Medal commemorating the marriage
12. Holyrood Palace
13. Edinburgh
14. The first fruit of the marriage
15. Nineteen-year-old Queen Anne
16. Twenty-nine-year-old King James

PREFACE

Biographers of King James VI and historians of his reign have shown surprisingly little interest in investigating in any detail his marriage and the events surrounding it. An entertaining symptom of this lack of attention is the fact that there has been a good deal of confusion as to the date and place of the marriage. Some have placed it in Copenhagen on 20 August 1589, some in Oslo on 23 November 1589. Others described both marriages, completely ignoring the matter of how he could have got married twice. A few writers have even created a third marriage, through confusing one of the old versions of the name of Oslo, Uppsala, with the Swedish town of that name. In reality, those who opt for two marriages are correct. A civil marriage took place in Denmark (though not in Copenhagen) then a religious ceremony in Norway — causing further confusion as it had originally been planned to hold the latter in Scotland.

It might be thought that the neglect indicated by such uncertainty as to these basic facts about the marriage is hardly significant, for many royal marriages were routine exchanges of goods (brides, that is), affairs worthy of the attention only of the incurably romantic (though in reality romance was seldom present). But James's marriage and its context are particularly interesting and even entertaining in a number of respects. It was Scotland's last royal marriage, coronation and ceremonial entry into Edinburgh before the union of the crowns of 1603 led to the removal of the Stuart dynasty to London. The marriage was also the occasion of King James's only travels outside Britain. Given that he was endowed with more intellectual curiosity than many an entire dynasty, his only direct exposure to a foreign society and culture should be seen as likely to be noteworthy in seeking to understand James as man and ruler — not least, of course, because he was destined to become the first monarch ever to rule over the entire British Isles.

Looked at from other angles, the story of the marriage is full of dramatic and, yes, even romantic, incident. A child bride whose life is imperilled by storms at sea. A young bridegroom so anxious to prove that damaging rumours about his lack of interest in girls were untrue that he secretly deserted his kingdom to set off on a bizarre attempt to rescue his damsel in distress. An improvised royal wedding celebrated with provincial simplicity when they meet. A journey from Norway to Denmark by sledge through frozen winter landscapes. A diplomatic incident on the Swedish frontier. Royal festivities and epic drinking in Denmark, with intervals of sobriety in which James indulged his passion for hunting and showed himself to be a culture-vulture, engaging in discussions with theologians, astronomers and other scholars, visiting castles, laboratories and cathedrals. The journey home to Scotland. The queen's coronation (with a touch of theological controversy) and splendid entry into Edinburgh. Macabre allegations of witchcraft being employed (in both Denmark and Scotland) to wreck the marriage.

With all this, and indeed more, there is something in the episode for practically every taste. But the aftermath brings us back firmly to reality: the royal couple did not live happily ever after.

Why, then, has the marriage received so little attention from historians? One explanation might be sought in lack of sources for the historian to work on, and certainly the one printed collection of papers relating to the marriage, published by the Bannatyne Club in 1828, might seem to support this: it is very thin and idiosyncratic. In fact there are many other available sources, rich and varied, both Scottish and Danish, from which events can be reconstructed and analysed. Part of the problem in discussing the matter in the past has been the failure to and exploit the rich Danish evidence.

This is where I came in. I stumbled on references to a Danish narrative account of events surrounding the wedding. Though published in Oslo in 1852 it had never been translated into English, but a hint at the wealth of information contained in it was provided by an obscure article by A H Millar in the *Scottish Review* of 1893. I decided that the publication of an English translation of the Danish Account was highly desirable as part of a new look at the marriage. Two considerations should perhaps have dissuaded me from becoming involved in such an undertaking: my inability to read a word of Danish; and my ignorance of Scandinavia and its history!

However, risking appearing the proverbial fool, I rushed in. If I have been saved from the consequences of my folly it is the result of two factors. Peter Graves not only provided a splendid translation of the Danish Account, but translations of much other Danish material; and other scholars, especially in Scandinavia, have proved most generous in offering their expertise.

PREFACE

The Danish Account

The Danish Account of the events leading up to and following the marriage of James VI and Anne of Denmark was first published by Professor P A Munch in *Norske Samlinger*, i (Christiania [Oslo], 1852), 451–512, from an eighteenth-century copy in the Count of Holstein-Ledreborg's library at Ledreborg. This copy is now in the Royal Library (Det Kongelige Bibliotek) in Copenhagen. Munch mentions another copy as also being in the Royal Library, but this has not been traced.

Two more copies survive in the National Archives (Riksarkivet) in Oslo. Manuskiptsamlingen, 15 folio, is evidently the copy made for P A Munch from the Ledreborg version, and used in printing the *Norske Samlinger* text: it includes the editorial introduction Munch published with the text, written in his own hand. Manuskiptsamlingen, 62 quarto, is written mainly in a German hand, and probably dates from the eighteenth century. It was formerly in the library of Carsten Anker (1747–1824), a Norwegian businessman, and was given to the National Archives in 1814.

Millar, *Wedding-Tour*, 149 stated that the original manuscript of the Danish Account was in the library of the University of Oslo, but there is no trace of either the original or a copy there today. Had the original been in Oslo, Munch would probably have known of it and used it, so it seems likely that Millar was mistaken.

The Danish Account is supposed to have been compiled for King Christian IV of Denmark, and the text makes this plausible both through what it includes and what it excludes. Its coverage of events is very uneven, and one interpretation of this is that the author left out details or parts of the story which Christian was already well informed about through personal involvement or other sources. Thus it details the early stages of the negotiations for the marriage but it omits the treaty finally agreed, and does not even mention the ceremony of Anne's marriage to James through his proxy, the Earl Marischal. Christian would already have seen the treaty, and been present at the ceremony, so there was no need to go over them again. The Danish Account summarises only briefly the hazards undergone by Anne during her voyage to Oslo, which is surely something her brother would want to hear about. Here the explanation may well be that two journals (in German) exist in the Danish archives detailing this episode: if Christian had read them, a further account was unnecessary.

SCOTLAND'S LAST ROYAL WEDDING

The Danish Account has much to say about events in Norway, the arrival of King James there, and his journey to Denmark; and it goes into the landing and coronation of Anne in Scotland in great detail: but it is (infuriatingly) rather thin on the doings of James and Anne in Denmark itself. Again, it may be assumed that Christian did not need information about this, since they had been guests at his court at the time.

Who was it who carefully prepared the Danish Account for King Christian? P A Munch speculated that it was possibly the work of Johan Sering, the Thuringian preacher who had been appointed Anne's chaplain. But this seems to have been no more than a guess based on the fact that of all the members of Anne's household mentioned in the Danish Account, Sering seemed the most likely to undertake such a clerkly task. But one might have expected a clergyman such as Sering to have more to say about questions of religious observance, which the Danish Account only touches on briefly. Another candidate for authorship might be Anne's secretary, Calixtus Schein (as he is not mentioned in the account, Munch did not know of his existence). But by far the most plausible conjecture is that the Danish Account was compiled by the secretary to the Danish ambassadors who accompanied Anne to Scotland, Dr Nicolaus Theophilus. In his capacity as royal librarian to Christian IV he had a court position which would make him an obvious choice, and he may well also have been responsible for the German diary of the ambassadors' proceedings in Scotland: there are close similarities between it and the relevant sections of the Danish Account.

In all probability the Danish Account was written in 1589–90, as the events it records took place. Thus it twice refers to Oslo as 'here'. The heading of the surviving texts refer to James as king of England as well as Scotland, which might seem to suggest that compilation took place in or after 1603, but it seems far more likely that the surviving texts derived from later copies which had updated James's titles.

Three 'insertions' of short documents in the text of the Danish Account have been made: the text of the marriage treaty; an account of the civil wedding in Copenhagen; and a letter from the king of Sweden relating to James's journey to Copenhagen. This seems the most convenient way of filling major gaps in the narrative.

David Stevenson, St Andrews

ACKNOWLEDGEMENTS

Help with miscellaneous queries about manuscripts and other material relating to James's visit, and with translations from Danish, Swedish and Latin, is most gratefully acknowledged from the following:

> Above all, to Peter Graves, for his labours in translating the Danish Account.
>
> Centre for Scottish Studies, University of Aberdeen, under the auspices of which work on this volume began.
>
> Göran Behre, Historiska Institutionen, Göteborgs Universitet.
>
> Professor Ian Cowan, Department of Scottish History, University of Glasgow, for the loan of microfilms belonging to the department of material in the Rigsarkivet, København.
>
> John Dahl, Norske Avdeling, Universitetsbiblioteket i Oslo.
>
> Dr Svend Gissel, Det Kongelige Bibliotek, København.
>
> Elin Graabraek, Vestfold Fylkesmuseum, Tønsberg.
>
> Professor R H P Green, Department of Classics, University of Glasgow, for finalising the translation of the Latin text of the procedure to be followed at proxy civil weddings.
>
> Harald Ilsøe, Det Kongelige Bibliotek, København most generously went far beyond my original inquiries and provided photocopies of a number of sources that I would otherwise have overlooked.
>
> Helge Kongsrud, Riksarkivet, Oslo.
>
> Tone Modalsli, Håndskriftsamlingen, Universitetsbiblioteket i Oslo.
>
> Dr Thomas Riis, København.
>
> Dr Wendy B Stevenson for drafting a translation of the Latin text of the procedure to be followed at proxy civil weddings.
>
> Professor Tony Upton, University of St Andrews, for work on translating the letter from the King of Sweden inserted in the Danish Account.

ABBREVIATIONS AND CONVENTIONS

APS	*The Acts of the Parliaments of Scotland,* ed T Thomson & C Innes (12 vols, Edinburgh, 1814–75)
BL	British Library
DBL	*Dansk Biografisk Leksikon* (16 vols, Copenhagen 1979–84)
DNB	*Dictionary of National Biography* (63 vols, 1880–1900)
Calderwood, *History*	D Calderwood, *The history of the kirk of Scotland* (8 vols, Wodrow Society, 1842–9)
CSPS	*Calendar of State Papers relating to Scotland and Mary, Queen of Scots, 1547–1603* (13 vols, London, 1898–1969)
Danish Account	The Danish narrative of events relating to the marriage, printed below in translation: see under *Norske Samlinger* below
Edin. recs., 1573–89	*Extracts from the records of the burgh of Edinburgh,* AD 1573–1589, ed J D Marwick (Scottish Burgh Record Society, 1882)
Edin. recs., 1589–1603	*Extracts from the records of the burgh of Edinburgh,* AD 1589–1603, ed M Wood and R K Hannay (Edinburgh, 1927)
Exchequer Rolls	*Rotuli Scaccarii Regum Scottorum. The Exchequer Rolls of Scotland, Vols xii and xiii, 1589–94 and 1595–1600* (1903–1908)
Fasti	*Fasti Ecclesiae Scoticanae* (10 vols, Edinburgh, 1915–81)
James the Sext	T Thomson (ed), *The historie and life of King James the Sext: being an account of the affairs of Scotland from the year 1566, to the year 1596* (Bannatyne Club, 1825)
Kancelliets Brevbøger	Laursen, L (ed), *Kancelliets Brevbøger vedrorende Danmarks indre forhold, 1588–1592* (Copenhagen, 1908)
Lee, *Thirlestane*	M Lee, *John Maitland of Thirlestane and the foundation of Stewart despotism in Scotland* (Princeton, NJ, 1959)

ABBREVIATIONS AND CONVENTIONS

Macray, 'First report'	W D Macray, 'Report on the archives of Denmark', *45th Report of the Deputy Keeper of the Public Records* (London, 1885), app. 2, no. 1, 1–56
Macray, 'Second report'	W D Macray, 'Second report on the royal archives of Denmark, and report on the Royal Library at Copenhagen', *46th Report of the Deputy Keeper of the Public Records* (London, 1886), app. II, no. 1, 1–75
Macray, 'Third report'	W D Macray, 'Third report on the royal archives of Denmark and report on the Royal Library at Copenhagen', *47th Report of the Deputy Keeper of the Public Records* (London, 1886), app. 5, 9–77
Marriage	J T G Craig (ed), *Papers relative to the marriage of King James the Sixth of Scotland, with the Princess Anna of Denmark* (Bannatyne Club, 1828)
Melville, *Memoirs*	Sir James Melville, *Memoirs of his own life* (Bannatyne Club, 1827)
Millar, 'Wedding-Tour'	A H Millar, 'The Wedding-Tour of James VI in Norway', *Scottish Review*, xxi (1893), 142–61
Moysie, *Memoirs*	David Moysie, *Memoirs of the affairs of Scotland* (Bannatyne Club, 1830)
NLS	National Library of Scotland
Norske Rigs-registranter	Lundh, O G, and Sars, I E (eds), *Norske Rigs-Registranter, 1588–1602* (Christiania, 1865)
Norske Samlinger	P A Munch (ed), Samtidig Beretning om Prindsesse Annas, Christian den 4des Systers, Giftermaal med Kong Jacob d. 6te af Skotland og hendes paafolgende Kroning, *Norske Samlinger*, i (Christiania, 1852), 450–512
Riis, *Auld acquaintance*	T Riis, *Should auld acquaintance be forgot. Scottish-Danish relations, c. 1450–1707* (2 vols, Odense, 1989)
RMS	*Register of the Great Seal of Scotland. Magni Sigilli Regum Scotorum* (11 vols, 1882–1914)
RPCS	*Register of the Privy Council of Scotland, [First Series], 1545–1625* (14 vols, London, 1877–98)
RSS	*Register of the Privy Seal of Scotland. Registrum Secreti Sigilli Regum Scotorum* (8 vols, 1908–83)

Scots peerage	J B Paul (ed), *The Scots peerage* (9 vols, Edinburgh, 1904–14)
SHS	Scottish History Society
Spottiswoode, *History*	J Spottiswoode, *History of the Church of Scotland* (3 vols, Spottiswoode Society, 1847–51)
SRO	Scottish Record Office
Thirlestane's Accounts	Audited accounts of Sir John Maitland of Thirlestane of money expended in 1589–90 on the occasion of James VI's marriage and visit to Norway and Denmark. British Library, Add. Ms. 22958
Vaus, *Correspondence*	Sir Patrick Waus of Barnbarroch, *Correspondence*, ed Robert Vans Agnew (2 vols, 1886)
Warrender papers	A I Cameron (ed), *The Warrender papers* (2 vols, SHS, 1931)
Williams, *Anne*	Ethel C Williams, *Anne of Denmark. Wife of James VI of Scotland: James I of England* (London, 1970)

Conventions

Personal names and place names have been standardised and modernised, except in a few cases in which the weird Danish corruptions of Scots names have defied identification. In most cases the standardised forms of Danish names reflect Danish usage, but in a few instances the well-established English variants have been employed, such as Anne, not Anna; Christian, not Christiern; Copenhagen, not København; Elsinore, not Helsingor; Frederick, not Frederik; Sophia, not Sophie.

The division of the translation of Danish Account into chapters and paragraphs has been modernised, but the headings contained in the original are retained within the chapters.

Money

£1 Scots = 0.5 dalers or thalers
      = 0.66 guilders or florins
      = 0.25 £ Sterling
      = 1.5 merks Scots

1 barrel of gold = £150,000 Scots

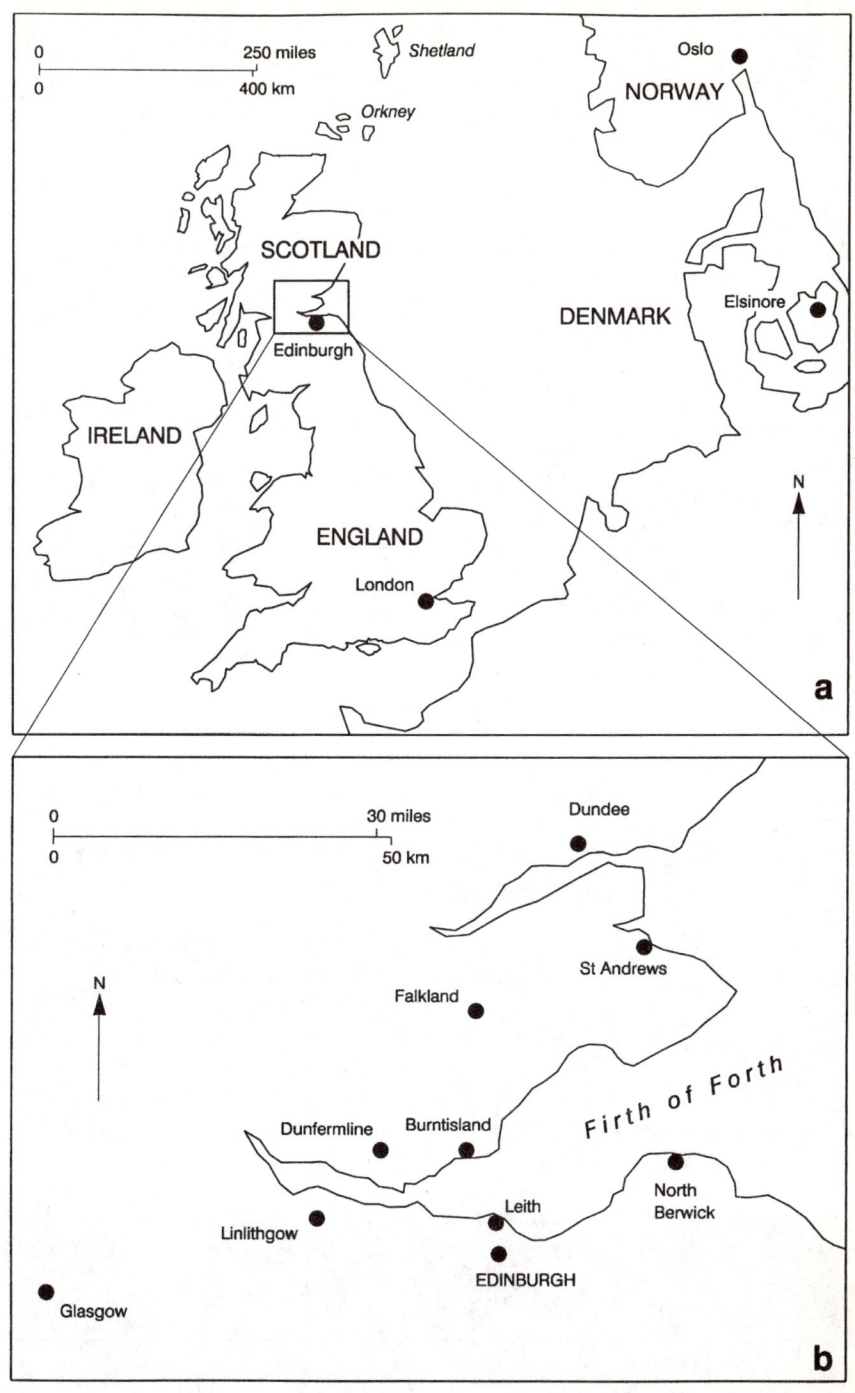

*Map 1. (a) Scotland, with South-east Scotland inset.
(b) South-east Scotland, enlarged.*

xv

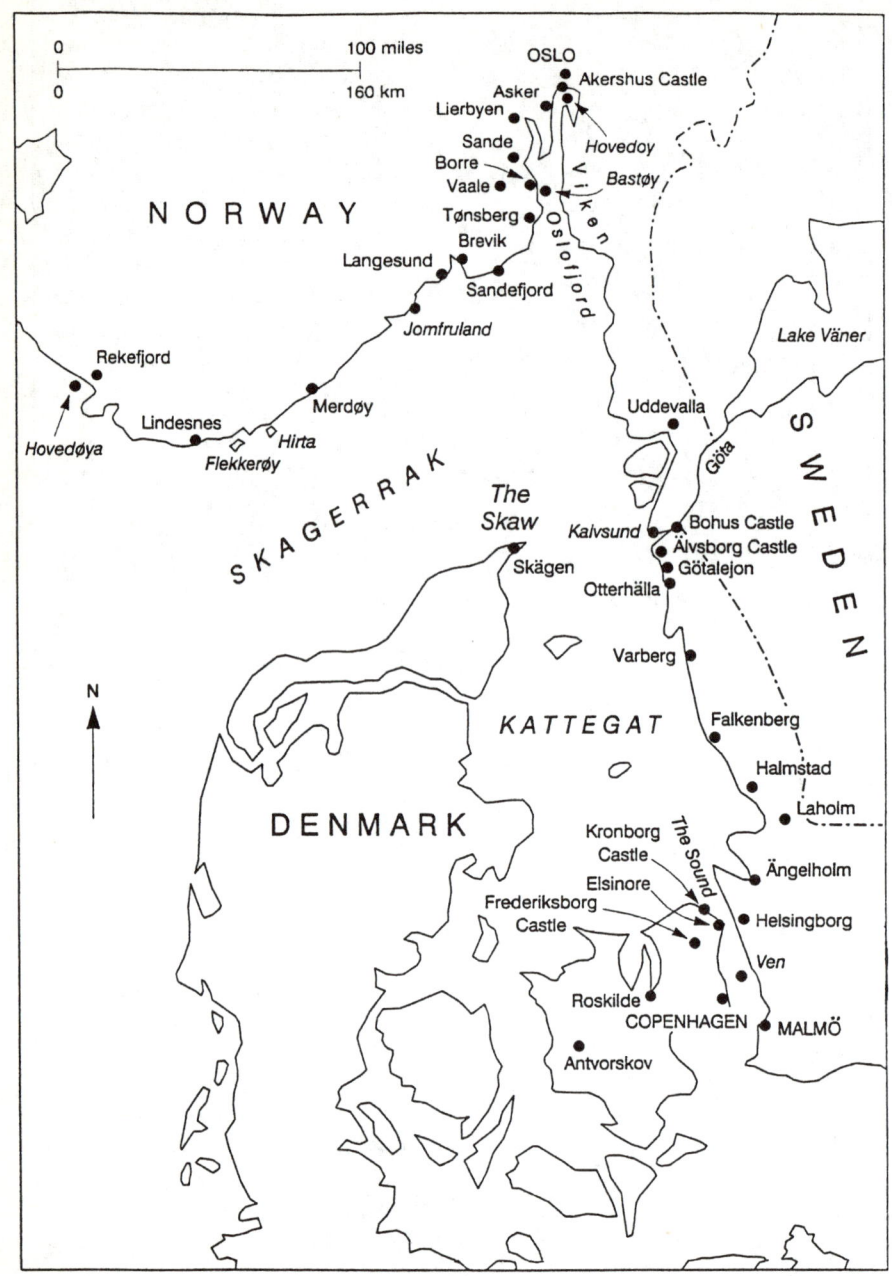

Map 2. Location Map: Denmark, Norway and Sweden.

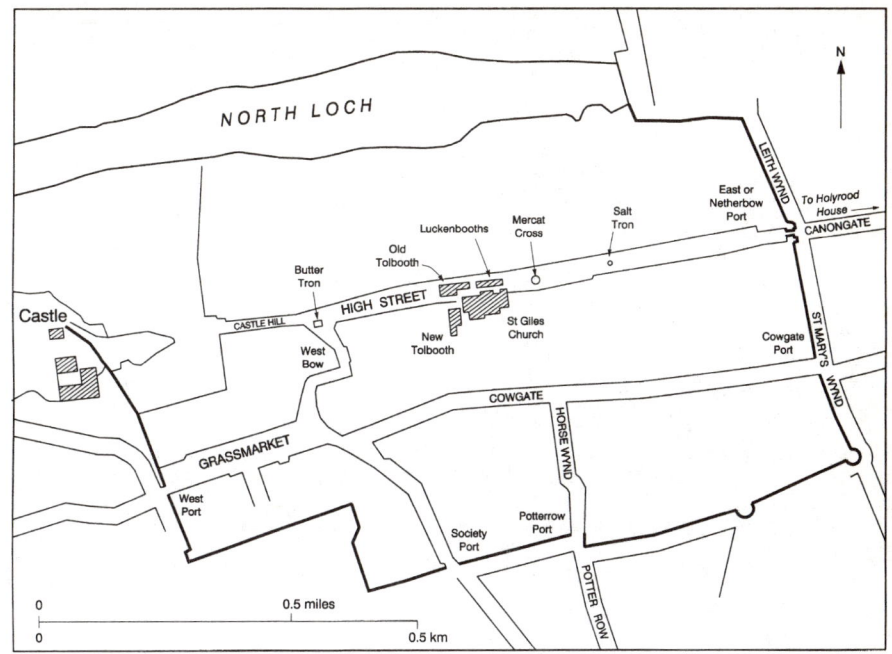

Map 3. Queen Annes's entry into Edinburgh.

The Queen was brought from Holyrood House in the east, round south of Edinburgh to the West Port. She then progressed through the Grassmarket up the West Bow to the Butter Tron, down the High Street past the Tolbooth and St Giles, the Mercat Cross and the Salt Tron, to the Netherbow Port. A short service in St Giles contrasted with the frequent stops on the rest of the ceremonial route for presentations, recitations, displays, plays and general celebrations by the townsfolk.

CHAPTER 1
THE QUEST FOR A BRIDE

Finding suitable marriage partners for monarchs has never been easy. A partner has to be acceptable in status, with sufficient eminence of blood to maintain or enhance the monarch's own standing among princes. Age and health must indicate the likelihood of providing good breeding stock. In addition there are political and religious considerations such as the need to gain or maintain influence or alliances, or even the hope of gaining control over another state. The latter motive had led the French to marry the heir to their throne to Mary Queen of Scots — and the English had for the same reason sought to claim her as a bride for their heir, the future Edward VI. The personal preferences of prospective partners might be considered — but were usually subordinated to practical calculations.

The sensitivity of the problem of choosing a partner for Mary's son, James VI of Scotland must have been increased by memories of the effects his mother's marital career had had both on Scotland and on her own fate. Mary Queen of Scots's first marriage (to the Dauphin Francis) had in the eyes of many almost reduced Scotland to being a province of France. Her second (to Lord Darnley) had seriously undermined her reputation within Scotland and had offended England. Her third (to the earl of Bothwell) had so discredited her that it had led to her enforced abdication and long imprisonment in England.

Admittedly the complications of finding a suitable partner for a male ruler were fewer than in the case of a female one, but Mary's recent outstanding examples of marry in haste, repent at leisure must have made James and his advisers very cautious in deciding on a suitable bride. Abstention from marriage was one way out, and it was probably an option that had attractions for James personally. But it was unacceptable. It was one of the most important functions of any monarch to beget an heir. James's contemporary, Elizabeth I of England, was an outstanding exception to this rule, of course, and in her dereliction of the duty of breeding she may well have taken to heart Mary Queen of Scots's example

SCOTLAND'S LAST ROYAL WEDDING

as a warning that a queen regnant should avoid the marriage bed. But pressure from his subjects to continue the dynasty (especially as it was, according to Scottish national mythology, the oldest in Europe) was clearly strong, and James must also have seen marriage and the production of an heir as necessary to advance his greatest ambition: his hope of inheriting the English throne on the death of the conveniently childless Elizabeth. Many in England were deeply unhappy at their queen's irresponsibility (though a Virgin Queen had some advantages from the point of view of image-makers) and an heir would add greatly to James's attraction as a potential successor to Elizabeth. It would indicate that through him the long-term succession in England could be secured. Without heirs, he would appear a stop-gap candidate, leaving the future of the throne uncertain.

On the other hand, even for a male ruler, marriage could be a disaster. Elizabeth's father, Henry VIII had a record of outstanding effort and little result. Investment in six wives produced only three surviving children — and of them only one was first class produce — that is, male. And even he (Edward VI) was sickly. Worse of all, none of the three themselves produced children.

What particular criteria were desirable in a prospective bride for James? Royal blood was perhaps more than usually important, to bolster the status of the Stuart monarchy after it's prestige had suffered two major blows: Protestant Reformation carried out in defiance of the crown, and the disgrace and downfall of Mary Queen of Scots. Religion was also central. In the age of Counter-Reformation, a Catholic bride would have been deeply disturbing to Protestant opinion in Scotland — and would have damaged James's prospects in England. In other respects as well a bride acceptable to the English as a prospective queen was required. James, though an independent monarch, had seen his country become almost a client state of England during his youth, with the English ready to intervene to protect her strategic interests in maintaining a Protestant regime on her northern border, and James knew his dependence on Elizabeth's support. He could not afford to make a marriage that would alienate her.

This created serious problems. Elizabeth was not the easiest monarch to please. Would any proposed bride for the Scots heir to her throne ever please her? She had been unhelpful over the marriages of Mary Queen of Scots, and was sensitive about the

THE QUEST FOR A BRIDE

matter of a wife for James as it raised the issue of the English succession after her death, something she was trying to ignore. Yet it was clear that she expected to have a major say in choosing — or more probably, vetoing — his bride.

James had to balance avoiding offending Elizabeth with satisfying demands that he provide for the succession to Britain's thrones. To further complicate matters, there was up to 1587 the almost ghostly voices of the imprisoned Mary Queen of Scots and her agents to be considered. She still had enough supporters in Scotland for it to be necessary to at least listen politely to hopeful suggestions about Catholic candidates, such as the duke of Lorraine's daughter.

James was reluctant to step into the religious, political and personal minefield of royal marriage, but he had no choice. In the mating game of kings personal feelings counted for little. Marry he must, James concluded, and hope to do it without annoying Cousin Elizabeth.

By the end of the 1570s there was much talk about possible brides for the teenage King James (born 1566). Early speculations and suggestions were wide-ranging. Possibilities in France (with both Catholic and Protestant bridal options available), Spain, Sweden and Denmark were all considered, but a Danish bride was the most likely outcome from the start. Denmark had a Protestant (though unfortunately Lutheran rather than Calvinist) dynasty; there were earlier dynastic links with Scotland through the marriage of James III to Margaret of Denmark; and not only were trading links between the two countries strong but it was only through Danish friendship that Scots ships could pass through the narrow Sound into the Baltic and trade there. And the king of Denmark, Frederick II, had two daughters of about the right age.

In 1580 it was alleged that the Danes themselves had made a discrete approach to the Scots on the matter of a dynastic marriage, and later in the year it was rumoured that Danish ambassadors were about to land to negotiate on the issue.[1] But such reports were more a testimony to the fact that the king's marriage was the subject of public discussion than to actual developments. From her English imprisonment Mary Queen of Scots indicated in 1583 that ideally she would like her son to marry into the Spanish dynasty, as it was Catholic. But she accepted that a Danish marriage would be more acceptable to English and Scottish Protestants. Indeed, she evidently had some thoughts of trying to persuade Queen Elizabeth to urge a Danish match on James, but to the relief of the Scots promised not to do so. Any approach from Mary would be likely to be resented by Elizabeth, and would be an embarrassment to James.[2] As far as both monarchs were concerned, Mary was an embarrassing left-over from the past (she was, after all, as James mother, by strict hereditary principles still rightful queen of Scotland). As far as possible, they pretended she wasn't there.

Action came at last in 1585, with the Danes taking the initiative — not least because they hoped negotiations for a marriage would help them to press for the return of Orkney and Shetland, which had passed to the Scottish crown a century before as pledges for payment of Queen Margaret's dowry. But the approach was still indirect. Make diplomatic contact with the Scots to talk about the disputed islands, informally seeking reactions to the possibility of a marriage. Since, however, there had been speculation about a Danish marriage for years, most Scots concluded from the start that the arrival of Danish diplomats meant negotiations on the matter. Thus, according to a Scottish chronicle, King Frederick II of Denmark suggested that James's 'gudlie stature, and ryp yeares requyrit the societie of sum condigne Princess to be his bedfallow.' He was willing to let James choose either of his two daughters, according to 'whilk should be the maist cumlie, and the best for his prencelie contentment.' This sounds much more like popular romantic rumour than hard diplomacy.

The Scottish response, according to the chronicle, was discouraging. It was announced that an outbreak of plague meant that there could be no safe access to vital documents that it would be necessary to consult in any negotiations. Therefore the Danish envoys were thanked for their message, and told that James himself would send an ambassador to Denmark later to negotiate. The Danes then, exceedingly well contented, departed with great joy. Or so it was said.[3]

The reality was rather different. The Danes kept up the outward pretence of only having come to negotiate about Orkney and Shetland. But everyone assumed otherwise — including Elizabeth and her ambassador in Scotland, Sir Edward Wotton. Rather surprisingly, at this point she told him to indicate to the Scots that a Danish marriage would have her approval. True to their instructions, the Danes didn't talk of a marriage, but the ambassadors must have heard much talk of a Scottish-Danish match, and found that many supported such an alliance. Yet while in Scotland they were given the impression at court that they were not welcome, and they certainly were not 'exceedingly well contented' when they left. The ambassadors, Manderup Parsberg[4] and Henrik Below,[5] with Dr Nicholaus Theophilus[6] acting as their secretary, left Scotland angry and insulted. They had been kept hanging around for months without an answer to their king's messages about the Northern Isles, had not been suitably entertained, had been treated with derision. It was even alleged that James himself had insulted Denmark and denounced its people for their rude manners, drunkenness and stupidity!

The reasons for this unfriendly reception of the Danes lay in the political situation. The Danish mission had been most unfortunately timed, for in the ascendant at the unstable Scottish court was James Stewart, earl of Arran, a strong supporter of Denmark's arch-enemy, Sweden. He had formerly served as a mercenary officer in Swedish armies, and his ambition was to arrange a Swedish marriage for James. Therefore he did all he could to make sure nothing came of the contacts with the Danes, while the ambassadors themselves sought to ignore Arran, suspicious of his Swedish connections, thus further alienating him. Arran poisoned the king and others against the unfortunate Danes, who were so furious at the insults offered to the honour of their king and country that they spoke of revenge. Sir James Melville, according to his own account, managed to get the treatment of the Danes improved by persuading the king that he had been misinformed about how contemptible a place Denmark was. He also alleged that the English ambassador, Wotton, caused much of the trouble by telling the Danes exaggerated stories about how rude the Scots were about all things Danish.[7] Elizabeth, it may be, was making encouraging noises while interfering behind the scenes.

Back in Denmark the ambassadors made known their discontent at the way they had been treated in Scotland,[8] but they probably sought to minimise what had happened to reduce the political damage done. A quarrel with James would not bring the return of the disputed islands any nearer, and James would be a good prize for a Danish princess — not so much because he was king of Scots, but because he would probably one day be king of England. Moreover news arriving from Scotland must have given the ambassadors great satisfaction. Within weeks of their departure the earl of Arran had been overthrown by an English-inspired coup. Moreover James soon sought to mend fences by sending Peter Young, his former tutor, to negotiate with the Danes in 1586. Again the mission was outwardly concerned with Orkney and Shetland, but this only thinly disguised approaches about a marriage. Now free of Arran's influence, James was serious about a Danish bride. Nonetheless, he was in no hurry, making excuses for sending only a relatively humble representative without power to settle anything, and indicating that decisions should await his reaching the age of twenty-one the following year. But Young was to bring back portraits of the Danish king and queen and their children.

The Danish royal portraits requested were probably in exchange for his own, sent with Young, for a portrait of the young king which is believed to have been sent to Denmark in the course of the marriage negotiations survives, and obvious time for James to send it was when Young was seeking Danish portraits. The picture, by the leading painter at the Scottish court, Andrian Vanson, has only recently emerged from obscurity and been returned to Scotland, and put on display in 1996 in James's birthplace, Edinburgh Castle. At first sight the portrait might not seem the ideal royal image to be used in marketing the king abroad. James looks even younger than his nineteen years. The face looks almost feminine, the hooded eyes are watchful, almost suspicious. The primly pursed mouth attempts a smile at the corners but it doesn't reach the eyes. There is dignity and intelligence here, and grand display of costume and jewellery, but no swagger of power or confident assertion, indeed perhaps some lack of confidence. It may well be that the problem is that it is too good a portrait for an advertisement: it tells more about the young man than it should.

However, as the eventual outcome of the negotiations was to show, the portrait can't have alienated the all too masculine and boisterous Frederick II and his courtiers too much. What the young Danish princesses, Elizabeth and Anne, thought is unknown — and really didn't matter.[9]

Shortly after Peter Young sailed, William Stewart of Pittenweem also set out for Denmark, ostensibly on private business. Stewart is perhaps best described as an adventurer — military, political and diplomatic. He appears repeatedly in the story of the marriage,

THE QUEST FOR A BRIDE

mainly through his knack for forcing himself onto the stage whenever possible. Though unpopular and mistrusted, he was clearly an astute manipulator. Probably the illegitimate son of a lairdly family, he had first emerged in the service of the Dutch fighting the Spanish in 1575. For a time he had led a partly Scottish regiment in Danzig opposing the Poles, before returning to the Netherlands. There had followed a brief period in the service of Frederick II of Denmark (whom he had previously offered to serve in 1575), which had ended embarrassingly when in 1578 Stewart's Scots soldiers in Elsinore had mutinied and looted the property of many courtiers. Not surprisingly the Danes raised no objections to the Scots leaving — provided the stolen property was returned. Stewart had then gone back to the Netherlands to fight for William of Orange, but in 1580 he had again entered Danish service, extricating himself from a command with the Dutch.

By 1582 Stewart was back in Scotland, being referred to as 'Lord Crownare' (colonel), and in the years ahead he was frequently referred to simply as the 'crowner' or 'colonel,' this rank acquired on the continent being a novelty in Scotland. He acted for a time as captain of King James's guard in the turbulent events of these years, earning himself notoriety through his hostility to Presbyterianism, but being rewarded by becoming commendator of Pittenween in 1583. When the series of political coups which marked the period in Scotland finally ended Stewart was on the losing side, being identified with the earl of Arran, and his journey to Denmark was supposedly intended to get payment for past services and perhaps resume his military career on the continent.[10]

However, with the opportunism of a born survivor Stewart saw in James's negotiations with Denmark an opportunity to wriggle back into favour at home, by somehow persuading the king to commission him to use his court contacts in Denmark to further the marriage. But there was more to his elaborate schemings than this. Stewart was a Danish mole who had been awaiting activation. In anticipation of the embassy promised by James, Frederick II had written to Stewart in September 1585 stressing the bonds of past service which tied Stewart to him, and urging that he get himself appointed as a member of the Scots embassy — or if not to find some pretext for coming to Denmark at the same time. Stewart could claim to be well qualified for such negotiations as he spoke German (the language of the Danish court): but as well as outwardly

7

SCOTLAND'S LAST ROYAL WEDDING

representing Scottish interests he would keep Frederick in touch with what was being said in private in the Scots camp.

Rumours of Stewart's involvement in intrigues and plots abound in his torturous career, but this particular piece of double-dealing was not discovered. However unprincipled it was, it may have proved beneficial to James as well as to Frederick. It helped negotiations make progress through giving the latter someone he felt he could trust (Stewart, of all men!) to reassure him about Scottish intentions. Anyway, Young and Stewart soon returned from Denmark with encouraging news of their reception and an invitation to send Scots ambassadors to negotiate in 1587.[11]

The king's choice of ambassadors for the 1587 mission was Sir Patrick Vaus of Barnbarroch and Peter Young. The fact that neither was a nobleman suggests James was still in no hurry and wished the negotiations to be low key. So too does the fact that there was a long delay before the new ambassadors sailed. Several months before he was eventually allowed to sail, Young was stressing to the king that honour required prompt action. Even if the marriage was to be set aside for the moment, there was the matter of Orkney to discuss. Another sign of James's lack of commitment was that his instructions to the ambassadors were 'uncertane and unresolut.' It is true that in March James ordered that no Scottish ships suitable for the voyage to Denmark were to sail until some had been chosen to carry the ambassadors, but the impression of urgency was misleading — no doubt deliberately. The ambassadors did not sail until the end of May, after Edinburgh had agreed to pay for a ship.[12]

The delays reflected James's financial problems and personal reluctance, but they were also in part the result of the execution of Mary Queen of Scots in England shortly before the Scots ambassadors left. King James had to walk a delicate tightrope. On the one hand he had to react with filial fury and make threatening noises: honour demanded that one made a fuss if someone chopped one's mother's head off. On the other hand, he wished to avoid breaking with Queen Elizabeth, and thus damaging his hopes for the English succession — and probably undermining the slowly emerging political stability of Scotland. With the matter of Mary's death dominating the politics of the day, the Danish match seemed relatively unimportant. Until the dust settled and it was possible to see how Mary's death effected relations with England, James would not want to enter into any new commitments.

THE QUEST FOR A BRIDE

Inadequately instructed, and aware of the complications to their negotiations that Mary's death might cause, the ambassadors submitted a list of questions to the king before they sailed, in the hope of clarifying the stance they were supposed to adopt in Denmark. James's replies were not always helpful — and on occasion reveal rather unseemly levity. When James indicated that no figure should be cited as to what size of tocher (dowry) he would be content with, he added 'ultra cupidam,' indicating a desire to get as much as possible. As to his future wife he was less fussy. If the elder of the Danish princesses, Elizabeth, was already contracted in marriage, then he would accept Anne, the second. Asked what to do if his proposed bride turned out to be seriously or incurably ill, James replied that the will of God must be borne with patience — again hardly an appropriate sentiment, however religiously correct. Nonetheless, the ambassadors were authorised to commit James to proceeding with the marriage with all possible diligence, and to negotiate about terms. But concluding a treaty was to be left to a future date, when noble ambassadors would be sent. The present ambassadors were to find out what King Frederick's attitude to Mary's execution was, and in discussing it they were to 'exaggerat the fact as farre as ye can.' James hoped for sympathy and support, thus seeking to make political capital out of his mother's death. But his ambassadors were to say nothing about James's own attitude, and were to avoid blaming anyone for the execution — so nothing could be said offensive to Elizabeth.[13]

Barnbarroch and Young arrived at Elsinore on 8 June 1587, but found King Frederick was away at Antvorskov (an abbey converted into a royal residence). After ten days a message arrived that they should go there to meet the king. An audience with him was arranged for 27 June, but then cancelled because he had toothache. He sent his chancellor, Niels Kaas,[14] together with Manderup Parsberg and Henrik Below (who had both been in Scotland the year before) to negotiate, but the Scots refused to proceed, as their commission instructed them to address the king personally. The Danes then brought up the matter of Orkney, but the Scots said they had no instructions on that matter — though still refusing to reveal what they did have instructions about. Quite what was going on here is hard to say. Frederick II really was unwell at this time, but he may have been giving the Scots representatives a taste of the poor treatment his own ambassadors had received in Scotland

SCOTLAND'S LAST ROYAL WEDDING

before: and he may also have been demonstrating displeasure at the social status of the Scots ambassadors. Moreover, while the Danes favoured a royal wedding, they were concerned not to appear too eager, so they could exert the maximum leverage for the return of Orkney in any negotiations.

Deadlock was broken however when it was agreed that the Scots would talk with Kaas (the most senior of the three Danes) alone. Under a promise from Kaas that he would only reveal what they said to Frederick himself, the Scots inquired whether the latter's elder daughter, Princess Elizabeth, was in good health — and whether she was contracted or promised in marriage. Kaas indicated that Frederick was favourably inclined to King James, and that Princess Elizabeth was not spoken for. Peter Young then revealed that the previous year he had really come to Denmark to inspect Elizabeth, and he now had been sent to ask for her hand.

On 29 July the Scots at last had an audience with Frederick, and were invited to dine with him. But early in the meal he retired to his chamber unwell, though he reappeared again later to drink a toast. As his illness was probably at least in part induced by the alcoholic excesses which were to hasten his death, and Danish toasts were notorious for their potency, this can hardly have improved his condition.

The Scots expected their brief meeting with the king to be the start of proper negotiations. In fact it was the high point of their mission. The following day they were told by Kaas and Henrik Ramel[15] that the king had not been able to see them more often because of illness, and he was about to depart to Elsinore. Not surprisingly, the Scots were astonished. Having said hello, Frederick was not even going to do them (or rather their own king, whom they represented) the courtesy of saying goodbye. And while too ill to do this, he was well enough to endure the rigours of travel.

The Scots had had no direct answer to their questions about the marriage. The Danish response was that the matter of Orkney should be settled first, though the Scots urged that the topics be regarded as entirely separate. If Frederick gave James his daughter in return for Orkney it would look as if he was selling her, and thus 'playing the merchant.' The gibe was a provocative one, for two years before the Danish mission in Scotland had had to endure whispering that their dynasty was disreputable in its origins, her monarchs being descended from merchants. It is a measure of

THE QUEST FOR A BRIDE

Scottish exasperation that they dared to hint that Frederick's attitude confirmed this. Further bickering followed. The Danes still insisted that Orkney must have priority. At the same time they insisted on their interest in the marriage — but then revealed that another marriage had been fixed up for Elizabeth after all. However, James could have her sister Anne — though Elizabeth, the more beautiful of the two, might be still available if James insisted!

What the Danes were probably trying to do was to force James into doing something more decisive, like sending a proper noble mission with full negotiating powers to Denmark. Ramel recalled that he had warned the Scots the previous year that Elizabeth might be married elsewhere if James did not hurry — and that Anne also might be spoken for. The Scots retorted haughtily that their kings were in the habit of only marrying eldest daughters, and then sailed for home thwarted. Whether the matter of Mary Queen of Scots had been discussed is uncertain. Reports that the Scots had sought Danish military aid if war with England broke out are unsubstantiated — and if any such Scots request was made, it would have been intended to demonstrate James's appropriate fury at his mother's death rather than reflecting any real expectation of war.[16]

On their return to Scotland Barnbarroch and Young reported, doubtless with some resentment, that they had been given fair words about the marriage, but kept hanging around, had only seen Frederick II once, and then sent home with nothing achieved — not even having seen the Danish princesses or their mother, Queen Sophia.[17]

While they had been away, the case of another candidate for James's hand had been pressed, and lack of progress in Denmark must have strengthened belief that this should be taken seriously. Guillaume de Salluste, seigneur du Bartas, a Huguenot soldier best known as a poet, had arrived to urge James to marry Catherine de Bourbon, the sister of King Henry III of Navarre.[18] The proposal had its attractions. Henry was supposed to be very rich; he was a Protestant; and he was heir to the throne of France — and indeed was to succeed to that throne in August 1589, the month of James's marriage to Anne of Denmark. Thus James could make a religiously sound marriage (sounder than a Danish one: the Danes being Lutherans, the Navarre dynasty Calvinist), could hope for a generous dowry, and could ally himself, as (hopefully) future king of England, with the future king of France. But such a marriage also had major drawbacks. Henry was an active Protestant champion, and was likely to have to fight for his French inheritance. Might Scotland find herself drawn into involvement in France's vicious religious wars? More immediately, such a marriage would bring on Scotland the enmity of the existing French regime, of Spain, and indeed of Catholic Europe in general, at a time when he still hoped to win Catholic support for his claim to the English throne. Denmark, on the other hand, while Protestant, was avoiding involvement in the partly religious-inspired wars of the age, and this was indeed one of the attractions of a Danish match.[19]

James's own attitude at this point is far from clear. It seems likely that he saw the Danish marriage as being the most sensible. The one thing that is obvious is that he still felt no personal inclination to give the matter priority. Probably it had already been noticed that he preferred male to female company — certainly this became a matter for gossip soon afterwards. But insinuations of homosexual inclinations — or even activities — only emerged much later in his life, and even then were to be unconvincing. It is of course all a matter of definition, and it is all too easy to label anyone not rampantly heterosexual as homosexual. But there are also many heterosexuals who socially prefer the company of men to women. It seems most probable that James was one of the latter, and one does not need to be a learned psychiatrist to detect in his background factors which might make him suspicious of women. He had never seen his mother since infancy. She had proved an incompetent ruler (just what prevailing wisdom would have predicted of a woman). Her second and third marriages had been disastrous, one leading to the murder of her husband (James's father), the other to dethronement, life imprisonment and execution. She had been denounced as an adultress and a whore. He might have a lingering attachment to her, and show favour to those who had been loyal in supporting her. But further complicating his attitude must have been lingering guilt. He sat on what was in the eyes on many her throne, while she languished in prison. He had (admittedly when far too young to be anything but the pawn of others) usurped her crown. He was a son who had betrayed and destroyed his mother. This could only be justified by accepting that at least some of the charges against her were true, and these charges were concerned mainly with her sexuality. She had married Darnley in passion, then within months was believed to have connived at his murder so she could indulge her infatuation with Bothwell. The prevailing — as for many centuries — mythology was that women were creatures of voracious sexual appetites and capacities, forces which were highly dangerous to society if allowed free play. They had to be kept under control by men: and it would be hard to find a better example of the disastrous consequences of women's sexuality out of control than Mary Queen of Scots.

No wonder James's attitude towards women was ambivalent. On top of his mother's saga, the doings of another woman who (like it or not) was a major influence in his life was hardly likely to endear the female sex to him. Queen Elizabeth — again a woman 'out of control' through unfortunate dynastic accident — heckled him, bullied him, made it clear she knew how to rule a kingdom a lot better than he did. Given a chance, women were domineering, and would humiliate men.

Women were a dangerous and distasteful phenomenon. In spite of sexual attraction, it was best to steer clear of them whenever possible. Marriage was necessary, but not something urgent, for James at least, until an heir was necessary.

There were, moreover, practical reasons which could be used to justify further delays. Following up the suggestion of Princess Catherine of Navarre as a partner might usefully indicate to the Danes that James had alternatives to what they might have to offer. The English, who earlier had seemed ready to accept a Danish wife for James, were now dithering, showing signs of favouring Catherine instead.[20] Such an alliance, the English calculated, might lead to Scottish involvement alongside England in intervening on the continent in Protestant interests. Moreover, trading disputes had strained English relations with Denmark, making a Scottish-Danish alliance seem threatening, [21] — and Queen Elizabeth probably also wished to show her displeasure at James negotiating about his marriage without consulting her, which she claimed he had promised to do.[22] To keep her happy it would be politic to pretend to take the prospect of a match with the house of Navarre seriously.

Another compelling motive for delay was James's acute financial difficulty. A suitably lavish embassy to Denmark to conclude a marriage would be very expensive, and a lot would need to be spent on repairing and furnishing Scotland's run-down royal palaces if a foreign princess was to be suitably received and housed. Finally, after the way Barnbarroch and Young had been treated in Denmark the situation was still too uncertain for the sending of a full-scale embassy to conclude a marriage. It might meet humiliating failure, as the Danes had not yet committed themselves.

In the event, the way forward proved to be through two semi-formal visits to Denmark by the usefully meddlesome William Stewart. Determined to keep himself at the forefront of Scoto-Danish relations, he was evidently willing to pay his own expenses again, and persuaded James that informal approaches by him through his Danish court contacts might be productive. King Frederick died in February 1588, but Stewart saw him shortly before his death. He arrived back in Scotland sometime that month with letters from Frederick declaring that James should have his second daughter, Anne, 'becaus hir moder thinckes hir maist meitt for him' — a face-saving indication that far from James being fobbed off with the younger daughter, he was actually being given her as a favour. 'Crowner' Stewart had achieved far more than the ambassadors the previous year, and thus won some popularity.[23] The secret of his success, the fact that he was a Danish agent, remained concealed.

Probably because of Frederick's death, a second mission by Stewart to Denmark took place late in 1588 (after a Danish representative had visited the Scots court), establishing links with the regents and council ruling in name of the young Christian IV. But though the death of Frederick led to this further delay, it may have furthered the match in other respects. The new regime in Denmark seems to have been anxious to conclude the marriage and thus cement friendship with Scotland in the time of a royal minority.[24]

Expectations in Scotland of an imminent marriage were strong: but still James failed to show any sense of urgency, and attention began to switch to the king himself in a potentially damaging way. It was now observed that he 'never regardes the company of any woman, not so muche as in any dalliance.'[25] A young king who showed no taste for the company of women, who didn't even indulge in mild flirtation, was a matter for concern. Exasperation grew. As early as July 1587 the three estates had shown themselves ready to support the king's marriage by agreeing to taxation for it, and in April 1588 this had been agreed at £100,000 Scots.[26] But still nothing had happened. Some blamed James's closest adviser, Sir John Maitland of Thirlestane, who held office both as chancellor and secretary. Many of the nobility resented Thirlestane's influence on the king, regarding him as an upstart and likely to damage their

THE QUEST FOR A BRIDE

interests through his stress on restoring order in the country and ensuring that even the greatest obeyed the law. It was rumoured that he advised the king that forcing the kingdom into better order should be the first priority, and that marriage would distract attention from this.[27] Still, the king showed a degree of continuing commitment to action by appointing the Earl Marischal to lead an embassy to Denmark. But though the earl evidently had two ships ready at Leith by the beginning of May 1589, orders to sail failed to arrive in the weeks that followed. Tension rose in Edinburgh, with fears that the king might still be considering the Navarre marriage, and in the end it was the burgesses of the capital who forced decision on the dithering monarch.

The flash-point came on 27 May, with two items of news coinciding. A Danish representative arrived at Leith to inquire (no doubt with some asperity) whether James was going to proceed with the marriage; and the Earl Marischal dismissed his ships, despairing of receiving orders to sail in the foreseeable future. The next day the provost, baillies and many burgesses cornered Thirlestane in his chamber and made their opinions clear. Blaming him for delaying the marriage as part of an English plot to keep the king single, they forcefully indicated that he and the rest of those regarded as the pro-English faction would die unless the marriage took place. As well as the succession issue, there was a more practical one. If a diplomatic break with Denmark took place, trade would be disrupted and (it was alleged) all the burghs of Scotland would be undone, for the entry of Scots ships to the Baltic could be prevented by the Danes through their control of the Sound. If the alternative match with Catherine de Bourbon took place, then the hostility of France might disrupt peaceful trade on that front as well.[28]

According to the conspiracy-obsessed Sir James Melville, the incident was even more bizarre than it seemed, because it was the king himself who had secretly incited the action of the burgesses, acting through the deacons of the crafts. Thirlestane had won the support of the majority of the privy council in opposing the marriage so as to avoid trouble with England, and James was trying to exert pressure on the council to change its mind.[29] This seems pretty implausible, but it is quite possible that some of those in high places who favoured the marriage had indicated that a demonstration in Edinburgh might settle the issue. In Thirlestane's opinion Peter Young was responsible for the incident, but the king would take no action against the demonstrators, doubtless infuriating his aggrieved chancellor by saying that those who had threatened the latter's life had done so out of love and zeal for their king — and understandable concern for trade.[30]

Money to help to send the Earl Marischal on his way was at last found by giving him most of a recent payment to James by Elizabeth of the irregular pension intended to keep him both solvent and friendly with England. As she had still not approved the match this use of her subsidy was unlikely to please her. Thomas Fowler, England's representative in Edinburgh, gloomily reported on 7 June that the ambassadors were ready to sail on the next wind, blaming William Stewart and Peter Young for pushing the king into action: they had persuaded James that Catherine of Navarre was old and crooked, and the king had at last managed to summon up some romantic enthusiasm for Anne of Denmark — Catherine was thirty-one, Anne fourteen, while James himself was now twenty-three. Thirlestane, stubborn to the last, said those who had negotiated with the Danes in the past were nothing but fools out for self gain — and that the ambassadors now being sent were merely fools of higher social status. Wise men feared a Danish match would bring to Scotland Lutheranism, along with the drunkenness for which the Danes were notorious — and the Scots had as much of the latter as they could use already. Anyway, Princess Anne was too young to be a steadying influence on James, whereas Catherine of Navarre was said to be 'staid' and might be able to curb James's greatest weakness — his irresponsibility in spending money.[31] But these were not arguments likely to win royal support. James can hardly have been taken by the image of Catherine as the ideal bride because she would be a motherly steadying influence who would control his purse.

CHAPTER 2

NEGOTIATIONS AND PROXY MARRIAGE

In spite of English sour grapes and Thirlestane's mutterings, events now moved fast. It was resolved that the embassy should consist of five men — the Earl Marischal; Andrew Keith, Lord Dingwall; James Scrymgeour of Dudhope; John Skene; and George Young. The inclusion of Peter Young and Barnbarroch was evidently suggested, but vetoed by the king, who held them partly responsible for the failure of their mission in 1587 — and anyway the earl said he would not go if Peter Young was to sail with him, as he would seek to claim all the credit for a successful mission for himself.[1]

To these five men was entrusted James's matrimonial future. George Keith, 5th Earl Marischal, (c. 1553–1623) had become a privy councillor in 1582, and his choice as head of the mission was based on three qualifications: his nobility, his knowledge of languages and his wealth. The last of these was essential as the ambassador was expected in the first instance to bear much of the costs of the mission, which had to be sufficiently splendid and lavish to reflect honour on his king and country. He had long been the leading candidate for heading the embassy — it had been said that he would lead it as far back as 1587[2] — largely because he was the richest of the king's subjects. The annual income of his father, who had died in 1581, had been estimated at £180,000 Scots,[3] considerably more than the son was eventually to accept as James's tocher (dowry). Thirlestane was withering about the earl, remarking that he and his nephew and fellow ambassador, Lord Dingwall, 'will not both make a wise man.'[4] But Thirlestane was embittered about the whole conduct of the negotiations, and thus far from an unbiased witness. Marischal was in reality a man of education and culture, who in 1593 was to found Marischal College in Aberdeen. But it seems that he did not possess the commanding physical presence James might have been expected to want in his personal representative, for the king on one occasion at least addressed him as 'My little fat pork.'[5]

Andrew Keith was the illegitimate son of Marischal's brother, and had made himself a successful career as a mercenary soldier.

SCOTLAND'S LAST ROYAL WEDDING

He had spent eighteen years in the service of Sweden, and had been created Lord Dingwall in 1584. Keith had probably reached Sweden in 1566, had supported the coup which brought King Johan III to power in 1569 and had became a trusted administrator. A good marriage had brought him land, and he had obtained from Scotland evidence of his noble (though illegitimate) birth to help his advancement. In 1575 he had been knighted and became Baron Forsholm.[6] As a result of Keith's military experience James had recently appointed him 'generall colonel and commander' in the wars within the realm for life, with an annual pension of £500 Scots, with the same privileges as his predecessors and the right to appoint colonels under him. [7] In practice this seems to have meant very little, and when he is referred to as 'under-marischal' he was presumably acting through a commission from his uncle, the earl. After his mission to Denmark he was to return to Sweden, just before King Johan's death in 1592. He supported Johan's successor, Sigismund, and evidently cut his links with Scotland by resigning his lands and lordship there to Sir William Keith of Delny.[8] But he was forced to flee from Sweden when Sigismund was dethroned in 1598, and died in Paris sometime before 1602.[9]

James and the Earl Marischal may have thought that appointing Dingwall to the embassy was an astute move, as he had such long experience of Scandinavian affairs. In fact it was an elementary blunder. The Danes certainly knew of Dingwall: but they knew him as a servant of their old enemies, the Swedes, who had fought in wars against Denmark. Perhaps Thirlestane's lack of confidence in the earl's wisdom was justified by this inclusion of his nephew in the mission.

James Scrymgeour of Dudhope, constable of Dundee and standard-bearer of Scotland, had more appropriate experience of contact with the Danes. He had been banished to Denmark when the earl of Arran was dominant in Scotland, being regarded as one of the latter's greatest enemies, but had been recalled in June 1585.[10] Becoming an advocate the same year, he had served James VI in a number of diplomatic missions to Europe. If contemporary gossip is to be believed, the king had reservations about his abilities. When he was first proposed as a legal expert to take part in the mission, James is said to have protested that there were many better lawyers. However, he was evidently won over by the arguments that Dudhope knew much about the Germans (here

NEGOTIATIONS AND PROXY MARRIAGE

taken to include Danes), could make long harangues in Latin, and 'was a gud trew stout man, lyk a Dutche [Deusch] man.'[11]

John Skene, the fourth member of the mission, was to be appointed joint king's advocate in August 1589, while he was in Denmark, and he was knighted shortly afterwards. To help defray the expenses of the mission to Denmark, King James suggested to Edinburgh that if it paid the lawyer 2,000 merks he could be useful to the town by representing the interests of the burghs in the negotiations. Edinburgh took the hint and paid up, but decided that rather that relying on an appointee of the king, Skene, to represent burgh interests, it would be better to nominate their own man to accompany the mission — William Fowler, poet and nominal parson of Hawick, who was given 500 merks.[12] Inclusion on the mission was to be advantageous to the careers of both men. Skene was to become a lord of session and clerk register in 1594, and Fowler gained a more immediate reward, being appointed master of requests and secretary depute to his new queen, Anne of Denmark, in Oslo in October 1589. [13]

George Young held the office of secretary-depute to James VI, and acted as secretary to the mission. Thus the five-man team comprised a great noble, a lesser noble, a gentleman lawyer; and two other lawyers. one of whom acted as secretary. They 'past foruard in thair ambassadge magnificklie,' sailing from Leith on 18 June 1589. The indefatigable Colonel William Stewart, determined not to be left out of the action, had been hovering in the background, and sailed from Aberdeen shortly afterwards, perhaps with some late instructions from the king.[14] Indeed, it is possible that he carried a comprehensive revision of the opening position to be taken in negotiations by the Earl Marischal.

The version of James's instructions to be followed in discussions of the marriage that is usually cited was obtained by English agents in Scotland. But the proposals actually made by the ambassadors to the Danes, as revealed in the Danish Account, differ greatly. The explanation is evidently that the terms were modified at the last minute, perhaps before the earl sailed, or perhaps just afterwards, the new terms being sent with Stewart. The changes probably arose from realisation that the original terms proposed for a treaty were wildly unrealistic, either through over-optimism or, as those tending to conspiracy theories believed, because Chancellor Thirlestane had deliberately drafted proposals which he knew the Danes

19

would reject, as he still opposed the marriage.[15] Probably, the Scots were, as was usual in negotiations, resolved to begin by asking for far more than they would be prepared to settle for at the end of the day, to allow for flexibility and concession during negotiations. But they quickly realised that the first set of demands was too inflated to be credible even in such a tactical context, and therefore the terms were changed drastically. To take just one example: it had originally been intended that a dowry of £1,000,000 Scots for Princess Anne be requested: in the revised instructions this was halved to £500,000: and in the event the Scots were to settle in the treaty for £150,000.[16]

At last decisive moves towards a marriage had been made, and anticipation grew in Scotland. News — and rumours — of developments came from merchant ships arriving from Denmark. The ambassadors had landed at Copenhagen on 29 June, and had been greeted with great honour — and no doubt relief, as it was said the nobility had been assembled awaiting the tardy Scots for twenty days. The Danes were treating the marriage as a certainty. The bride was said to be busy learning French so she could talk to her husband — a rather surprising choice of language. Perhaps it was assumed that just as civilised Danes at their court spoke German, so the Scots court would speak French. Sixteen ships were ready to carry Anne to Scotland. Rich provision had been made of clothing, jewels and furnishings for horses, coaches and women (an interesting trio). More than 300 tailors and embroiderers had been at work for three months preparing for the great event and assembling Anne's trousseau. Or so rumour alleged. James's mouth no doubt watered at such stories of the wealth of his prospective in-laws, but indications that the arrival of his bride might not be long delayed also caused some panic. James still had no palace in a fit condition to receive her, let alone food and furnishings for the necessary celebrations. He had not even got suitable clothes for himself ready. Broad hints were dropped that financial help from Queen Elizabeth was urgently necessary if he was not to be disgraced.

As to James's own attitude to the prospect of becoming a married man, reports were mixed. He was growing in affection for Anne and talked of her virtues: or, he was a cold wooer, still not in a hurry for marriage. Such contradictions may well reflect ambivalences in James himself, as he waited in nervous anticipation for his unseen bride.[17]

NEGOTIATIONS AND PROXY MARRIAGE

Meanwhile, James had a country to govern, and he moved north east to deal with the problems caused by unruly Catholic nobles there. On 22 July official news from Denmark at last arrived, brought by three of his ambassadors, Lord Dingwall, Skene and Young, along with William Fowler. They landed at Aberdeen, presumably knowing the king was in the north, and next day travelled to see the king at the laird of Boyne's house. Their report indicated that the Danes had made magnificent preparations on the assumption that the marriage would go ahead, but were complaining about the excessive demands made by the Scots. They had already spent much, and now the Scots were making huge demands concerning the dowry and other matters. Kings, said the Danes loftily, should marry for love and alliances, not money. Moreover, Anne was so in love with James that she would die if the match was broken off. The Danes were playing the romance-is-all card. Implausible, but good publicity.

The Scots ambassadors had, it seemed, been outmanoeuvred, their attempts at hard negotiations being met by the pretence that the Danes were offended, as they had thought that the marriage was already settled and there was little to negotiate about. As should have been predicted, the Danes also expressed offence at the presence of the 'Swedish' Lord Dingwall on the mission. The Earl Marischal had felt that in the circumstances it was necessary to refer matters back to James. Meanwhile, to pass the time, he had set off on a tourist jaunt to see the cities of north west Germany!

Instead of a wife James had received news of further complications. There were still rumours about his lack of enthusiasm for matrimony, and that Queen Elizabeth was trying to prevent him marrying. But by this time James seems to have made up his mind. On 3 August Dingwall and his colleagues were dispatched back to Denmark with instructions which were evidently to accept what the Danes had offered. James had recognised that he could not withdraw at this stage without loss of honour and protests within Scotland. To save face over his climbdown he blamed Colonel Stewart for committing him too deeply — and claimed haughtily that he would not play the merchant for his wife by quibbling over the tocher. Another dig at the mercantile origins of the Danish dynasty. They had claimed that his demands were exorbitant: his response was that he would not resort to such base haggling. But while thus still indulging in the posturing of diplomatic exchanges, by now James's personal inclinations were firmly in favour of the marriage.[18] He astonished everyone by changing from the cold wooer to the passionate lover. Having at last accepted marriage, he would fulfil his romantic role with enthusiasm.

Events in this prolonged stop-go long-distance romance now accelerated with a speed that threw James into a brief frenzy of activity. The negotiations (described in the Danish Account below) were quickly completed. On 28 August Colonel Stewart, no doubt determined that he should be the first bearer of the glad tidings, landed at Leith and hastened to Stirling to tell the king that he was a married man. The ceremony, with the Earl Marischal acting as James's proxy, had taken place on 20 August. James greeted the news with a mixture of joy and amazement, and rushed to Edinburgh to supervise the preparations for Anne's arrival, which was expected shortly. Holyrood Palace had to be in a fit state to welcome his bride: and Holyrood Abbey had to be ready for the royal couple to get married in.[19]

James and Anne were from one perspective married already, from another about to be married. Civil law was satisfied that a valid marriage had taken place in Kronborg Castle. Canon law, the law of the church, insisted its formalities and ceremonies were what really constituted marriage, and these were still to come. Confusingly, however, none of the sources (or, it seems, later historians) make the distinction between civil and canon law. Writers who record two 'marriages' two ceremonies give no explanation. Thus an English representative first referred to the marriage as having already taken place, then went on to say it would be held at Holyrood on 29 September. [20]

It had been agreed that the Danes would see to the civil marriage, and the Scots would look after the religious side of things. No description of the civil marriage itself has survived in either Danish or Scottish sources. But a paper does exist drawn up in advance to outline the conduct of the ceremony. This can be used to reconstruct events with some confidence. Impersonal preliminaries took place in the morning — the swearing by the Scots to the contract agreed. Then, after a meal — which the Scots took on their own, indicating that this was a low key affair rather than a show occasion — came the personal. It was probably at this point that the Earl Marischal on his king's behalf gave Anne jewels worth £12,600 Scots.[21]; and it may be that some music written specially for the marriage was performed at now as well — the *Harmonia Gratulatoria Nuptis et Honori...Iacobi VI* composed by Abraham Praetorius, cantor in Copenhagen.[22] Finally, the royal couple, with the Earl Marischal as James's proxy, entered a bedchamber, each preceded by twelves of their countrymen bearing coloured torches, and were symbolically put to bed. Even if they was still no marriage in the eyes of the church, symbolic consummation was regarded as permissible.

CHAPTER 3

STORM-TOSSED LOVERS

By the time James first heard (28 August) of his marriage, preparations for Anne's voyage to Scotland were reaching a climax. The previous day Christian IV had written to James telling him of the arrangements made. Anne would be accompanied to Scotland by Peder Munk, Breide Ranzau, Dr Paul Kniblo, and Niels Krag.[1] The delegation was a suitably distinguished one. Peder Munk was Admiral of Denmark and a member of the council of regents.[2] He commanded the fleet which was about to sail, but was to gain little honour from the mission. After the failure of the attempts to reach Scotland he put the blame on his fellow member of the regency council, Christoffer Valkendorf.[3] Munk had quarrelled with him previously, and now alleged that Valkendorf's incompetence had led to some of the ships in the the fleet not being in a seaworthy condition. Neils Krag was a noted philologist, historian and diplomat, whose career evidently benefited from the Scots contacts he was now establishing. In 1592 he and Steen Bille were to be sent to Scotland to negotiate on disputes concerning of Queen Anne's property. Krag's resolute stand for the queen's interests won him the favour of James VI, who is said to have 'admitted him to the Scottish nobility' on 1 August 1592. In 1594 he was appointed royal historiographer in Denmark, and tradition claims that Scottish influence lay behind the appointment: Peter Young had discussed with him errors relating to Danish history in George Buchanan's history of Scotland, and urged that Krag be commissioned to write a history of Denmark which would correct them.[4] Paul Kniblo was a Dutchman in Danish service,[5] while Breide Rantzau was a councillor of the realm, a member of one of the greatest of Danish noble families.[6]

Reports that Anne and her fleet had sailed on 1 September intensified excitement in Scotland — though in reality she did not sail until 5 September. Then came anticlimax, as the days and weeks passed and no fleet was sighted in the Forth. The reasons for the delay were well understood: contrary winds, which were making the journey to Scotland difficult. At last on 15 September

STORM-TOSSED LOVERS

some definite news arrived. Lord Dingwall landed and reported that his ship had sailed from Elsinore with the Danish fleet and had last seen it near the Skaw, the northernmost point of the Danish mainland. Naturally this raised apprehensions: if the Scottish ship had got through, why were the Danes unable to do so? Presumably they had been trapped by westerly winds — and soon after Dingwall's arrival more contrary winds arose. At James's instigation 24 September was declared a public fast, with prayers for Anne's preservation. By early October merchant ships were arriving which had sailed from Denmark long after the Danish fleet, and in a superstitious age men began to discern ominous portents of disaster in chance accidents. When the Danish fleet had been preparing to sail, guns firing salutes had twice burst, causing deaths and injuries, while in the Forth a ship under sail collided with and sank a boat crossing from Burntisland to Leith. Nearly all those on board the latter were drowned, including Janet Kennedy, wife of Sir Andrew Melville, the master of the king's household. A former servant of Mary Queen of Scots in England, Janet had been summoned to be a member of the new queen's household. Such disasters were seen as sinister straws in the contrary winds.

Desperate for news, on 28 September James dispatched Colonel Stewart in search of the Earl Marischal, with a letter to him which insultingly (no doubt through impatience) began with the phrase already cited — 'My little fat pork,' demanding information and wishing him a speedy voyage. Stewart also carried a letter to Anne, expressing his fears and anxieties about her fate in the storms, tactfully written in the French language she had been reported as learning.

Stewart found the Danish fleet at Flekkerøy off the southern tip of Norway on 4 October. Munk and the Danish envoys accompanying Anne had just written to Queen Sophia and the Danish regents about the delays caused by storms, and on Stewart's arrival they penned a letter to James. Four times they had been driven back to harbour by storms, and on the last attempt to get to Scotland the seasick Princess Anne had not eaten for three days. Marischal and the other Scots ambassadors had reluctantly agreed, after two days of argument, that the voyage should be abandoned for the winter. Then Stewart had arrived and demanded in the king's name that his bride be delivered. On 7 October, however, the previous decision was confirmed. In the minds of all concerned must have been the thought that while failure to deliver Anne promptly might

25

bring disapproval, a princess drowned or dead from exhaustion would bring disgrace. Were there frightening recollections of how, long ago in 1290, the child Margaret Queen of Scots, the Maid of Norway, had died in Orkney after an autumn voyage from Norway? That event had led to disputes for the Scottish throne and the long Wars of Independence with England.

Anne must have expected to reach Scotland after a voyage of only a few days. Instead, it took fifty days of storm and stress even to get her to Oslo. She must have been weakened by seasickness and demoralised. Ships needed repair and re-provisioning. The decision to abandon the voyage was humiliating for the Danes, but wise.

Having decided to play safe, the Danes wrote to James to tell him that Anne and the Scottish ambassadors had been sent to Oslo in the few ships that remained seaworthy. One of the Scots ships set off immediately for home with the message — and arrived in Scotland on 10 October, demonstrating how simple the voyage could be, if only the Danes had managed to get their timing right. The news it brought dispelled James's worst fears: but it brought him no wife. Steen Bille[7] and Andrew Sinclair[8] gave first-hand accounts of dramatic events. Anne was in good health in spite of prolonged storms and great danger. Many of the Danish ships were now leaking so badly that they were hardly fit to sail to Scotland. Some of the great ships, intended to impress the Scots with Danish naval strength, now wallowed in Norwegian fjords, seeking suitable weather to take Anne on the last leg of her journey to Oslo; the rest were returning to Copenhagen. The Scots had urged that Anne be transferred aboard the lighter Scottish ships which could make it to Scotland, but the Danes refused, and in view of the intensity of the equinoctial storms had recommended that her voyage be delayed until the spring.

Clearly each side had its own priorities. The Danes saw their's as lying in ensuring Anne's safety and in maintaining national honour, by having their fleet deliver Anne to Scotland with suitable pomp, while the Scots saw the priority as being the prompt delivery of a bride to their impatient king. Eventually the Earl Marischal had agreed with the Danes that seeking safety in Oslo made sense. The fact that the ship which carried Bille and Sinclair to Scotland with this news had only taken three days for the passage indicates that it had had favourable weather and must have

STORM-TOSSED LOVERS

added to the frustration of all concerned. Impatiently James muttered complaints about Thirlestane and others who had delayed the marriage until so late in the year — and doubtless about his fat little pork and the Danes who always seemed to choose the wrong moment to set sail.[9]

By now James was playing the frustrated lover with a zeal that suggests genuine emotion as well as politic calculation. Every day was like a year while his love and joy was parted from him, according to this passionate and true lover.[10] His romantic enthusiasm led him to pen two sonnets stuffed with classical allusions, 'A complaint against the contrary wyndes that hindered the Queene to com to Scotland from Denmarke,' as well as a number of other love poems.[11]

However, at least the delay provided time for one complication to be resolved: the attitude of Queen Elizabeth to the marriage. Even before news of the event arrived, the English had realised that the marriage was likely to go ahead, and had decided not to oppose it. James's decision to go ahead without the humiliation of virtually asking Elizabeth for permission to marry had paid off. On 18 August instructions were issued to the English agent in Edinburgh that it was not to be said that Elizabeth was against the marriage. Two days later this became, rather less grudgingly, that Elizabeth would allow the marriage since James was resolved on it.[12] This was hardly surprising — Elizabeth had no real reason for objecting to the match, and James and his representatives urged its advantages as a Protestant alliance on her. Colonel Stewart even claimed that Scotland and Denmark once joined together could persuade the king of Spain to make peace with England.

James was eager to have English support not just for political reasons but also in order to persuade Elizabeth to give him additional financial help at so expensive a time. Her assumption that her agreement to his marriage was necessary might be insulting, but had to be ignored as he needed to be bailed out. Not ungenerously in the circumstances, Elizabeth sent him £2,000 sterling's worth of gilt and silver plate to grace the royal tables or to be used as gifts.[13]

This was most encouraging to James, but it was embarrassing as well. He had talked of urgent need for help. But the conventional privilege which tolerates the late arrival of brides looked in this case likely to have to be stretched to cover months, so the urgency had vanished. Similarly the hectic preparations made in Edinburgh

SCOTLAND'S LAST ROYAL WEDDING

for Anne's arrival[14] were wasted. So too were the urgent requests which had been dispatched to landowners urging them to send the king supplies of fat beef (on the hoof) and mutton, wild fowl and other foodstuffs for the celebrations welcoming 'the Quene our bedfellow' who was 'hourlie louked for to arrive'.[15]

James now determined on a romantic rescue operation. The hereditary admiral of Scotland, the earl of Bothwell, would be sent with a small fleet to seek out Anne and bring her to her new husband and home. Unfortunately while the admiral was willing in principle, he demanded money to equip his expedition, and this James was unable to provide. Melting down Elizabeth's recently arrived plate would hardly be tactful.

Here Thirlestane saw an opportunity to regain his credit with the king, weakened by recent events. He and his friends would gather and pay for the ships, and he himself would lead the matrimonial rescue expedition. In this project lie salvation for himself as well as for Anne. He was generally thought to have opposed the marriage, and certainly he had delayed it. If the bride did not arrive soon his unpopularity would intensify further, and if the king had to wait throughout the winter for her, his complaints about the delay being Thirlestane's fault would surely intensify.[16] Thirlestane's political career, based entirely on royal favour, was unlikely to survive such a winter of royal discontent.

Thus far Thirlestane's offer to go and bring Anne to Scotland makes sense. On the other hand, his Norwegian venture would mean that he and the king would be separated for a considerable period of time, and that was something which a politician so dependent on favour would hardly risk. Hostile voices might well gain the king's ear. Thirlestane was not so foolish as to make such a blunder, and it seems highly likely that when he put forward his proposal to go to Norway he had already reached a secret agreement with the king that they would sail together. But this element of the plan had to be kept secret because there would be almost universal opposition to it. For the king to leave his kingdom on a winter voyage with an inevitable element of risk would be seen as folly, dangerous both for the king and for the precarious stability of Scotland. It was irresponsible.

Which man first proposed to make the joint voyage? If it was the king who first resolved to sail to claim his lady, then Thirlestane had had to make sure he went too (by offering to make the preparations), for the sake of his political survival. But equally, if Thirlestane first thought of putting the king under an additional obligation to him by financing the voyage, he had to protect his interests by taking he king with him.

On balance, it seems most likely that the initiative came from the king. The delay in the arrival of his wife was damaging to his own reputation as well as to Thirlestane's, reviving gossip about how uninterested in marriage he seemed. Anne was his betrothed, virtually his spouse (he already referred to her as the queen): it looked bad that he sat doing nothing when she was threatened by tempests and risked being marooned in the wilds of Norway through a hard winter. Politically, some gesture had to be made to show how keen he was to experience matrimonial bliss, how he was in command, not a mere victim of circumstances. To calculation was added genuine feeling. However briefly, James does seem to have been in love, though with a girl he had never met. Sadly, perhaps that was the only circumstance in which he could ever love one.

Nonetheless, he was a lover, and thus honour bound to go to the rescue of his damsel, who was so clearly distressed.

Inevitably, the scale of the preparations for Thirlestane's departure soon began to rouse suspicions. The ships being seemed to be taking on board an amazingly lavish cargo of delicate foods and wines, and the number of officials and royal servants making preparations to sail seemed inappropriately large. The privy council met several times in Leith to supervise preparations, while orders were sent to many ports to supply ships at their own expense. Rumours spread wildly, but the king blandly denied everything, letting as few as possible into his secret. In Edinburgh there was bitterness at the idea of a king deserting his kingdom (it was realised he probably would not return before the spring if he did sail), and threats as to what he would find on his return if he sailed. Some of the nobility suggested keeping a close watch on his movements, and stopping him embarking by force if necessary. Betting on James's intentions became widespread. Thomas Fowler, the English representative, wondered that Thirlestane would be so foolish as to plan such an enterprise without consulting any of the old nobility.[17] But Thirlestane himself was gambling. If his venture succeeded, he would get the credit — with the queen as well as the king — for at last bringing the royal couple together, and thus secure his position.

SCOTLAND'S LAST ROYAL WEDDING

The king continued his hidden preparations, drafting instructions for the government of the country in his absence and justifications of his actions. By 17 October he had let his privy council into his confidence, and it was beginning to prepare for government in his absence.[18] On Sunday 19 October, in the dark of early evening, he planned to slip on board ship at Leith, but a storm made this impossible. Not until late evening of 22 October was he able to sail, leaving orders dated at Leith that day. [19]

The declaration he left explaining his actions is an extraordinary document seeking to justify an extraordinary decision. In a long reign full of decisions, good and bad, James can seldom have made a more bizarre one. The reasons in favour of the enterprise have already been outlined, but it can only have been irrational obsession (otherwise known as love) with Anne which led him to so dangerous an act. A king's place, unless leading armies of invasion or very occasionally making royal visits with serious diplomatic purposes, was in his kingdom. Government was personal government, much dependent on the character and authority of the individual. Take away that presence, and stability was in danger. If such generalisations could be applied to any kingdom, they had particular force in Scotland at the end of the 1580s. Though the last few years had seen relative stability, the earlier years of the decade had been marked by a succession of coups. Though most welcomed the emergence of an adult monarch after long years of turbulent royal minority, there were still elements in the nobility willing to use force to advance their political ends, and some Catholics in the north ready to plot with foreign powers. An insecure order had been achieved. Respect for James was slowly growing. For the king to endanger all this by secretly deserting the kingdom for (as it turned out) over six months was surely a folly explicable only by royal infatuation.

Possibly, however, James recalled that his mother had been brought up in France and married while there, and more to the point his grandfather James V had visited France to marry and bring home his bride. A precedent had been established. Why shouldn't he too get an overseas trip out of his marriage? True, the Danes hadn't invited him, but now he had a good excuse for simply turning up.

Knowing how great the controversy would be when a king vanished, James did all he could to calm fears and ensure that the true situation (or rather, his version of events) would be publicised and regarded as credible. He wrote out the declaration to be issued after his departure in his own hand so its contents could not be doubted. He had, he related, been found fault with by all for delaying his marriage so long. He was alone, without father, mother, brother or sister, king of Scots and heir apparent of England. His isolation was held to make him weak, and he was disdained for not providing for the succession. Indeed, the 'lang delay' (which James thus admitted to) led many to say that he was unable to provide for the succession, as if he were of barren stock.

Seldom do kings discuss with their subjects rumours of royal impotence. Anyway, James related that these and other reasons had led him to hasten his marriage. As to his own nature, God was his witness, he could have abstained from marriage longer were it not for the good of his country. Thus even when setting off to claim his bride, James seemed to show lack of enthusiasm for doing his patriotic sexual duty. However, it seems probable that James was not meaning to indicate distaste for the whole business, but rather to make the point that in leaving his kingdom he was not carried away by passion. He was acting rationally. It had been determined that he should marry in the current year by the three estates. Since Anne could not come to him, he would go to her. This was his own princely decision. First he had intended to sail with Bothwell. When that plan fell through James had said he would sail even if only one ship was available. Thirlestane had then made his offer to provide ships, to counter the rumour that he opposed the marriage, to serve the king, and for fear he would sail by himself. James claimed he had not told Thirlestane he intended to sail with him: the impression given is this was a last minute surprise sprung on Thirlestane, who therefore could not be blamed for the king leaving.[20]

Thus James's declaration was as much directed towards arguing that Thirlestane was innocent of involving the king in the venture as towards explaining the king's own actions. And on neither count was it convincing. So much protestation about Thirlestane's innocence was likely to intensify belief in his involvement, and the idea that James had to sail because he had undertaken to the estates to marry in 1589 was ridiculous.

A king who has been accused of personal timidity who now hazarded a winter voyage on notoriously dangerous seas. A king generally indifferent to women who set out on a romantic quest. A king who prided himself on his kingcraft, his grasp of the realities of power and its limitations, risking losing the respect and authority he had begun to gain from his subjects by unnecessarily absenting himself from his kingdom. But at least passion did not prevent James from taking account of the political problems that would be caused by his absence. He made careful arrangements for government in his absence. His privy council should meet regularly in Edinburgh, with the king's closest relative and most senior noble, the duke of Lennox,[21] as president. Second to him in authority in the state was to be the admiral, the earl of Bothwell — perhaps chosen on the basis that this turbulent man was one of those most likely to cause trouble, but could be bought off for a time with a grant of legitimate authority. Groups of nobles were appointed to attend the council in turn to help govern the country, while Lord Hamilton was to have special authority in the difficult Border area, acting in consultation with local notables.

In the event this delegation of power worked. Order and stability were maintained in James's absence. His calculated risk paid off. The decision to sail had been a bad one, but was retrospectively justified by its results.[22]

In a letter to his council James declared that he hoped to be back in Scotland with his bride within twenty days. Whether this reflected what he really thought, or what he calculated was most likely to be conducive to stability in his absence, is impossible to say. Like his subjects, he must have realised that there was a strong possibility of his having to — or deciding to — winter abroad. Whatever the risks, the attractions of such an eventuality must have been very much in his mind. The experience of possibly visiting a foreign court, touring a strange land, may have been as enticing as that of meeting his bride. It would be a break, welcome if irresponsible, from the difficulties of government in Scotland. More positively such a venture may well have been seen by James as an assertion of his status. He had ambitions to play a part on the European diplomatic scene, but had grown up in the shadow of Elizabeth and England, and could be perceived as a client king. His marriage to a foreign princess was in itself a political as well as a personal rite of passage, showing his independence. To go further, and actually visit a foreign court and making personal contacts useful for advancing his diplomatic dreams of a Protestant

STORM-TOSSED LOVERS

alliance would do more to establish him as an independent ruler, with policies of his own, free from Elizabeth's apron-strings. His Danish visit represented a political coming of age, enhancing his status at home as well as abroad.

No complete list of the entourage which accompanied James on his voyage is known, but clearly it was large and splendidly equipped. The Earl Marischal's entourage had had to be sufficiently magnificent to honour the king's personal representative. James's own would have to be sufficient to make the splendour of a king in person clear even when he joined the earl's party. Included on the new voyage were six additional ambassadors to Denmark.[23] Maitland of Thirlestane; Sir Lewis Bellenden of Auchinoul and Broughton, justice clerk and governor of Linlithgow Palace;[24] Robert Douglas, collector general and provost of Lincluden;[25] Sir Patrick Vaus of Barnbarroch; Sir John Carmichael of that Ilk;[26] and Sir William Keith of Delny, master of the wardrobe. In one sense extra ambassadors might well have been needed to placate the Danes. Foreign royal visitors usually announced their intentions before dropping in. And a royal visitor whose presence carried derogatory implications about Danish seamanship through their inability to deliver one of their own princesses to Scotland might receive a cool welcome. Perhaps it was just as well that James's first destination was Norway rather than the Danish court, so the latter could have time to adjust to news of his presence before any face to face meeting took place. After all, when he landed he was a foreign sovereign entering a country without the permission of its own king.

CHAPTER 4

MARRIAGE IN NORWAY

> As on the wings of your enchanting fame
> I was transported ou'r the stormin' seas.[1]

Thus King James described his voyage to meet his new queen — who can't have been much impressed as she did not know English. Perhaps that was just as well, as the verse is poor stuff.

By 27 October James's ships had been seen off the coast of Norway, and on the 29th they were off the island of Flekkerøy. All were in good health, it was reported, and James had not been seasick.[2] His further progress was delayed by bad weather, but Steen Bille (who had been in Scotland and accompanied James on his voyage) set off for Oslo to bring news of the king's arrival. A cannon fired in salute by the king's ship on his departure was fully loaded by mistake, and killed a boy on another ship — or severed the arm of a kinsman of Bille's, by another account. Thus the omens remained bad.[3] A rather better one was that, according to the Danish Account, James insisted when he landed on Fleckkerøy on sleeping in the same farmhouse as Anne had done some weeks before, declaring that he desired to sleep where she had slept. No doubt there were jokes that when bride and groom shared a bed it was usual for them both to be in it at the same time, but it was all the same a suitably romantic gesture.

With James now landed in Norway the Danish Account takes up the story of his movements and actions, but there is a good deal to be added from other sources. James took three weeks to reach Oslo, arriving only after delays caused by 'mikle foull wather of a stormie wintar.'[4] On his way he stopped at Tønsberg, and it has been suggested that he probably 'resided at the mansion of Jarlsberg Hovegaard, an ancient royal residence about half a mile from Tønsberg.' The Danish Account however says he stayed in Jørgen Lauritsen's house for six nights. Certainly he attended worship in the Marien Kirke on 16 November when his chaplain, David Lindsay,[5] preached to him. Subsequently a little wooden panel was attached to the pew used by James, recording his visit in letters of gold. The church has been destroyed, but the panel survives, commemorating the unexpected visit of a foreign monarch to the little town.[6]

James's entry to Oslo took place on 19 November, the Scots party being escorted by Axel Gyldenstierne, the Danish governor of Norway and commander of Akershus Castle,[7] and Danish, Norwegian and Scottish nobles who had come to meet him. James went straight to the Old Bishops' Palace, to meet his bride. The building had been seized by the crown after the Reformation, and was occupied by the burgomaster of Oslo, Christen Mule. Dating originally from about 1200, the palace had been much altered. By the sixteenth century it housed kitchens and a chapel on the ground floor, with upper stories protruding and supported on wooden columns, thus forming a colonnade round the building. The second floor contained bedrooms, the first the great hall, the scene of the royal meeting.[8]

The 'official' version of the meeting in the Danish Account blandly says that James stayed with Anne for about half an hour, before leaving for the house he was to lodge in. A Scottish chronicler is less smooth, and indicates both James's impatience to meet his bride — and that in the first moments of their meeting differences in national customs caused dispute between them. James

> immediately at his coming passed quickly with boots and all to her highness. The rest of his company went to his own lodging taken against his coming. His Majesty minded to give the queen a kiss after the Scots fashion at meeting, which she refused as not being the form of her country. Marry, after a few words privately spoken between His Majesty and her, there passed familiarity and kisses.[9]

Having her husband erupt into her presence without even bothering to take his boots or coat off, and then break the codes of manners she was used to by trying to kiss her in public, perhaps did not conform to Anne's vision of what her first meeting with her husband should be like. Still, it displayed a flattering ardour. And after James had taken her aside and no doubt pointed out that obedience was due to a husband, and she needed to get used to Scottish customs, his meeting with Anne was evidently successful. 'A joyfull meiting on all sydis' was one report.[10] James got his public kisses and familiarity, and no doubt felt himself to be the macho hero of the hour sweeping all aside to claim his bride. From then on, in all probability, anticlimax, with his ardour evaporating on contact with reality.

SCOTLAND'S LAST ROYAL WEDDING

James probably rested for the next few days, though he ratified his marriage contract on 21 November.[11] Two days later he was back in the great hall of the Old Bishops' Palace for a church wedding ceremony. Now that he had joined his bride, it was appropriate that this take place without waiting until the couple returned to Scotland. For those hastening to prepare Holyrood for such a ceremony without adequate resources this was no doubt a great relief. The burden of organisation fell on the Danes instead.

The ceremony was conducted 'with all the splendour possible at that time and place.' The Danish Account thus indicates that all that could be done without proper advance preparation in Oslo in winter had been done, but the implication is clearly that James's marriage had not been as magnificent as it should have been.[12] Policy was also involved, however, in James's marriage on the cheap. It had been his responsibility to arrange — and pay for — a suitably regal ceremony in Scotland, the Danes having paid for the civil affair. But he had now turned up as an uninvited guest to get married in Norway. Therefore the Danish council had sent orders that if the religious ceremony did take place in Oslo it should be kept cheap.[13] Did they suspect that one of his motives for coming had been to avoid paying for his own marriage? If so, it is possible they were right. Perhaps a small-scale 'special circumstances' wedding in provincial Oslo was better than a scruffy one in Edinburgh displaying royal poverty.

It is not surprising to find the banquet that followed the wedding described unenthusiastically as reasonable, given the circumstances.[14] The Danish Account, perhaps in embarrassment, does not even mention the banquet. This may have been the occasion at which the rector of Oslo, Jacob Jacobsen Wolf, added to the festivities by reciting his Latin verses commemorating the wedding.[15]

If financial considerations stinted the wedding feast, they also dominated the following day. James made the customary 'morning-gift' to his bride. The Danes had insisted that Anne be granted property in Scotland equal in value to twice her dowry. The marriage contract had specified that she should have the palace of Linlithgow, the castle of Falkland and a third of the king's property. Subsequently the Danes had, it seems, complained that this was not enough — or perhaps that it was too vague. Consequently James now granted her the Lordship of Dunfermline north of the Forth in addition to the other properties — now defined as the

MARRIAGE IN NORWAY

palaces of Linlithgow and Dunfermline and the county of Fife.[16] That James had indeed tried to evade granting Anne as much as the Danes had stipulated seems indicated by a clause in his draft instructions to his ambassadors. If absolutely necessary, they were to offer a third of his property to Anne — but they were to avoid putting a value on this.[17] The Danish council, on the other hand, had sent instructions that the details of the gift were to be fully settled while James was still in Norway.[18]

Now that his marriage had been successfully accomplished, James issued an act exonerating the Earl Marischal and his colleagues for their proceedings as ambassadors.[19] William Fowler was appointed master of requests and secretary depute to Queen Anne — her secretary being Calixtus Schein, who had come from Denmark with her.[20] Another Scot in becoming a member of the new queen's household moved at one stroke from a disgraced exile to being a royal official. David Cunningham of Robertland had played a leading role in organising and carrying out in 1586 one of the most notorious assassinations of the time in Scotland. The earl of Eglinton, long at feud with the Cunninghams, had been ambushed, together with some of his servants, and shot and hacked to death. Robertland, regarded as the leader of the assassins, had fled to Denmark, and had found powerful friends there. Christian IV and the Danish regents had already written to James asking that he be pardoned. Now, in Oslo, Anne's ladies in waiting, and perhaps the new queen herself urged that a pardon be granted. The Earl Marischal and Thirlestane added their support. James gave way to this pressure, and Robertland is said to have become Anne's master-stabler — though a 1591 household list makes him sewer, the official responsible for tables and seating at meals, and for the serving and tasting of dishes.[21] To have a known murderer as your food-taster seems an odd way of trying to avoid being poisoned.

Long before James's arrival in Oslo the Danes had resolved that Anne should return to Denmark for the winter — by land. Travelling south before crossing to Denmark, she would only have a very short sea journey to make after her recent terrifying experiences. Queen Sophia had travelled north in November to meet her daughter at Varberg, coming no further as that would have meant entering Swedish territory. But news that James had landed in Norway had reached Oslo before Anne had left, so the journey had been abandoned and Sophia returned to Denmark.[22]

37

SCOTLAND'S LAST ROYAL WEDDING

Now the plans were revived. James accepted suggestions that he should not seek a winter return to Scotland with his bride. At first James had proposed wintering in Oslo, but the Danish court had been horrified by the suggestion. It would be highly unpleasant for everyone, and the winter was already showing signs of being a severe one. By 1 December the harbour at Copenhagen was already closed by ice. Perhaps, it was surmised, James did not want to suggest coming to Denmark without being invited. It seems likely that this was the case — James wanted to visit Denmark but was being careful not to be presumptuous.[23] To assure him that he would be a welcome guest two councillors, Korfit Wiffert and Jørgen Brahe, were dispatched from Copenhagen on 26 November, arriving in Oslo on 10 December.[24] They brought letters from Christian IV and Queen Sophia begging James to come and spend the winter with them. The long dark nights would make it difficult for him to return home, and the cold and ice would be much greater in Norway than in Denmark. The royal party was to travel south by land, and arrangements were being made for its safe passage across the corridor of Swedish territory which reached the sea at the mouth of the Göta River.[25]

Even before the formal invitation arrived, James had begun his preparations for a prolonged stay abroad. Whether or not he stayed in Oslo, he had no immediate intention of returning to Scotland, and prudence indicated that he should cut the size of his retinue. It had made a suitable grand show for the wedding (though there had been hardly anyone there to appreciate it), and James would doubtless have liked to reach the Danish court with it in full strength, but he could not afford it. This, no doubt, was a relief to the Danes, who would be expected to show hospitality. Therefore on 30 November about fifty Scots left for home, leaving only forty or fifty to accompany the king.[26] Yet again, the Scots seemed able to cross the winter seas though the Danes couldn't — though of course far greater risks could be taken with the lives of courtiers than princesses.

Some of those who left gained immediate reward for their services. One of them was Vaus of Barnbarroch. As a leaving present James issued him with a new charter for his lands, which in future were to be held from the crown for the nominal annual payment of one rose — the symbol of love. Quite why of all those involved Vaus was singled out for this romantically symbolic gift is obscure.[27]

MARRIAGE IN NORWAY

That James was enjoying his foreign jaunt he indicated in a letter dated 1 December, the day after most of those sent back to Scotland had left, addressed to Lord John Hamilton and entrusted to Colonel William Stewart. 'In a worde, all thingis ar succeidit with me sen [since] my pairting according to uishe [wish],' he wrote, before signing off 'Youre maister in the aulde mainer, James R.'[28] The general report those returning to Scotland brought was similar. James was in good health and contented with his wife; all things were answerable to his heart's desire.[29]

Before he left Oslo there was also the need to reward in a suitable manner Danes who had welcomed and entertained him, and the silverware supplied by Queen Elizabeth, which he had brought with him, allowed him to make suitably lavish gestures. Bishop Jens Nilssøn, as the Danish Account relates, received two gilded silver plates. Thirlestane was in charge of the king's 'cupboard' containing the plate, and he was ordered to select from it a basin and a laver (jug), with six cups and their covers, and a covered 'saltfatt' (salt cellar), as a gift for Steen Brahe. Thirlestane was then to choose the next best pieces of the same types to be given to Axel Gyldenstierne. The rest of the contents of the cupboard were to become Thirlestane's own property, in recompense of his work and great expenses in accompanying the king and giving out silver work at his command.[30] In exhausting this source of gifts before he left Oslo James was no doubt counting on the fact that he now had Anne's dowry at his disposal and could use it in Denmark for similar royal munificence.

Most of James's entourage departed ahead of him, on 15 December, perhaps to help prepare for his arrival in Denmark. Queen Sophia had ordered Gert Rantzau to prepare rooms in Kronborg Castle, beside Elsinore, for the royal couple and the nobles accompanying them. The rest of his retinue was to be accommodated in the town of Elsinore.[31]

CHAPTER 5

WINTER JOURNEY

James and Anne left Oslo by sledge at eight o'clock on the morning of 22 December, a week after the young bride had celebrated her fifteenth birthday. At their departure James stood up in his sledge and bade all present good-night in both Scots and Danish, according to the Danish Account. Either the royal command of Danish was defective or the royal head was befuddled by the excessive drinking for which the Danes were notorious. Or perhaps, in the pitch dark of a northern winter morning, good-night seemed appropriate.

The Danish Account briefly narrates the progress of the royal party southwards, but several incidents on the journey deserve further discussion. One episode is included in the Account — rather surprisingly, as it generally glosses over controversial matters. James reached Bohus, on the Swedish border, on 1 January 1590. On Sunday 4 January Queen Anne heard a sermon in German in her own apartments. In the church there was a Danish service. After it was over, a chair was prepared for King James, and Henrik Gyldenstierne,[1] the governor of Bohus Castle, went to the altar and ordered that the candles be removed. Mickel Basse (Bartz),[2] the priest, objected that this was an infringement of the freedom of the church. But the candles were duly removed, and only then did James and his retinue entered the church for a service in Scots. The Danish Account does not mention such events in connection with James's earlier attendances at church services in Norway, but it seems likely that what was notable about what happened at Bohus was not that ornaments were removed, but that a priest ventured to protest. A letter of March 1590 records that when James attended church in Denmark the tapers, candlesticks, altar cloths and vestments were all removed by his chaplain so nothing should offend the Calvinist king and his councillors.[3]

Does the removal of such trappings indicate that at this stage of his life James found them offensive? In later years he was of course to favour the more elaborate worship of the Church of England over the stark worship of the Church of Scotland. Or was the purging of Danish kirks for Scottish worship insisted on not so much by the king as by David Lindsay, his chaplain, representing the Presbyterian-inclined general assembly of the Church of Scotland? Since his baptism as a Catholic as an infant, James had only been exposed to the plain Calvinist worship of the Scottish church. In Norway and Denmark even though the churches were purged of anything offensive that was moveable before he worshipped, he must have seen the Lutheran church interiors in much their normal state, and learnt of the worship that took place in them. What influence did such experiences have? Did they induce thoughts of more elaborate church furnishings and worship for Scotland? It is impossible to answer, but these were the only occasions that James had to experience first-hand the ways of any church other than the Scottish Calvinist one before his move to England in 1603.

Dispute over religious practices may also explain an odd traditional anecdote about James's journey. At 'Quille,' it is said, a blind old man, 'Gjedda' or 'Gaedda,' was parish minister. When he greeted James the king showed little respect and laughed at the minister's long white beard, whereupon the old man retired to his room and refused to come out until the royal party had left. The anecdote makes the insult personal, and indicates behaviour on James's part which is out of character. Was the minister's indignation really a reaction to re-arrangements of his church insisted on for James's worship?[4]

The Danish Account mentions the religious incident at Bohus. It remains completely silent about a second, diplomatic, incident that occurred there, merely recording without explanation that the royal couple remained a full week at Bohus before proceeding south. Why this delay? The answer lies in a diplomatic blunder too embarrassing to the Danes to be recalled in a report to their king. The Danes at the time held much of what is now southern Sweden, and a narrow strip of land along the west coast which almost provided a land link with Norway. But at one point, south of Bohus, a corridor of Swedish territory reached the west coast. Internationally, it was a very sensitive area. The Danes wanted it because it would give them an unbroken land link between their territories in Sweden and their Norwegian kingdom. Moreover, if they controlled the whole west coast, they could confine Swedish shipping to the Baltic, only letting Swedish ships out through he Sound on their own terms. For these very reasons, the Swedes had fought hard — and successfully — to maintain this free opening to the seas of the rest of the world. A generation later the Swedes were to found Gotenburg at this spot to exploit its strategic potential.

James and his party had to cross this Swedish corridor, but the king was evidently unaware of the careful preparations necessary, the niceties to be observed to preserve both Swedish and Danish face. The Danes, of course, well knew the possible difficulties. All that was necessary must be done to avoid provoking an incident. For the Swedes to refuse a royal guest of the Danes permission to travel south, thus flaunting their sovereignty in the area, would be a public humiliation for Denmark.

The Danes had, therefore, been careful to apply in good time on behalf of James for passage through Sweden. The instructions to Korfit Wiffert of Malmö Castle, Jörgen Brahe of Landskrona and Dr Paul Kniblo, dated 26 November, which had dispatched them to Norway to meet James, had also told them to ask the Swedish governor of Älvsborg (Jören Ericksson Ulfsparre) for permission for James to pass through Swedish territory.[5] By 30 November the Danish council had also written to Erik Gustavsen Stanbuk, governor of Vestland, to ask for passage for James and his party. The next day the council sent to its representatives in Oslo telling them of this, and asking them to indicate to James that it would not be beneath his dignity to apply himself to the Swedish governor of Älvsborg for safe passage.[6]

This was reasonable: a king wanting to cross another king's territory should surely send greetings and formally seek permission. But James failed to take the Danish hint that royal protocol required that he himself approach the Swedes. Given that King Johan III of Sweden was notoriously touchy and suspicious, this was folly. Johan's reaction to James's discourtesy was predictable. He ordered Jörgen Ulfsparre to keep the king of Scots out of Swedish territory, by force if necessary. Only after he had applied for, and received, a safe conduct from Johan himself was this young whipper-snapper of a foreign king to be allowed entry. When James did ultimately cross the Swedish corridor, he was to be shown all due respect — but beyond that was to be made to pay for what he needed.[7]

It may not have been until they reached Bohus that James's Danish hosts found out that their journey had not been cleared by the Swedes. When James realised the situation, he hastily sent Captain William Murray to Stockholm to obtain the necessary safe-

WINTER JOURNEY

conduct from King Johan — and, no doubt, offer apologies.[8] Meanwhile, the Danes and their Scottish guests were humiliated by having to wait at Bohus.

At least Johan sent the necessary orders promptly, not wishing to push his moral advantage too far. James immediately hastened through Swedish territory, accompanied by a Swedish captain and 400 men,[9] — even though Queen Anne was ill. The writer of the Danish Account, in his efforts to avoid mentioning the whole unfortunate incident, makes James seem simply heartless in treating his bride with so little consideration. But clearly he and his Danish hosts were impatient and humiliated, and wanted to get the matter settled as soon as possible.

Once through the Swedish corridor, the royal party moved on to Varberg — where a further delay of six days occurred. Again the Account gives no explanation. Perhaps Anne was still unwell, or perhaps arrangements for the reception of the Scots king in Denmark were not yet complete. Part of the problem may have been that travel arrangements had been disrupted by the sudden death of the governor of Varberg Castle, Anders Bing, on 16 December.

His death caused some consternation in official Danish circles. His widow proposed to follow the local custom in bitterly cold winters when the ground was frozen hard and transport difficult. This was to leave the corpse unburied until the thaw in spring — or, in this case, at least until after the Scottish royal guests had been suitably entertained. However, the Danish court decided that having the royal visit coincide with a funeral was better than having to admit that the deceased governor was being stored deep-frozen. Such a custom might be made necessary by the climate, but it was evidently considered not socially acceptable. Bing's widow was therefore instructed that under no circumstances was her husband's funeral to be delayed. He was to be buried in the church at Varberg until spring, when he could be disinterred and reburied at his own parish church. Instructions were also sent to Jørgen Brahe to hasten ahead of James's party to take over responsibility for the necessary arrangements for receiving James at Varberg.[10]

Bing was buried on 10 January. James and Anne did not take part in the funeral procession, on the pretext that they were too tired from travelling. But they were present when the procession left the castle, and James wrote a Latin epitaph for Bing during the funeral service (on Sunday 11 January). He ordered that this be

SCOTLAND'S LAST ROYAL WEDDING

inscribed on the tomb, to honour a worthy man and in eternal memory of James's own presence.[11]

The stop at Varberg marked a change in modes of transport for James and Anne. The Danish council had arranged for carriages to be waiting there to meet him, so the sledges which had carried them from Oslo were abandoned.[12] A final delay occurred at Helsingborg, where the royal party had to wait for three days for a 'tempest of weather' to abate and allow them to cross to Elsinore.[13] When Anne had left her homeland four months before she must have done so with the expectation that she would never see it again, but now she was returning briefly to the palaces and people of her childhood.

CHAPTER 6

DANISH DIVERSIONS

On 21 January a small boat decked in red velvet came to collect the royal couple and carry them to Elsinore. There a formal procession was marshalled, with each of James's Scots councillors paired with a member of the Danish council.[1] The procession made its way to Kronborg Castle, where James was greeted by Queen Sophia, his mother-in-law, by his young brothers-in-law King Christian IV, by Duke Ulrick, Christian's younger brother, and by the four regents of the regency council.

Thus having journeyed 'throw manie woods and wildernes, in confermed frost and snaw' James reached his destination, and he stayed there until spring. One Scots account simply notes of his months in Denmark that James 'maid guid cheir and drank stoutlie till the springtyme.'[2] While this picture of single-minded hedonism is an exaggeration, there is a good deal of truth in it. James was on his holidays and determined to make the most of it.

The Denmark in which he found himself was a small nation in European terms, but still one of greater wealth and international significance than his native Scotland. As well as Denmark itself, its kings ruled the kingdom of Norway, territories in north Germany, and much of what is now southern Sweden. To wealth based on land and her own trade was added the unique asset of the Sound Tolls: customs duties levied on all ships sailing through the narrow Øresund, the Danish-controlled passage in and out of the Baltic. James must have envied the power and wealth of the Danish monarchy, the relative political stability and orderliness of the land. In all-European terms he might still be on the periphery in Denmark, but he was a good deal nearer the centre than in Scotland.

While noting the power of the Danish monarchy he may well not have been able to see (as historians do, with the benefit of hindsight) how its power relative to that of the nobility was increasing in the long term as the result of changes in land holding following the Reformation. He would probably have been more impressed by the power of the nobility, especially during a royal

SCOTLAND'S LAST ROYAL WEDDING

minority in which its representatives were acting as regents. Further, the monarchy was still — in theory at least — elective.

Danish society contained perhaps 250 noble families, and whereas many of them were modest in their resources and quite a few were slipping into an impoverished state, a distinct élite higher nobility of relatively few families was emerging and coming to dominate society and politics. But though this differentiation within the nobility was increasing the power of a small group of families, it also made them more and more dependent on the monarchy, as they identified with its interests rather than with that of the nobility as a whole. Their seeming domination was to turn out, in the long term, to be partly an illusion. But for the moment it was accepted that an elected king governed with consent of his council of state, made up of such higher nobles and churchmen.[3]

A prestigious monarchy and a rich, powerful and cultured noble élite thus existed side by side. There must have seemed to James something of a paradox here. On the one hand a strong monarchy with power and prestige; on the other hand noble power institutionalised through elective monarchy and the council in a way in which it was not in Scotland. As a king he would have taken it for granted that the nobility had a major part to play in ruling a country. But the balance of power between them varied from one polity to another. He must have pondered whether the king of Denmark was better off, with a fairly law-abiding nobility with such institutionalised power, or he himself as king of Scots with nobles whose rights in the state were ill defined, but who in practice were frequently disobedient and sometimes threatening.

The entrenched power of the Danish nobles was something which certainly was not clearly perceived by their Scots counterparts. The Scottish nobility evidently had considerable reservations about their king developing too close an interest in Danish society, because what the titled nobility of Scotland perceived in Denmark was a society without a properly graduated, hierarchical nobility. Scandinavia was slow to follow the rest of Europe in creating elaborate hierarchies of ranks (dukes. marquises, earls, lords and so on) through which to order and formalise noble status. Sweden only began introducing such titles in the 1560s, and Denmark was to delay the process for another century.[4] Confusing titles, the trappings of power and status, with the reality, some at least of the Scottish nobility saw Danish society as lacking a proper aristocracy. That the king should marry a representative of such a society was a bit worrying: that he should actually go and visit that society, giving him time to study what was seen as a state with strong monarchy and no real nobility, was deeply worrying.

The feature of Danish society which aroused most widespread comment from Scots, however, was not its political system, but the drinking that seemed central to national culture. There was general agreement in Europe that the Danes drank more heavily than any other people on the continent. Drunkenness was regarded with national pride among the Danes. Here was something they were better at than anyone else. Being entertained by the Danes was sometimes feared — honour would require acceptance of the massive amounts of drink hospitably offered. King Frederick II had given an outstanding lead to his people here. His drinking was famous or — infamous — leading to incidents like the one in which the befuddled king had managed to fall, horse and all, from a bridge into a river. Earlier, he had got involved in a drunken fight at his sister's wedding. Celebration at the christening of Prince Christian in 1577 had featured a mock battle between the Philistines and the Hebrews. It had veered violently off course when the Philistines, drink taken, decided that they were tired of always being defeated, as the script required. They therefore proceeded to beat up the Hebrews. The Danish nobility, determined not to miss the fun, then piled in enthusiastically.[5]

The firing of cannon as healths were drunk in the Castle of Elsinore (Kronborg) is of course mentioned in *Hamlet*,[6] and Ben Jonson referred to 'The Danes that drench / Their cares in wine.' Thomas Nashe, however, refused the Danes per-eminence in drinking, coupling them with the Dutch — though he was evidently thinking of the commons rather than élites: both were 'simple honest men' who 'will be drunke and snort [snore] in the midst of dinner' and Nashe warned 'he hurts himself only that goes thither.'[7] But it is Fynes Moryson, the English traveller, who provides the best international comparative survey of drinking of the age. The Scots were heavier drinkers than the English. While they were not high on the European league table, 'I cannot altogether free them from the imputation of excesse, wherewith the popular voice chargeth them.' (Some things, it seems, don't change over the centuries). But the Germans scored more highly: 'this nation in generall, and every part or member thereof, practising night and

SCOTLAND'S LAST ROYAL WEDDING

day the faculty of drinking, become strong and invincible professors therein.' The Saxons were the worst of the Germans, but 'the Danes passe (if it be possible) their neighbour Saxons in the excesse of their drinking.'[8]

James appears to have done his best to maintain the honour of Scotland when it came to drinking, but while in Denmark he was also keen to see the sights and talk to famous men he knew by repute. The Danish Account does not give a full itinerary, but other sources help fill out the picture of his activities. His base was the royal residence of Kronborg Castle, dominating Elsinore — which was described by Fynes Moryson as 'a poore village, but much frequented by seafaring men.' The town derived its importance from being the centre for collection of the Sound Tolls, and the castle's cannon had a key role in enforcing the control of the Sound. A few years after James's visit Moryson had great difficulty in getting in to the castle because of the 'scrupulous and jealous nature' of the Danes. But disguising himself as a merchant and giving a large tip did the trick. Built round a courtyard, the best views were on the north side where the hundreds of ships passing through the Sound could be seen. Here Moryson found two rooms still called the King of Scotland's chambers. The apartments had been hung in red cloth, and the chairs and stools covered in it. Thus on his Danish holiday James was privileged to have rooms with a sea view — and within cannon shot, if not stone's throw, of it.[9] Doubtless he got the rooms with the views not out of courtesy alone. From his windows he could see enacted every day a living pageant of Danish power in action as ships of all nations were stopped and taxed.

James evidently stayed at Kronborg from his arrival on 21 January until early March.[10] Presumably he was at once resting after the strenuous journey from Denmark, getting to know his Danish in-laws, and waiting until the weather began to improve, the days get longer. On 7 March he ventured to Copenhagen. Moryson is again invaluable in describing what James found there. It was a city of 'no beauty or magnificence,' built of clay, timber and plaster, reasonably well fortified — it was the only walled city in the country. But even the freestone royal castle failed the Moryson magnificence test.[11] James's destination was not the castle but the 'royal academy' or university. Arriving with his retinue, as the Danish Account relates, he was greeted with two hours of discourses.

First to speak was Hans Olufsen Slangerup, professor of theology since 1586.[12] Following him there spoke Anders Christensen, who had been appointed professor of medicine in 1585, and was an innovator in being the first to teach practical anatomy there.[13] Finally Povel Mathias, the bishop of Zealand thanked the king for his visit. In return James emphasised his enthusiasm for the academic treat which had been laid on for him, saying that he had always been interested in literary — meaning intellectual — matters.

Later the king sent gifts to the bishop for the university — seven large books and a gilded cup — as well as a monetary gifts to the doctors who had presented him with a book (Slangerup and Christensen?) and to the hospital in Copenhagen.[14]

From Copenhagen James made his way to Roskilde, where he was on 11 and 12 March. At last he had reached a place that the critical Fynes Moryson was ready to approve — even if he merely calls it a fair and pleasant village.[15] The description ignores the main importance of Roskilde. Its great cathedral was the burial place of the Danish kings. The indefatigable Bishop Povel Mathias had hastened from Copenhagen to assemble the priests of his diocese to honour James, and he gave a Latin oration before them, at which James is said to have expressed himself well pleased.[16] But so far as James was concerned, the highlight of his visit was the opportunity to debate with the leading Danish theologian of the age. Niels Hemmingsen was an old man, having been born in 1513. He came from a fairly obscure family but had been able to study abroad through the help of an uncle (a blacksmith) and, later, of noble patrons. He had became professor of Greek in Copenhagen about 1543, and professor of theology in 1557, while his numerous works had been widely translated. The fact that though Lutheran in his basic theology, he was considerably influenced by Calvinist ideas adds interest to his conversations with the Calvinist King James. But he firmly maintained the Lutheran rejection of the central Calvinist doctrine of predestination.[17]

James excitedly declared that seeing and talking to Hemmingsen was one of his three most remarkable experiences in Denmark, according to a Danish priest, Christern Nielsen Brun, who may well have been at the assembly in Roskilde Cathedral. The other two outstanding experiences listed by the king were seeing the magnificent monument to Frederick II in the cathedral, and seeing churches free of idols and idolatry.[18] It may, indeed, have been after witnessing a communion service at Roskilde that James, according to Danish tradition, asked his Presbyterian ministers whether they did not find the Danish services with vestments and candles innocent and un-popish.[19] The two comments attributed to James — about lack of idolatry and about the acceptability of Danish church furnishings — may simply be different accounts of the same incident. But they do emphasise the religious education James was receiving on his travels. Primed by his own Calvinist chaplains, he had doubtless expected to be faced by unacceptable idolatry in Lutheran Denmark. Instead he evidently found nothing to object to in Danish services, and presumably felt the zeal of his religious mentors in whisking away the contamination of candles and altar cloths before he worshipped to be unnecessary. Moreover, while the Scots may have got away with such high-handed purging in small-town churches in Norway, it is likely that it was impossible to do so in the greater churches in Denmark. Certainly James was exposed to church music including instrumental accompaniment as well as singing at Roskilde. Payments to a musician for song books, and to 'Symon the violar,' who presented his own book to the king, were probably made at Roskilde. Other payments were to the keeper of the kirk, to the virgoner (player on the virginals) and musicians, and to the ringer of the bells in Roskilde.[20]

From Roskilde the king moved on to the great castle and palace of Frederiksborg, where he is recorded as giving money to the poor on 13 March. He can next be traced playing cards at Horsholm, south of Elsinore, on 19 March,[21] and he was up early enough the next morning to have landed on the island of Ven by 8 am.

This was another intellectual pilgrimage for James. Ven (or Hven) had been given by Frederick II to the foremost astronomer of the age, the great — if bloody-minded — Tyge (Tycho) Brahe.[22] On the island Brahe had constructed an astonishing laboratory, Uranienborg, and was developing a whole range of activities to back up his core scientific work. His main legacy was to be the compilation of lists of the precise positions of thousands of stars. Even though his work was done without the aid of the just-about-to-be invented telescope, they were so accurate that they were to play a key role in developing understanding of the motions of planets. Though James's attention was no doubt focused on Brahe and astronomy, he is also recorded distributing largess to the printer in 'Tichobravis Ile,' and to the masons, wrights and workmen constructing a paper mill and a corn mill.[23] Typically, it was not enough for Tyge Brahe to establish his own publishing press: he had to make his own paper as well.

Detail of James's reactions to Uranienborg are sadly lacking — why couldn't he have written a long gossipy letter to someone about it? It is known that he smiled on seeing in Tyge's library a portrait of his former tutor, George Buchanan, presented on an earlier visit by Peter Young.[24] As a memento of his visit James left a Latin couplet, presumably inscribed in a book:

> The Lion's wrath is noble
> Spare the conquered and overthrow the haughty.

The fierce or rampant lion is obviously the lion of Scotland, so James was announcing his ideal of himself as king, merciful to the submissive but determined to suppress the disobedient. Maitland of Thirlestane also contributed a verse indicating his admiration for Uranienborg.[25]

James's conversations with Tyge left a deep impression on him, as he recorded in 1593 when he granted Brahe's works copyright in Scotland for thirty years. After praising the scientist's learning he continued:

> Nor am I acquainted with these things from the relation of others, or from a mere perusal of your [published] works: but I have seen them with my own eyes, and heard them with my own ears, in your residence at Uranienborg, during the various learned and agreeable conversations which I then held with you, which even now effect my mind to such a degree, that it is difficult to decide, whether I recollect them with greater pleasure or admiration.

For good measure James also sent Brahe a couple more Latin epigrams.[26]

The king left Ven at 3pm — so he hadn't had much time for the 'various…conversations' he claimed to have had with Brahe. Probably he returned directly to Kronborg. He is recorded hunting on 27 March, and an English agent writing from Kronborg on 5 April reported that James had returned from a progress in which he had visited some of the king of Denmark's towns and houses, and had had good hunting according to the fashion of the country.[27]

Thus James's sight-seeing was interspersed with hunting. Gambling and drinking were also high ranking among his activities. Signs of the effects of the latter appear in some of his letters. Though James often wrote to close friends in an informal way, drink seems to

SCOTLAND'S LAST ROYAL WEDDING

have reinforced this tendency in Denmark. Two letters to Alexander Lindsay, a brother of the earl of Crawford, would seem to indicate as much. Lindsay was James's vice-chamberlain and a personal friend. He had been with James on his travels, but had been among those sent back to Scotland from Norway. He may have indicated that he feared that this was a sign that he had lost royal favour. James wrote to reassure him — and to urge him to marry Jean Lyon, the widow of the earl of Angus.

> Sandie,
> We are going on here in the auld way, and very merry. I'll not forget you when I come hame, — you shall be a Lord. But mind Jean Lyon, for her auld tout will make you a new horn,
>
> J.R.

The 'auld way' is evidently an alcoholic one, and the closing words are cheerfully obscene, it would seem.

Lindsay may have responded by indicating that the promise in the letter of elevation to the nobility, though gratifying, was worryingly vague, for James wrote again on the matter — more specifically, but no more soberly:

> Lett this assure you, in the inuiolabill worde of youre awin prince & maister, that quhen Godd randeris me in Skotlande, I sall irreuocablie, & with consent of Parliament, erect you the temporalitie of [the bishopric of] Murraye in a temporall lordshipp; and lett this serue for cure to youre present disease. From the castell of Croneburg, quhaire we are drinking & dryving ou'r in the aulde maner.

The 'disease' was presumably anxiety. 'Driving over' means passing time idly.[28] A not entirely sober servant in James's household confirms an alcoholic atmosphere. Great honour was being done them by the Danes, who provided brave entertainment. Time was passed merrily in hunting — but they were dying of thirst, cobwebs growing in their throats. James spoke often of Dives, thus comparing his lifestyle in Denmark with that of the rich man in the story of Lazarus, who was luxuriously clothed and 'fared sumptuously every day.' Presumably courtiers forbore to remind James that Dives was consigned to hell to pay for his earthly pleasures — or perhaps James himself was indicating that his Calvinist conscience was not entirely at ease with his lifestyle. The king, the report continued, was relieved at how little trouble there was within his own entourage or between Scots and Danes, as men who were continually drinking could seldom agree for long.[29]

DANISH DIVERSIONS

James's gambling led to a constant trickle of payments to him by Thirlestane to give him stakes to play with. If James ever won, he seems to have kept the winnings for his own pocket. Other payments record James rewarding servants at places he visited, making payments to the poor, and presenting suitable gifts to leading Danes: sometimes jewels, more often gold chains for men, rings for their wives. Financing the king in this lifestyle was obviously expensive, though bed and board were provided by his Danish hosts. At first the king's other daily expenses were paid by Thirlestane personally — with promise of subsequent repayment. Up to February 1590 Thirlestane had paid out nearly £6,000 Scots for preparing the ship which had brought James to Norway, and £5,000 in other expenses after the king had landed. But arrival in Denmark relieved the chancellor's pocket. In February the dowry of £150,000 Scots was paid, and as a bonus Queen Sophia made James a gift of £20,000 — perhaps intended to cover his expenses while in Denmark.[30] In spite of having the dowry to draw on, however, James was not above begging further favours from Queen Elizabeth: he did a deal whereby a George Mair, a Scotsman who was burgomaster of Elsinore, would provide furs and other necessities for Queen Anne free if James, in return, got the merchant the privilege of exporting some English cloth to Denmark free of customs duties.[31]

By April James was ready to return home: the perils of winter were past. But he allowed himself to be persuaded to stay on for a few extra weeks, in order to attend the wedding of his queen's sister, Princess Elizabeth, who was to marry Duke Henrik Julius of Braunschweig-Wolfenbüttel (Henry of Brunswick). For James the main attraction was probably not more royal ceremony and celebration so much as the opportunities that would be provided of meeting Brunswick and other German princes who attended the wedding. To a king ambitious to play a part in European diplomacy this was a golden opportunity to make himself known. Sadly, information as to what contacts he made is fragmentary — though it is known that he exchanged letters with the duke of Holstein, and that the duke of Brunswick presented him with a horse. Young Duke Philip II of Pomerania came to the wedding with Duke Ulrick of Mecklenburg and met James. Maitland's accounts of payments made from the tocher include items relating to jewels given to the princes at the Brunswick wedding. Four great diamonds and two great rubies in Thirlestane's care were also given away among other jewels presented to Queen Sophia, young Christian IV, and the princes.[32] One of James's representatives commented on James's stress on asserting his own importance and independence by emphasising his alliances and blood-connections with royal dynasties, and exchanging gifts was part of this. He 'would no longer be kept as a novice, but would be known.'[33] Playing on the international scene was increasing his confidence.

A meeting with one prince is commemorated by James's inscription in Duke Ulrick of Mecklenburg's *album amicorum* or autograph book — using the same couplet he had written for Tyge Brahe. Anne signed with a German inscription accepting that all was in the hands of God. Was this merely a pious generalisation or did it have specific reference to her own circumstances? She probably faced the prospect of having to leave again for Scotland with resignation rather than eager anticipation; and the same sentiment may have been her reaction to the prospect of a life wedded to King James.

Gert Rantzau used the blank leaves of a book of psalms for autographs, collecting those of Mecklenburg, James, and Anne, perhaps on the same occasion as the signing of the duke's own book. James omitted his epigram this time, but Anne again acknowledged all to be in the hands of God — this time in her newly-acquired French.[34]

Attending the wedding of Elizabeth and the duke of Brunswick on 19 April must have been one of the high points of James's stay in Scandinavia, so it is most frustrating that the Danish Account simply notes his presence in passing — and then equally abruptly records the fact that James and his queen sailed for Scotland two days later. Scottish sources are little more informative, though the gift to James of a hagbut (a kind of musket) and sword by Henrik Gyldenstierne is recorded, and payments to Danish kettle-drummers, trumpeters and violars hint at the ceremonial at the king's departure. Clearly it was a noisily festive occasion.[35]

Among the items taken on board before the king sailed were the remains of his dowry and the monetary gift from Queen Sophia. Of the total of £170,000 Scots, £108,000 remained on James's return to Scotland and was handed over to the comptroller. James had been extravagant — but his honour and that of Scotland had required lavish giving. That the remainder of this windfall was frittered away in the years that followed, instead of being treated as a valuable capital asset, is less excuseable.[36]

James had been on holiday. But all his cares had not been left behind in Scotland. From his arrival in Oslo his entourage had been split by dissension over precedence. If too much drink was not the problem, there were other causes of trouble. At the centre of the disputes were Thirlestane and the Earl Marischal. The bitterness against Thirlestane, the upstart who had the king's favour, had been exported in the person of Marischal, representative of the established nobility. A new dimension was added to the fears of the old nobility by the king's (and Thirlestane's) direct exposure to a Danish society which lacked a titled nobility and possessed a strong monarchy. What lessons might they learn from the example of Denmark? Marischal had thought he held the trump card which would put Thirlestane in his place. In Scotland Thirlestane had held precedence above all the nobility through holding the office of chancellor. But in Norway and Denmark, Marischal claimed, he outranked the jumped-up laird. As ambassador he was the king's personal representative, and had been the king's proxy at his civil wedding. He therefore claimed precedence immediately after the king.

The Thirlestane faction prevailed, however. Whatever precedence Marischal might have claimed as the king's proxy had lapsed, along with his authority as ambassador, once the king himself was present. Moreover, as if to punish Marischal and his supporters for their divisive posturings, Sir William Keith, the earl's kinsman, was deprived of his office as master of the wardrobe, being replaced by George Hume, after James complained that Keith wore richer clothing than his king. Marischal's request that Anne's dowry be used to pay the expenses he and his colleagues had incurred on their mission was also turned down, after Thirlestane insisted that the money should not be touched until they returned to Scotland — though in fact of course James himself spent much of it in Denmark.

Paranoia grew among the Marischal's faction, with rumours that the chancellor, in the subversive atmosphere of Denmark, was drafting new forms and fashions of government. The privy council would be abolished. Nobles would be barred from the exchequer. The court of session would be purged. Nobles would only be allowed to come to the royal court when sent for — and even then would only be allowed to bring a few servants. Granting of knighthoods would be strictly limited. Further, moving from rumour to fact, James sent Sir John Carmichael back to Scotland ahead of him with 4,000 thalers from the dowry to raise a paid royal guard of 200 men. This, it was feared, was intended to enforce the innovations in government, and in particular to bar the nobility from their traditional free access to the king. In all, an aristocratic nightmare.[37]

Obsessed with these visions of Danish-inspired absolutist conspiracy, the nobility overlooked the fact that in many respects they ought to welcome Danish influence. The Danish nobles might lack the outward pomp of titles, but they had the power. King Christian was reputed to be able to do little without the consent of his councillors.[38] Arguably, James had more to fear from the true example of Denmark than his nobles did.

In many ways James's European honeymoon had been a success. He had clearly, indeed startlingly, demonstrated his commitment to the Danish match. He had introduced himself personally at least to the fringes of the extended family of European royalty. In doing so he had shown himself ready to escape Queen Elizabeth's apron strings and act for himself. Not only had he upheld Scotland's honour abroad, his own subjects would surely treat him with more respect now he had been seen acting upon a European stage, and through the rite of marriage he had confirmed that he was a man, no longer a youth dependent on others. Thirlestane too could rejoice. The gamble of sponsoring the royal marriage jaunt had confirmed him in the king's favour — and won him the queen's. The uppity nobility had again been forced to back down, with the side-lining of the Earl Marischal.

Both king and chancellor were soon to find, however, that success created its own problems.

CHAPTER 7
SCOTTISH CELEBRATIONS

By the time James and his bride sailed triumphantly into the Firth of Forth in the spring of 1590 Scotland had had plenty of time to prepare for the new queen's arrival. She had first been expected the previous autumn, and there had been a number of false alarms since James had set off to find her, first suggesting that he would return with her immediately, then that he would sail early in 1590. Much that had been done proved unnecessary, being overtaken by events.[1]

Once it became clear in April that the royal couple's arrival was imminent, every effort was made to give the best possible impression to the Danish delegation accompanying James. While the 'strangers' were in town, beggars were to be removed from the streets of Edinburgh — as were those similar disfigurements, midden heaps. All vennels or closes were to be kept clean. As soon as the king's ship was sighted, bonfires were to be lit in front of the houses of the burgh.[2]

As soon as he arrived James added his own efforts to create a sanitised Scotland for his guests. No one, he decreed, was to molest, harm or injure the foreigners (perhaps the most basic concern all tourist authorities), and subjects were to act peacefully and avoid feuds.[3]

Five Danish and three Scots ships made up the little fleet which arrived at Leith. It would have been bigger if other ships had not set off to pursue a pirate vessel which had been sighted, the prospect of profit compensating for missing the pomp of the landing of the royal party. Led by the Danish ambassadors — Peder Munk, Breide Rantzau and Steen Brahe — the Danish party consisted of about 224 people, more than enough to be a severe strain on James's finances as their host. Entertaining them would cost £800 Scots a day, it was estimated, and hasty arrangements were made that whenever possible leading Danes should be boarded out with the nobility.[4]

The royal party landed in the late afternoon or early evening, to the accompaniment of salutes of cannon fire from the ships. At the lodgings prepared for the couple in Leith, James Elphinstone delivered a Latin oration, and the couple then passed to the parish church for a sermon — or perhaps the queen stayed behind, for by one account she was spared the sermon as it was in English (Scots) and thus would be incomprehensible to her.[5]

Provision of lodgings at Leith might have seemed simply a thoughtful gesture, so that the queen, tired from her voyage, would have no further travelling to do on the day that she landed. But she must surely have been exasperated to find that she saw no more of her new homeland than the port for nearly a week. There might have been plenty of time to arrange for the queen's arrival, but money had been so short that work on preparing Holyrood House was still in progress.[6] The Danish ambassadors quickly became impatient at what they saw as Scots tardiness — though the Danish Account's repeated emphasis on the ambassadors' wish to expedite matters may have been partly intended to impress the Danish authorities with their business-like efficiency. They were to stay for the queen's coronation, and were dismayed to be told it would not be until 17 May. In the meantime they decided to check up on the queen's 'morning gift' from James and other revenues being assigned to her. It was their duty to see that she got all she was entitled to. This at least got them out of the way, travelling round Fife and the Lothians. Not only did this temporarily stop them pestering James, but responsibility for hospitality to them and their followers could be passed to local nobles and lairds.

The old Scottish feudal custom of handing over a symbolic sample of the soil or turf of land when transferring possession of it evidently came as a surprise to the Danes. One would like to be able to read the thoughts of Peder Munk, admiral of Denmark, when at Falkland he had a stone and a handful of earth solemnly thrust upon him. But more worrying to the Danes was that they found Falkland, Dunfermline and Linlithgow were of much less value than they had been led to believe, and the palaces in some decay.[7]

The coronation duly took place at Holyrood on Sunday 17 May, described by the Danish Account with all the detail of ceremonial that the Danish court would require. But at one point a tactful economy with the truth is evident. One of the ministers conducting the ceremonies, Robert Bruce, made a short speech on passing Anne the sceptre. He acknowledged her as queen on behalf of the estates of the realm, and pledged obedience to her in all concerning the honour of God, the comfort of His church, and her welfare. Bruce's colleague David Lindsay then translated this into French so Anne could understand it. She assented to what had been said, and then went on to take her (strongly anti-Catholic) coronation oath. So far the Danish Account. But the Scots narrative of events adds an extra sentence at the end of Bruce's English speech that does not appear in the French version: 'and we creave from your Majestie the confessione of the faith and religion quhilk we professe.'[8]

There are two possible interpretations of this discrepancy. One is that the Danish author omitted the sentence as he knew that it would cause massive offence in Denmark. Anne had been promised the free exercise of her Lutheran faith, yet this sentence could be interpreted as meaning that pressure was being applied to try to get her to accept the Scottish Calvinist faith and confession. The other interpretation is that this sentence was no part of Bruce's speech, but was added in the Scots source to give the impression that she had accepted Calvinism, to satisfy Scots readers!

Luckily, no one at the time seems to have commented on this evident Calvinist attempt to embroil the queen in sectarian conflict, but another religious controversy effecting the coronation did lead to argument. Some of the Edinburgh ministers had wanted to ban unction — the anointing of the queen with oil — from the coronation, as a superstitious ceremony. But James had then threatened that if Robert Bruce refused to anoint the queen, the coronation would be delayed until a bishop could be present to administer unction. In these circumstances the Presbyterian-inclined ministers decided to submit. Their campaign against episcopal authority in the church had been largely successful. Bishops still existed, but had been successfully marginalised (as the fact that none had been summoned to the coronation indicates). Now the unction issue might lead to one being hauled out of obscurity and being given a leading role in the coronation. Better anoint the queen themselves, however distasteful the idea was, than let a hated bishop do it. As to the wider matter of the absence of bishops from the coronation, James had presumably agreed with the ministers that they should be kept away to avoid dispute. Certainly the cover story that there were no bishops because there had not been enough notice given of the coronation for them to come to Edinburgh is implausible.[9]

SCOTLAND'S LAST ROYAL WEDDING

Yet another religious squabble effected the final event in Queen Anne's formal reception in the new kingdom, her ceremonial entry to Edinburgh (Leith and Holyrood lay outside the boundaries of the town). It had been intended to hold the entry on the same day as the coronation, Sunday 17 May. But ministers objected that it was largely a secular event. Its pageantry and festivities would profane the Sabbath, and the king was persuaded to change the date to the following Tuesday, 19 May — doubtless to the exasperation of the Danes at further delay, but to the relief of the burgh, as preparations were not yet complete, in spite of all inhabitants being summoned to help on pain of fines.[10]

The ceremonial entry to a town was a well-established genre of Renaissance pageantry.[11] Many of the elements of such entries had became fairly standardised, and indeed the 1590 Edinburgh entry had so much in common with entries arranged by the burgh in 1561 (for Mary Queen of Scots) and 1579 (for James VI) that it has been remarked that it is as if the pageant imagination was bankrupt, with each event repeating themes presented on previous occasions.[12] This is perhaps too harsh. A fairly large degree of repetition of standard elements was only to be expected. Events in the 1590 pageants which have many parallels in other pageants included the use of 'whifflers,' walking ahead of the procession to clear the way through the crowd; 'moors' (here acting as the whifflers) or other exotic or outlandishly dressed figures; keys handed over by figures descending from above in some mechanical contrivance, accompanied by recitations of verses or by singing; tableaux of figures representing the virtues or other personifications, carrying their 'attributes' (symbolic objects by which they could be identified) and delivering appropriate speeches; portraits expounding royal genealogies; wine running at fountains with Bacchus presiding; the throwing of sweetmeats to the crowd; and the propine or gift to the person being honoured.[13]

As with the coronation, the Danish Account goes into great detail about the entry, for this was the sort of thing the Danish court would want to hear about. But the Account is only one of several descriptions of the entry, and (as the notes to the Account indicate) at a surprising number of points it is difficult to reconcile these sources. Some are clearly confused in places, and at some points there are inexplicable contradictions between sources. Perhaps in the midst of the noisy and elaborate festivities it proved impossible to record and interpret every event with complete accuracy — especially as Bacchus's fountain flowing with wine was resorted to for refreshment. Perhaps too there is a warning here: the planners of pageants and scholarly commentators may understand all the elaborate symbolism involved, but spectators often only partly comprehended what was going on, leading to garbled accounts of what took place.

For the entry Anne was brought by coach round the south of the burgh from Holyrood in the east, so she could make her entry through the West Port (Gate). Her coach then wound its way — with frequent stops — through the port and the Grassmarket, up the West Bow to the High Street, and down to St Giles's Church for a sermon and psalm singing. Here certainly preparations had been last minute. The 'scholar's loft' had been elaborately refurbished for the use of James and Anne, and work on this had continued through the previous night, poor boys being employed to hold candles so the wrights (carpenters) could see what they were doing.[14] Out of the church to more pageantry, down to the Netherbow and presentation of the burgh's gift of gold and diamonds to Anne, then out the Netherbow Port and down the Canongate back to Holyrood.

The ceremonies were at last complete and the royal couple could settle down to their lives together, though it was not until 27 May that the Danish envoys and their servants sailed. Anne must have seen them leave with deep melancholy, but to James and the Scots their departure must have been a vast relief. Supporting the Danish guests had been a strain. One estimate was that the cost was 1200 merks — about £200 sterling — a day.[15] A 'common contribution of certain noblemen and barons' was arranged, but even those who had promised to contribute could be slow in paying up.[16] The burgh of Edinburgh, having already financed the queen's entry, was one of the last to entertain the Danish ambassadors on a rota basis. On 24 May they had held a banquet for the ambassadors, though it 'seems to have been more remarkable for abundance than elegance.'[17]

A final expense James was probably glad to pay — that of giving the Danish ambassadors a suitable send-off. Before they boarded ship on 25 May they received gold chains and other gifts said to have been worth 4500 crowns, as well as having their ships stocked with food and wine. The Danes had been expensive, and had complained continually about the morning gift, and they had been exhausting, demanding guests. They had required company for their revels so far into the night that James had not been able to get more than three hours sleep a night.[18]

Still, if James and his subjects had had to spend much, there was some compensation: Anne's dowry, and presents on his wedding. Queen Elizabeth sent 'a fair cupboard of silver gilt cunningly wrought, and some cups of gold massive,' while ambassadors from the Netherlands presented 'a golden buist [box]' containing a promise written in gold lettering on parchment of an annual pension, and great cups of gold — two of which were so heavy they were hard to lift. Sadly, within a few years James's financial problems led him to have this gold and silver treasure melted down, just as the capital represented by the tocher was squandered.[19] A less tangible gift but an encouraging one for a king obsessed with becoming king of England also came from Queen Elizabeth. She marked his marriage by having him made a knight of the garter. To assure him that this honour was truly fit for a king she pointed out that no lesser men had been made knights at the same time: the only person elevated with him was King Henry IV of France — the former Henry III of Navarre, whose sister Catherine had once been considered as a wife for James.[20] Given that James is said to have had a particular fear of assassination, engrained by the bloody politics of mid sixteenth century Scotland, he probably was glad in retrospect to have avoided involvement in France's even bloodier dynastic conflicts. Henry had moved from the throne of Navarre to France on the murder of Henry III of France, and he himself was eventually to be assassinated.

1. Prospective bride: Princess Anne as a child — or possibly her elder sister Princess Elizabeth. By Hans Knieper. Both princesses were 'on offer', but by the time King James had made up his mind to a Danish match only Anne was available. (Courtesy Det Nationalhistoriske Museum pä Hillerod, Denmark.)

2. Father-in-law, deceased: King Frederick II of Denmark, father of Princess Anne. By Hans Knieper, 1581. The death of the overbearing, hot tempered and frequently drunk Frederick in 1588 may have hastened the marriage negotiations. (Courtesy Det Nationalhistoriske Museum pä Hillerod, Denmark.)

3. Mother-in-law: Queen Sophia, widow of Frederick II and mother of Anne of Denmark and Christian IV. (Courtesy De Danske Kongers Kronologiske Samling, Rosenburg, Copenhagen.)

4. *Brother-in-law: Christian IV of Denmark, Anne's little brother. He was to become one of Denmark's most ambitious and flamboyant kings.* (Courtesy De Danske Kongers Kronologiske Samling, Rosenborg, Copenhagen.)

5. Wooden tablet commemorating James VI's Visit to Tonsberg in 1589. The tablet used to mark the spot in the church where he sat to worship. The sudden arrival of a foreign king in the little town was clearly an event to be remembered. (Courtesy Vestfold Fylkesmuseum, Tonsberg, Norway.)

6. Sir John Maitland of Thirlstane peers out with suspicious appraisal. Switching rather late to support for the Danish marriage, he was confirmed in royal favour by the move — but then fell out with the new queen. Portrait by Adam de Colone. (Courtesy the Thirlestane Castle Trust.)

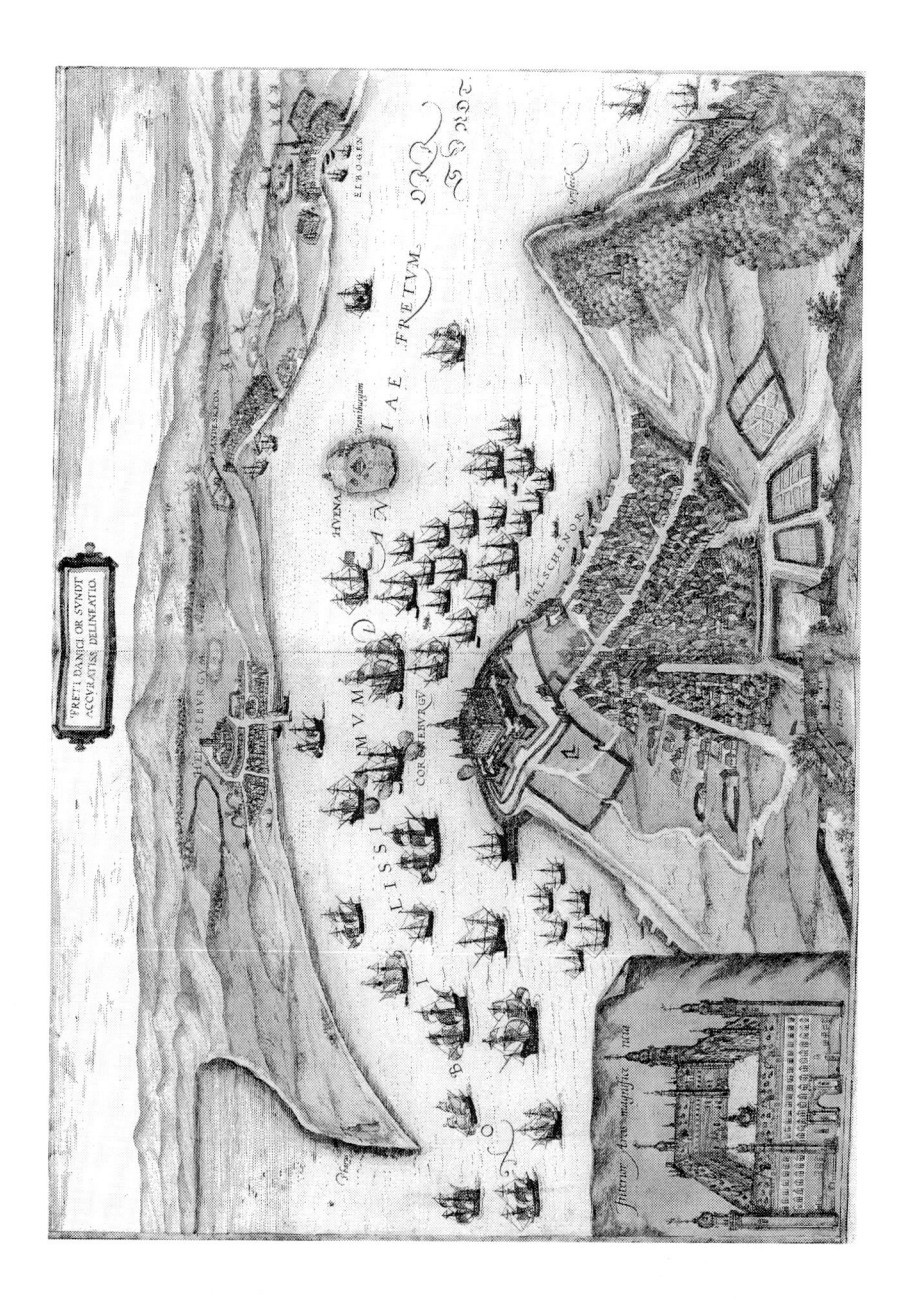

7. *Kronborg Castle and Elsinore. 'Coronburgum' dominates the town of 'Helschenor' and the Sound controlling entry to the Baltic. James VI was given rooms in the castle overlooking the Sound, so he could be impressed by the passing ships paying dues to the Danish crown. In this engraving some ships are firing salutes in acknowledgement of Danish power in these waters, and a gun from Kronborg replies. Across the sound James could see Helsingborg, from which he had crossed to Elsinore, and Tyge Brahe's island of Ven ('Hvena') lies in the sound itself.* Civitates Orbis Terrarum, *iv, plate 26.* (Courtesy the British Library.)

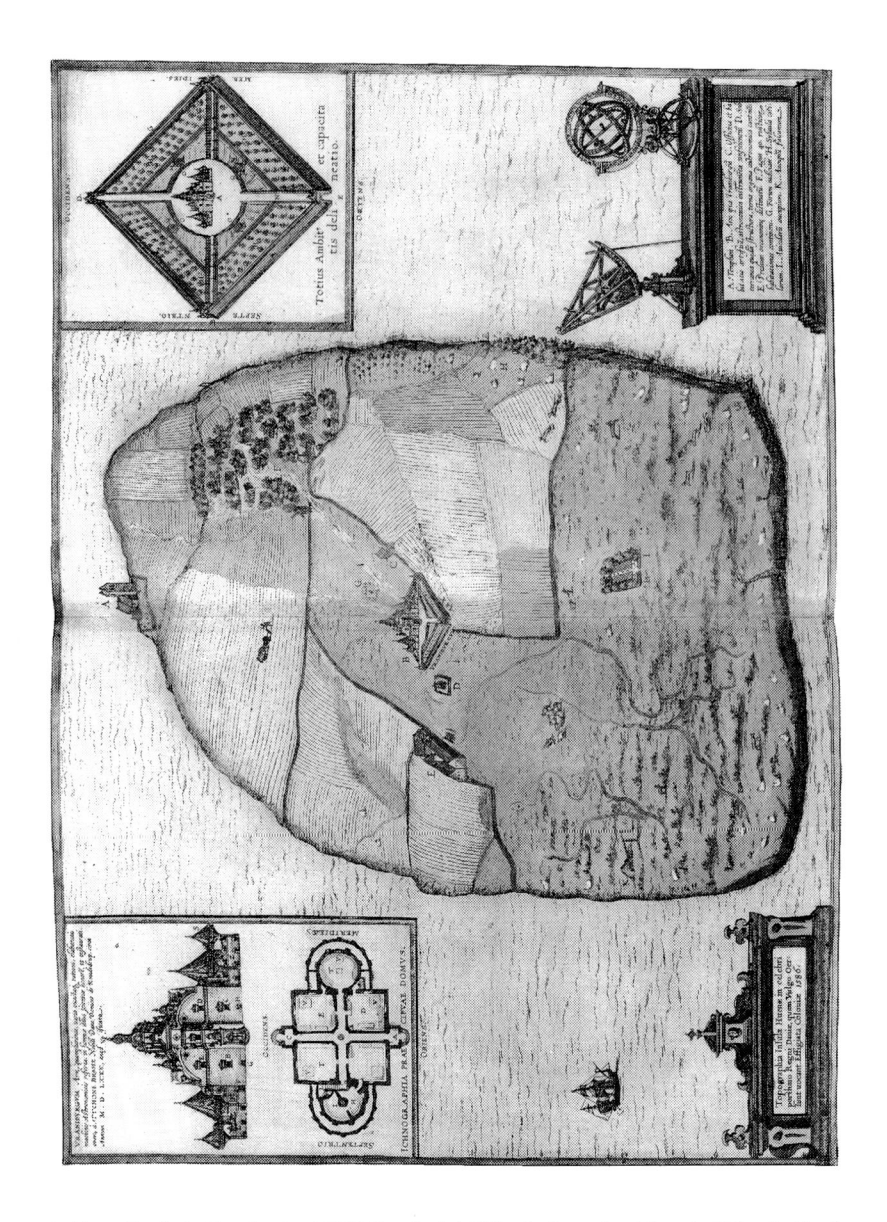

8. *Tyge Brahe's Empire in 1586. Frederick II had given the island of Ven to Brahe to encourage his remarkable astronomical observations, and Brahe had developed it into a sort of northern Renaissance scientific gentleman's paradise on earth. The centre of the island was dominated by Uranieborg, castle and observatory. The cultivated north of the island, with its little peasant village, provided for his material needs. Sjerneborg (Star Castle) was another observatory, built (partly underground to protect instruments from wind) south of Uranieborg ('D'). In a workshop astronomical instruments were built ('C'). Additional facilities included a tannery and a printing press, though work on the paper mill and corn mill, which James VI was to see under construction on his visit of 20 March 1590, had not yet begun. At the 'Forum Judicale' Brahe doubtless dispensed justice as owner of the land, while for his leisure pursuits falcons were kept for hunting, and the south of island abounded with rabbits, deer and foxes.* Civitates Orbis Terrarum, *iv, plate 27.* (Courtesy the British Library.)

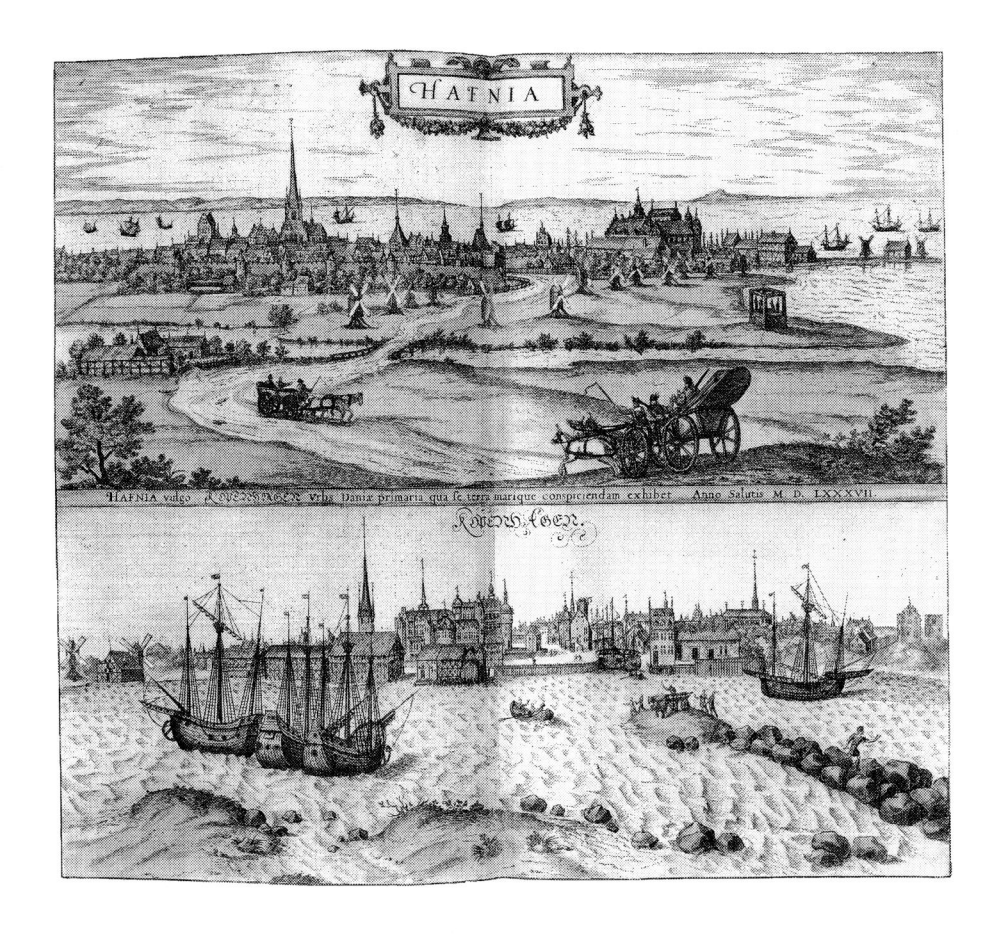

9. *Views of Copenhagen (Kobenhavn, or Hafnia)*. Civitates Orbis Terrarum, *iv, 28*. (Courtesy the British Library.)

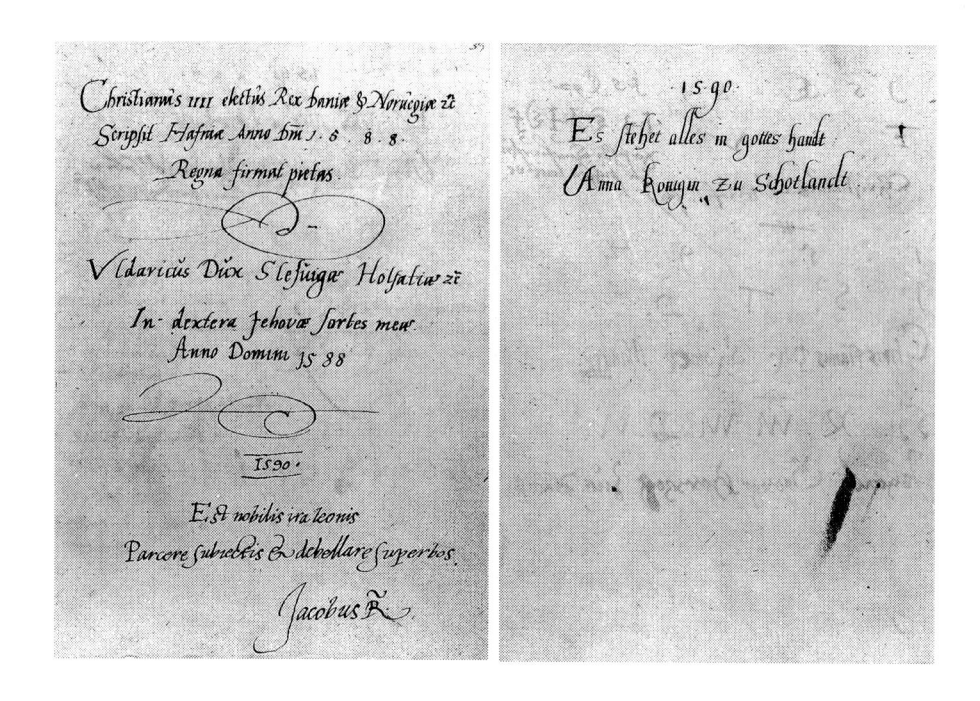

10. Signatures of James and Anne in the autograph book of Ulrich, Duke of Mecklenburg. Anne, writing in German (her first language), signs with her new title, 'Konigin zu Schotlandt.' Above James's signature, an earlier meeting of Mecklenburg with the duke of Schleswig-Holstein, and the accession of Christian IV, are commemorated. (Courtesy Det Kongelige Bibliotek, Copenhagen.)

11. Medal commemorating the marriage. Trashy royal memorabilia is nothing new. The two portraits are absurdly different in scale. The sentiment may be loyal but the execution is crude. (Courtesy the British Museum.)

12. Holyrood Palace, lying just east of Edinburgh was the main residence of the kings of Scots. The engraving dates from the mid seventeenth century but shows the palace much as it was when Queen Anne arrived in 1590.

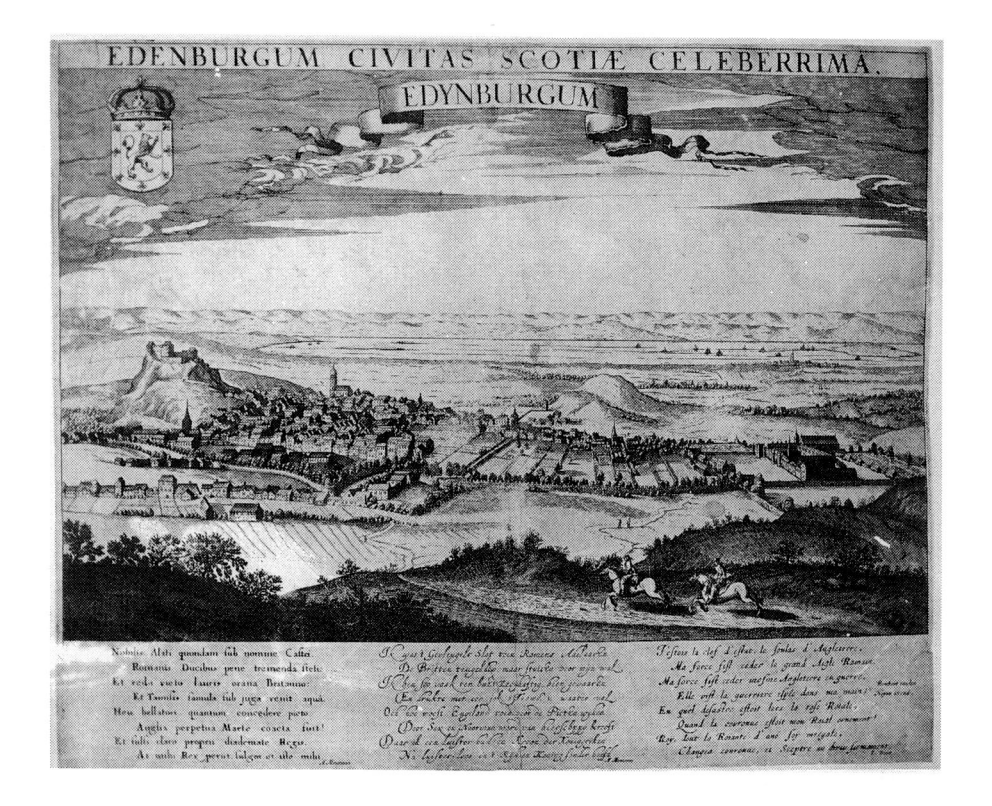

13. *Edinburgh in the mid seventeenth century. In this view from the south, the castle lies on the left, the palace of Holyrood on the right. For her ceremonial entry to Edinburgh Queen Anne was brought round outside the town walls from Holyrood to the West Port, just south of the castle, and then driven through the Grassmarket, up the West Bow, along the High Street to the East Port, and thence back to Holyrood. In the background lies the Firth of Forth, with the hills of Fife beyond. On the south shore to the right of the engraving Leith, where Anne had landed in Scotland, can just be seen.*

14. *The first fruit of the marriage. Prince Frederick Henry, aged two, almost disappears within his finery. The cherries symbolise sweetness or beauty of character.* (Courtesy the Earl of Rosebery.)

15. Ninteen-year-old Queen Anne. Portrait attributed to Adrain Vanson, 1595. (Courtesy the Scottish National Portrait Gallery.)

16. Twenty-nine-year-old King James. Portrait attributed to Adrian Vanson, 1595. The central setting of jewels in the king's hat form the letter A, referring to Anne. (Courtesy the Scottish National Portrait Gallery.)

CHAPTER 8

AND THEY DID NOT LIVE HAPPILY EVER AFTER

There is a great deal of information surviving about the marriage of James and Anne. But it tells us almost nothing about one of the key players. It is known that Princess Anne was frightened and seasick (not surprisingly) when at sea in the storms of autumn 1589. Her startled protest at James trying to kiss her at their first meeting is well known. And that she was unwell on the sledge journey south to Denmark is recorded. But that is just about all that is known about her feelings or reactions to events. At her coronation and her entry to Edinburgh a symbolic dummy could have been substituted for her person, so far as the historical sources go. Nothing is known of the fifteen year old's appearance during these events or her reactions to the rituals in which she played a central part. The Danish ambassadors, in their efforts to check that the properties promised were being settled on her showed concern for her financial welfare. But they make no comments on Anne's personal responses to taking her place in a new court in a foreign land. This may not be very remarkable: the trade in princesses was a matter much more of politics and property than of personalities. Yet in view of evidence that does emerge rather later, it seems ominous. Anne may well have already shown a tendency towards melancholy, in spite of the Danish servants and ladies in waiting who remained with her. Certainly she never sought to capitalise on her youth and sex to make any impact beyond the court. A visitor to court in June 1590 noted 'Our Quein carys a marvelus gravity, quhilk, with her partiall solitarines, contrar to the humor of our pepell, hath banis[h]ed all our ladys clein from her.'[1] As at Anne's first meeting with James in Oslo, it seems, she found Scots informality hard to adjust to. But it is hardly surprising that the young girl's reaction to her sudden arrival in an alien court as queen should lead her at first to withdraw into the little circle of those she knew, her Danish servants.

For all his initial romantic enthusiasm, James was not the lover to woo this rather lost child into acceptance of her lot and persuade her to play a more public role. James had no malice towards her, and indeed retained at least vestiges of fondness for her and concern for her welfare. But he had little desire for her company. Nonetheless, it turned out to be a good marriage. It produced male heirs to the throne.

James probably at first thought of his wife as something of a nonentity. He must have been disconcerted, therefore, to find once Anne had got settled in Scotland, that he had acquired a wife who was strong willed and fiercely determined to have what she saw as her rights recognised. She had a will of her own, and was prepared to fight for her own interests — financial and spiritual. She soon began to make some Scots friends, and through them was drawn into Scottish politics. It may be doubted how much she understood the complexities of factional infighting at court (did anyone?) and how far she merely supported those who became her friends, above all the countess of Huntly. Soon Anne's political involvement became entangled in a fight for her rights.

Maitland of Thirlestane, now promoted to Lord Thirlestane, in recognition of his services, remained at first the dominant figure at court, protected by the favour of the new queen as well as the king. His manoeuvres to turn his original opposition to the marriage into enthusiastic support had paid off splendidly. But Queen Anne quickly turned against him. She may well have been influenced by the many sly voices at court which sought to undermine the upstart, but she had personal reasons as well. Thirlestane, with his talent for upsetting people, evidently made comments to James about her which she regarded as disparaging — perhaps about her ill-informed attempts to intervene in public life — and this she bitterly resented. Moreover an ambiguity in the wording of part of her marriage settlement brought her interests into direct conflict with his, and this was seized upon by Thirlestane's opponents to poison her mind against him as someone who had sought to deprive her of her rights.

The problem was not (for once) the result of Thirlestane's tactlessness and arrogance, but of coincidence. The morning gift bestowed on Anne by James the day after their wedding had included among a number of properties the lands of the lordship of Dunfermline north of the River Forth. What precisely did this mean? Was it 'those lands of the lordship which lie north of the Forth, and no other lands of the lordship?' Or was it 'all the lands of the lordship of Dunfermline, which place lies north of the Forth'? In other words, had Anne been given all the lands of the lordship,

AND THEY DID NOT LIVE HAPPILY EVER AFTER

or only those north of the river? The intention had evidently been the latter. She was only to get part of the lordship. But the Danes insisted that she had been promised all of it. James had given way and assured them that the southern lands of the lordship, which had been alienated to others, would be redeemed and given to Anne. However, the property handed over to Anne in 1590 omitted these lands. James no doubt hoped that the ambassadors would not notice his sleight of hand and the matter would be forgotten. But the issue was brought to the attention of the Danes at the time of their departure from Scotland, evidently by John Lindsay of Menmuir. He urged that the Danes send further ambassadors to demand that Anne was granted her full rights.[2] Menmuir's intervention was no scrupulous reaction to malpractice, but an attack on Thirlestane. It was designed to embarrass him and, above all, to turn the new queen against him, for by coincidence Thirlestane had possession of many of the disputed lands. Naturally he was reluctant to give them up, so his enemies could portrayed him as a greedy noveau riche trying to cheat the innocent young queen out of her property. The coincidence that he held these lands was a gift to his enemies. Making the marriage had brought his career to its peak, with his ennoblement symbolising his triumph. Now it was to make a major contribution to his downfall.

Indignant at a daughter of Denmark being cheated, the Danish court intervened with relays of envoys to Scotland. In 1592 ambassadors arrived to carry out a minute investigation of Anne's rights. Eventually Thirlestane and others were forced to yield, surrendering their rights within the lordship of Dunfermline to the queen.[3] Not surprisingly the Danes remained suspicious, fearing further Scots sharp-practice, but when new Danish envoys arrived in 1593 they soon found reason for immediate worry about Anne's safety rather than her fortune. They were present during one of the wild earl of Bothwell's raids on the court, when he burst into the king's chamber with drawn sword. After checking on the queen's safety, the Danes demanded to know what was going on. On asking whether the king was being held captive or was at liberty, James evasively — and rather oddly — replied that he would leave it to his council to decide. While the Danes puzzled unhappily over this bewildering response, James got on with sorting out yet another political crisis.[4] No wonder the Danes left with deep foreboding about the situation in Scotland, and doubtless private thoughts that for James to follow 'the example of Denmark' in politics would be no bad thing. Christian IV was so concerned about the instability in Scotland that he sent James gunpowder, and promised to send three fully equipped warships if order was not restored by the spring. Rather less helpful was another gift from Christian — a well-travelled lion, which he himself had been sent by the king of Poland. Perhaps Christian felt James could do with a tactful reminder of his own motto about the wrath of the lion as a virtue in a ruler.[5] And of course a lion was a particularly suitable present for a king of Scots as the lion was the heraldic device of the kingdom. It also neatly got rid of an unwanted gift.

At least when Danish representatives returned in 1594 they came on a happier errand, for they attended the baptism of Anne's first child, Prince Henry Frederick.[6] The 'Frederick' commemorated Anne's father. The 'Henry' was more important. While it, in turn, stood for the prince's other grandfather, Henry, Lord Darnley, it was no coincidence that it was also the most commonly used name of past English sovereigns, and the name of Queen Elizabeth's father (and founder of the protestant regime she presided over), King Henry VIII. In naming his son and heir, James flattered his great southern patron — and underlined his claim that his family should succeed her on the English throne. Dynastically, the marriage had served its purpose admirably, by the prompt production of a healthy son. It was a triumph for Anne. In the months before the birth she must have recalled the stories of how, at her own birth twenty years before, her furious father had burst into her mother's bedchamber and denounced her for producing a second daughter when she had not yet produced a son. But for Anne all had gone well. Danish royal breeding stock had been vindicated.

The Danish envoys had congratulations to offer her and James, but were obsessed by the long delays in celebrating the baptism of the new prince. The king's ambition to put on a good show for an international audience as usual came into conflict with difficulties in raising money for such events. Almost last minute orders that the chapel of Stirling Castle, which was to be the scene of the ceremony, was to be completely rebuilt for the occasion suggest some lack of prior planning.

Anne had shown determination in insisting on her property rights, and proof of her ability to bear sons further strengthened her position. She also demonstrated that she had a will of her own

AND THEY DID NOT LIVE HAPPILY EVER AFTER

over religion. The marriage treaty had guaranteed her right to Lutheran worship, and a Lutheran chaplain, Johan Sering, had accompanied her to Scotland. There is no evidence that she was hindered in her religious observances, but the position of this two-person Lutheran cell in Scotland was obviously artificial. Calvinist ministers no doubt made their dislike of the arrangement clear — and they certainly must have added to whatever distaste Anne had for the ministers through their criticisms of the lifestyle and extravagance of king and queen alike. Many members of the court including Anne's closest friend, the countess of Huntly, were 'court Catholics,' followers of the old faith who avoided persecution by being discreet about their beliefs, secret in their observances.

Nonetheless, Anne might well have remained loyal to the religion of her youth if it had not first been deserted by Johan Sering. His pleas that he be replaced as promised and allowed to return to Denmark or his native Thuringia were ignored, and eventually he converted to Calvinism. Anne then refused to accept him as her pastor — though he nonetheless accompanied her to England in 1603 in that capacity. Deserted by the man entrusted with upholding her faith, she turned the other way, to the Catholicism of many of her friends, as the only alternative to obnoxious Calvinism. Her conversion evidently took place in about 1600, when she took instruction from a priest clandestinely serving some of Scotland's aristocratic Catholics.

On James's attitude to his wife's conversion reliance has to be placed on deduction from events rather than direct evidence. He must have been horrified, but doubtless he had seen it coming, as she reacted against Calvinism. Moreover, at least by the time she converted he had managed to gain the initiative in his long struggle against the most furiously anti-Catholic of the Presbyterian ministers in the Church of Scotland. Nonetheless, a Catholic wife was a serious embarrassment. James decided on damage limitation, giving expediency and common sense precedence over religious bigotry. Kingcraft, he called it. Don't let the matter become public issue. He couldn't get Anne to change her mind, but he did persuade her to accept freedom to practice her religion quietly, discretely, with the small coterie of court Catholics. The compromise worked. Anne's Catholicism remained an open secret, confined to court. For all his neglect of his wife, perhaps James felt some understanding and sympathy for her stand.

SCOTLAND'S LAST ROYAL WEDDING

Moreover, James's ever-calculating mind probably saw that some advantage might be gleaned from her potentially catastrophic conversion to Catholicism. James was increasingly obsessed with gaining as much support as possible for his bid for the English throne on Elizabeth's death. While wooing mainly Protestant approval in England, he was constantly fearful of some last minute upset through English Catholic intervention with foreign help. Therefore he was seeking to reassure Catholics that though he was a Protestant, they had nothing to fear from him. What better way of doing this than by quietly demonstrating to the Vatican that he had accepted his wife's Catholicism and was protecting her freedom to exercise her religion?[7]

Presbyterian ministers continued to try to stir up outrage about the way Catholicism was protected at court, but the political damage done by Anne's conversion was limited. However an early attempt by her to do more for her new faith than practise it quietly could have had disastrous consequences.

Having won her battle for all the lands of Dunfermline some years before, Anne now developed conscientious scruples. These lands had been the property of Dunfermline Abbey. She was living off ill-gotten gains plundered by Protestant heretics from the Catholic Church she. Now she was a Catholic, she must return them to their rightful owner. The young queen could hardly have come up with a better idea for destabilising Scotland if she had tried. Religion was one thing, but what the queen was now threatening was to question something far more basic to the souls of Scotland's nobles and lairds. Property rights. Wealth was mainly derived from ownership of land, and huge areas of former church lands had been passed into the possession of the crown and nobility. There were few great men in Scotland whose power was not partly based on land plundered from the church. Now, in effect, Anne was blithely announcing that all former church property should be returned to its rightful owners.

Legally, the question of former church lands was a mess. Many landowners had worries niggling at the back of their minds about their rights to such property being open to challenge. The Protestant nightmare of Catholic Counter Reformation was intensified by fear for land as well as souls. Nobody wanted the issue raised, for fear of what the outcome might be. Hang on to what you've got, and prevent anyone looking into how you got it, was the prevailing

AND THEY DID NOT LIVE HAPPILY EVER AFTER

sentiment. And, as King James knew well, many of his great subjects would fight rather give up land. Further, raising the land issue would draw attention to Anne's religious conversion in a most public way, inevitably leading threatened landowners to ally themselves to Protestant outrage. A queen with too tender a conscience would be a disaster for the whole country.

Luckily, Anne was dissuaded from consciencious folly. Perhaps surrendering the lordship of Dunfermline had been no more than a passing twinge of conscience, or she backed down when she realised the problems such a gesture would cause. Or perhaps James explained that the crown and nobility had been looting the Catholic church for generations before Protestantism had emerged, so it was quite respectable! Moreover, Anne must have realised that the increasingly extravagant life-style to which she was addicted could not be maintained if she gave away much of her property. Indeed, the very idea of giving away Dunfermline indicated lack of financial foresight. Where money was concerned, she was as irresponsible as her husband.

Little is known of the lives of most of Anne's Danish entourage in Scotland, but a few achieved not so much fame as notoriety. The sad Johan Sering, in unwelcome exile, deserted the Lutheranism he was supposed to defend. Margaret Vinstarr, a lady in waiting, became the mistress of the laird of Logie, who supported the earl of Bothwell in some of his antics. When Logie was arrested in 1592 and imprisoned in the king's house in Dalkeith, Margaret imperiously instructed his guards to bring him to the queen's chamber one night, and then ordered them to remain at the door while she herself took him in to see Anne. She then smuggled Logie through a chamber in which the king and queen were sleeping, and helped him climb down ropes she had prepared to a waiting horse. King James was, not surprisingly, furious, and demanded that Margaret Vinstarr be dismissed and sent back to Denmark. Anne stubbornly refused: she herself would go home rather than be deprived of any of her ladies. The interview ended with both James and Anne in tears of vexation and rage.[8]

Another glimpse of a Dane at court aptly illustrates that proud element in Danish culture, the art of drinking. The anecdote concerns a Danish gentleman whose name is lost but whose exploits were still remembered with awe two hundred years later.

SCOTLAND'S LAST ROYAL WEDDING

They inspired Robert Burns to write his ballad *The Whistle*. One of the Danes who came to Scotland with Anne, the story runs, was a giant of a man, and 'a matchless champion of Bacchus.' At the beginning of every drinking session he laid an ebony whistle on the table. The last person at the table still able to blow it, as they drank relentless bumper after bumper, kept it as a prize. This champion of champions among drinkers was said to have produced evidence that he had retained unbroken possession of the whistle after contests in north German courts, and the courts of Sweden, Russia, Poland — and even in Denmark itself. Scots courtiers suffered defeat after defeat in seeking to win the prize, until Sir Robert Laurie of Maxwellton entered the fray. For three days and three nights the two men drank — and at last Maxwellton emerged as victor, the only man able in drunken stupor to get a peep out the whistle. At this point oral tradition loses interest in the defeated and sodden Dane. But the whistle he had forfeited continued to be contested for occasionally, being won in 1789 by a descendent of Maxwellton, in the contest Burns commemorated.

The story can be shown to be inaccurate in that the Lauries lacked both a baronecy and the lands of Maxwellton until much later than the 1590s, But there is no reason to doubt the essentials of this anecdote.[9]

The Scots thus allowed the Danes to influence them in respect of drinking habits — and the English were also to do so, in 1606 when Christian IV visited James and Anne at Whitehall. Even if Sir John Harrington's notorious account of a court entertainment is exaggerated, it clearly was an occasion true to Danish tradition. During an elaborate court masque, a tipsy queen of Sheba approached Christian with a rich offering of food, but tripped up at the last minute and threw 'wine, cream, jelly, beverage, cakes, spices and other good matters' all over the king. Nonetheless he gallantly got up to dance with her, but was so drunk that he fell over and had to be carried away and laid out on a bed of state. Hope and Faith were both sick; Victory was led away to sleep it off after her drunken ranting became tiresome; Peace lost her temper, and laid into her attendants with her olive branch.[10] Perhaps too good — or bad — to be entirely true.

What of 'the example of Denmark, so feared in political matters? Did James's Danish travels influence the way he ruled his kingdom?

AND THEY DID NOT LIVE HAPPILY EVER AFTER

In the short term many contemporaries believed that they did, but it is hard to distinguish where rumour and paranoid distortions of irrelevant developments end and reality begins. James had returned from Denmark in 1590 to a highly charged political atmosphere, in which belief that Thirlestane's influence on the king was a threat to noble rights had been intensified by the stories carried back from Denmark about how he and his faction had humiliated the Earl Marischal. Rumours still spread that James and Thirlestane were studying the Danish political system and planning reforms in Scotland based on it. For months the king had been separated from his rightful advisers, with Thirlestane whispering poison in his ear. Royal instructions sent back to Scotland ahead of the king had ordered that no nobles should come to court unless they were sent for, and that when they did come they should only bring six men each with them. This was interpreted as ominously limiting rights of access to the king, and abolishing the entourages whereby nobles sought to assert their status — and intimidate their opponents.[10]

Once the king returned, any changes he made were instantly blamed on Denmark. It was noted that the king's chamber was kept more private than before.[12] One visitor to court in June 1590 reported

> things are beginning to be greatly altered here; the Court wondrous solitary, and the patron [pattern] of the Court of Denmark is greatly befor the King's eye, and the eye of our reformatours.

The king had dismissed the best of his old servants; measures were in hand to change the court of session, and many other changes were planned. The king's only adviser on such things was Chancellor Thirlestane.[13]

James and Thirlestane did indeed believe that learning from Denmark would be valuable, and clearly James was attracted by the idea of a court in which access to him was controlled by him, and if necessary exclusion enforced by his new guard led by Sir John Carmichael. This in many ways was the key issue. Were nobles, through their status to continue to have automatic right of entry to the king's chamber whenever they felt like it? Or was the king to choose who would be summoned, whose requests for access would be granted?

The attempt at limiting access was made, but failed. On the one hand the king just did not have the resources to maintain a royal guard to protect him from whatever nobleman wished to elbow his way into his chamber: already by 1591 it was reported that he could not pay the guard.[14] On the other hand, the nobility's reaction was so hostile that enforcement of limited access probably came to be seen as too damaging to continue trying to enforce it. Bothwell's habit of bursting into the court in the middle of the night with his armed followers was carrying concepts of the nobility's right of free access to their king to extremes — but his ability to do so underlined the king's failure to enforce his will.

One grim legacy of the royal marriage and the storms which had caused such delays in Anne's arrival in Scotland was a number of executions in both Scotland and Denmark. Scapegoats were needed. Why had gales caused such disruption, putting the couple in danger? It was assumed the marriage had divine approval, so what had gone wrong? In Denmark there were at first attempts to find a rational explanation. Admiral Peder Munk had been in command of the Danish fleet which had failed, so he was the first to be blamed. He had failed to carry out his mission. Munk quickly found a way to pass the buck. Not he but Christofer Valkendorf, governor of Copenhagen and treasurer, who had the task of supervising the state of repair of naval vessels, was the one to blame. His neglect had meant some ships had become unseaworthy. Munk was successful in his arguments, and Valkendorf was tried for his alleged failures. But he too found scapegoats. Some witches were being tried, and they confessed to conspiring to raise storms to drown Munk and Princess Anne. The confessions were no doubt obtained by the usual cruel methods, and as the scattering of the fleet was a mysterious matter still being debated the witches would have been questioned about it and forced to 'confess.' Valkendorf was declared innocent. The witches were not so lucky, and a series of executions took place in 1590–2.[15]

In Scotland too there were investigations into allegations of witchcraft connected with the royal marriage. These began late in 1590, some months later than in Denmark, with the famous case of the witches of North Berwick. Here attempts to drown a royal personage (James or Anne, or both) were put in a much wider context of the struggle of good and evil. Back in the autumn of 1589, the story related, about a hundred witches had met in North Berwick kirk, where the devil appeared in the pulpit. Activities included dancing and singing, opening graves and removing some

AND THEY DID NOT LIVE HAPPILY EVER AFTER

bones, swinging cats in circles by their tails then launching them into the sea, and kissing the devil's 'erse.' When some of the 'witches' were interrogated, the central charges against them was that they had made pacts with the devil, and sought to harm the king, whom the devil was said to have referred to as his greatest enemy. Confessions were exacted by some of the most horrific tortures imaginable: the boot, to smash the lower leg bones; thumb screws to crush the prisoners' thumbs; pulling out of finger nails; tightening knotted cords round the head; and sleep deprivation, which was highly effective in leading to confessions.

Several features in the confessions and the trials that followed were new to Scotland. Above all, the giving of allegiance directly to the devil was novel. This myth about witches had spread widely in Europe, and now it reached Scotland. How it got to the country is impossible to say. A neat solution has been provided by attributing it to the Danes. James, and perhaps some of his courtiers, had absorbed ideas of the demonic pact, and brought it home from Denmark.[16] Certainly there must have been discussion of witchcraft at court in Denmark, with preparations for the trials of those accused of trying to drown Princess Anne well under way before the royal couple left for Scotland. However, there is no sign of the demonic pact in the Danish trials, and thus no evidence that it was part of the 'example of Denmark' brought home by James. On the other hand, another feature of Scandinavian witchcraft may well have influenced the North Berwick trials. 'Nautical *maleficum* appears to be a Norwegian, and to a lesser extent a Danish, speciality.' In the 1540s, for example, witches were alleged to have tried to prevent Christian III's fleet leaving harbour. Surely it is not just coincidence that nautical witchcraft became a fashion in North Berwick in a Scoto-Danish context of maritime problems?[17]

Witches hatching plots against the monarch and other members of the royal family were also new to Scotland. So too was the news that the devil thought James his worst enemy. This was a coup for royal propaganda, for it carried the message that Satan's attitude to James proved him a champion of the battle against evil. Such a boost for James's image was well timed, as he continued his attempt to win control of tiresome nobles and loud-mouthed churchmen. Moreover, the witch scandal was useful in that it tainted the earl of Bothwell. When the witches confessed they conveniently implicated him as an agent of the devil. Not only did

SCOTLAND'S LAST ROYAL WEDDING

James stand out as a leader in the fight against evil, the troublesome Bothwell was the servant of evil.[18]

There is no sign that Anne took any interest in the grim little witch hunt, though she was one of those who were supposed to have been intended as a victim. Doubtless she had enough to do settling into a new court and deciding who she could trust, and who would be false friends — and how to acquire some of the Scots tongue to be able to communicate with those around her. She was to prove a good friend, stubbornly defending those in trouble. But she was also a good hater — and an effective one, as the case of Maitland of Thirlestane showed. She blamed him above all others for the problems surrounding her Dunfermline lands, and was not placated by his surrender of the disputed property. She wanted vengeance, and would only be satisfied with his downfall. James was willing to satisfy her for his own reasons. Growing confidence meant that he was no longer inclined to allow one man so dominant a place in his affairs, especially one with such a talent for alienating others. As he had indicated in Denmark, he no longer regarded himself as an apprentice king. Thirlestane lost the secretary-ship a year after James had returned home, and though he remained chancellor until his death in 1595 his power had by then faded away.[19]

Anne had got her way in the contest with Thirlestane, but she lost the most passionate campaign she ever waged. She must have heard about the old Scottish royal tradition whereby a child heir to the throne was entrusted to the earl and countess of Mar, to be brought up by them at Stirling Castle. Moreover, in Denmark too the parting of royal children from their parents was common. She herself had been largely brought up by her mother's parents. The dowager countess of Mar, who would look after the infant heir, was the nearest James had had to a mother to stand in for the imprisoned Mary Queen of Scots, and in his eyes giving Henry into her care was almost like entrusting him to a grandparent of the child.

Nonetheless, once Prince Henry was born, Anne reacted with outrage to the plan to hand over the infant to the dowager countess. In the end she had to give way — now and with later children. Princes and princesses were parcelled out to appropriate nobles. That the earl and countess of Mar were personally disliked by Anne probably accounted for a good deal of her anger. Frequently James gave her what she wanted for the sake of peace, but on this issue he was implacable. Herself of royal birth, she should know better

AND THEY DID NOT LIVE HAPPILY EVER AFTER

than make a fuss where sticking to established traditional practice was concerned. He himself been brought up (no doubt successfully, at least in his own eyes) by the Mars. To ignore Mar's rights in the matter would be seen as an attack on noble privileges.

Thus Anne lost most of the childhoods of her children, and this became a long term grievance. Naturally she blamed her husband. Her marriage had already experienced strains: now the couple moved much further apart. She would perform her public duties, but otherwise live her own life — though the fact that her family continued to grow indicates at least occasional dutiful royal beddings.[20]

Whether it occurred to Anne — or anyone else — that there was one way in which she could recover her children is unknown. If James inherited the throne of England on Elizabeth's death, the royal family would undoubtedly move to England, and English etiquette did not banish royal children from their mother. For this reason Anne must have been delighted at the Union of the Crown in 1603. Occasional visiting rights gave way to closer and more frequent contacts with her children. But she had lost much of the infancies of Henry, Elizabeth, Margaret and Charles, and her three final children all died in infancy.

1590 had seen the end of the Danish phases of Anne's life. 1603 saw the end of the Scottish phase as well. She had no wish to see Scotland ever again, and illness gave her a good excuse for not accompanying James on his visit to his homeland in 1617. Memories of, and affection for, Denmark, however, remained strong.[21] She was reunited with her brother Christian IV during his visits of 1605 and 1614, though the latter was brief and his welcome from James half-hearted. The Danish king's arrival had been without warning, perhaps revenge for James's unannounced arrival in Norway back in 1589.

Anne developed her own court circle in England, and led a luxurious life within it. Already in Scotland she had shown herself to be a big spender, with a taste for expensive clothes and jewels. In England she had resources at her disposal vastly greater than before, and proved up to the challenge. Her finances were constantly in a mess, and the elaborate court masques she came to love were hugely expensive. But in time even extravagance palled. She was often ill, and her letters 'home' suggest melancholy and a continuing sense of exile. She died in 1619, and James followed her to the grave in 1625.

SCOTLAND'S LAST ROYAL WEDDING

The marriage that had begun in storms had had its own storms, with the row over bringing up Prince Henry as a culminating hurricane. Thereafter major fights were rarer, as husband and wife drew apart and concentrated on their own separate lives. By the time they died the closer relations with Denmark that had briefly flourished had also gone. In the early 1590s several Danish embassies had come to Scotland. Their missions mainly dealt with the awkward matter of James's morning gift to Anne, but the ambassadors had maintained and developed links between the two countries. They had met Scots who had been in Denmark in 1589-90, and old friendships were revived. Other links, mainly between learned men, were maintained through correspondence for some years, but then died out. 'The heyday of personal contacts' between Scottish and Danish élites was over. Christian IV's 1605 and 1614 visits were to England: Scotland no longer had a royal court.[22]

Perhaps the storms of late 1589 foretold more than the nature of the marriage. Its most important long-term result was the birth in 1600 of Prince Charles, who took over the position of heir to the thrones of Britain on the sudden death of Prince Henry in 1612. As a royal marriage the match had efficiently served its purpose, providing not only a male heir but a back-up when he fell by the wayside. But Charles's reign was to culminate in the ultimate of storms, the great civil wars of the Three Kingdoms. Judgement based on the maxim that 'by their fruits shall ye know them' can point out that what began in a bleak winter meeting in Oslo was a step down the road which led to disaster and even the temporary abolition of monarchy. Even historians smug with the advantage of hindsight, however, can hardly blame the young couple of 1589 for that.

The Danish Account of the Marriage

THE DANISH ACCOUNT OF THE MARRIAGE OF JAMES VI AND ANNE OF DENMARK

Translated by Peter Graves

An account of Princess Anne's marriage with King James VI of Scotland. The courtship, travels, beginning, progress and conclusion in Norway, Denmark and Scotland of James VI, King of England and Scotland, and Lady Anne of Denmark. Also the coronation of Her Majesty and the departure of the King of Denmarks's ambassadors from Scotland in 1589 [1590]

I — THE MAKING OF THE TREATY

Since the mighty and noble prince, King Frederick II, king of Denmark, Norway, the Wends and the Goths etc., after devout consideration had agreed to and promised the marriage of his daughter, the noble lady and princess, Lady Anne, to the noble prince and lord, James VI, the chosen and crowned king of Scotland, in accordance with his majesty's [James VI's] high desire; and since — on account of King Frederick's fatal and tragic demise — a not inconsiderable time had passed before this was brought to pass, the aforementioned mighty and noble King James VI in the year 1589 once again despatched envoys to Denmark in order to negotiate the alliance and entry into marriage of himself and the princess, Lady Anne, noble sister of Christian IV, elected king of Denmark, Norway, the Wends and the Goths. And, since that young prince and lord [Christian IV] was still a minor and not come of age, with the result that his princely grace could not be fully responsible for the kingdom, they were to negotiate with the noble Princess Sophia, mighty queen and regent etc. of Denmark, Norway, the Wends and the Goths and with the most wise council of the realm and the regency council, in order to bring such highly important matters to a conclusion. And the Scottish king's ambassador laid the following articles before the Danes. 9 July 1589:

The Demands of the Scottish envoys[1]

1. That the Danes should give the noble Scottish king a morning gift [dowry] of 250,000 daler[2] with Lady Anne.
2. That the Scots might have and enjoy the same privileges and freedoms throughout the whole of Denmark as native Danes have.

The Danes should likewise have and enjoy the same privileges and freedoms throughout the whole kingdom of Scotland as native Scots.[3]

3. That Scottish merchants should hereafter have customs and excise exemption from the extraordinary duty which is now levied in the Danish Sound and at Danish customs posts: namely, each hundredth penny.

4. That, when his majesty of Scotland has need of them, his majesty of Denmark will (at his own expense) send 5,000 foot soldiers and at least 1,000 cavalry to Scotland[4] and will keep them there at his own expense as long as his majesty of Scotland may have need.

5. That Denmark will grant to his majesty of Scotland three men of war with all their equipment and appurtenances; also that Denmark will lend him seven other ships to be sent home again at a pre-arranged time.[5]

6. That his majesty of Denmark should not make any approaches to his majesty of Scotland or his successors with regard to the redemption of the Orkney Islands as long as one of the two mighty lords lives.[6]

7. These highly esteemed kings should also enter into an alliance against the Catholic princes should the latter perpetuate any plot or incursion hostile to either of these mighty kings or their most praise-worthy kingdoms.

It is our friendly request that the noble Queen Sophia and likewise the noble and chosen prince, young Prince Christian, and also the mighty governing lords and most wise council of the kingdom of Denmark will communicate their answer and their comments.

1. George, earl and hereditary marischal of the kingdom of Scotland.
2. Andrew Keith, Lord Dingwall. 3. James Scrymgeour of Dudope.
4. John Skene. 5. George Young, secretary depute.

To which the Danes gave their answer on the following day, which was 10 July.[7] It was as follows:

1. Regarding the morning gift [dowry], namely 250,000 daler, which the envoys of the mighty and noble king of the Scots demand on behalf of their lord: it was already decided by the late King Frederick II of blessed memory (our former and most gracious king and lord) to give with his noble daughter and princess a morning gift of 75,000 daler or 100,000 guilder — which is commonly called a barrel of gold — not including the princely gems and other decorations which it is fitting for princesses to wear. It would not, therefore, be seemly for us to deviate in any way from the decided intention and will of our former most gracious king and lord without important reasons; nor to bind ourselves to anything further for which we must later provide a satisfactory and complete account. We desire therefore, that we be

THE DANISH ACCOUNT

excused from this, and also that the person of the noble lady herself rather than the morning gift or money be taken into consideration. If, at some later date as a result of these present beginnings, we may assume the relationship by marriage of many mighty princes and lords, even this resolution may be reconsidered with the greatest goodwill.

2. As to the privileges and freedoms which it is requested that Scots should receive in our kingdom: the most-wise lords ought to bear in mind the old treaties and alliances already entered into by these esteemed kingdoms of Denmark and Scotland. These themselves do not allow for any change. For which reason there is no necessity to renew [alter] them now; nor may this easily be brought to pass during the present minority of our young king.

3. With regard to the excise and duty that is levied in the Sound and at other customs posts: as it has been customary since ancient times we may not in this matter be party to any lessening of it; for that would be to diminish the royal rights and ancient dignity of this esteemed kingdom as well as to encroach upon the jurisdiction and authority of this kingdom and that of our chosen lord and king and his successors. We request with all respect, therefore, that such matters should not be raised. But when his grace comes to the age of majority (by the grace of God), and if his majesty is then approached once again about the matter, then the most wise council of the kingdom of Denmark offers (at your stipulation and request) to assist diligently in finding a favourable solution.

4. This is Denmark's answer to your fourth proposal: the kingdom cannot undertake such a service, particularly now during the minority of our young lord. But, when this business is brought to a good result and conclusion, then it is not to be doubted that the mighty and esteemed lords, each according to his circumstances and situation, will be supportive and helpful to each other in this matter as in any other; and they will do so from pure mutual and common love and good affection rather than from any obligation or bounden sense of duty which, with time, might rather lead to disagreement and disunity than to firm friendship and brotherly concord.

5. The council of the kingdom of Denmark does not doubt that the esteemed lords and royal envoys may by their own wisdom easily understand that it would not be proper to weaken the royal fleet either by gift or by loan during our gracious lord's youth. It presumes, therefore, that the most-wise envoys will desist from such a request of their own accord.

6. With regard to the Orkney Islands: it is not unknown to the good lords that the late King Frederick (of esteemed memory) broached this topic through the ambassador he dispatched four years ago, and therefore the council of the kingdom can neither grant nor agree to

this proposal. But, so that their respect for his royal majesty of Scotland may be recognised (and assuming that this business is brought to a good conclusion), they promise to allow this item to stand until our chosen and most gracious lord reaches the fullness of age. Then it will be free for his majesty to negotiate the matter with his majesty of Scotland. In which negotiation the council of the kingdom of Denmark will be found amenable and of all good-will towards his majesty of Scotland — though without prejudicing in any way the rights and freedoms of this kingdom.

7. As to the alliance that should be entered into with regard to religion, the council of Denmark answers as follows: the same thing was also demanded in the past of our blessed and departed lord by certain other lords; to this his majesty replied that it was not possible without the greatest of difficulty to bind oneself to such agreements unless the whole reformed community desired to do the same. Which he urged vigorously, saying he would be glad to see it come to pass. He was, however, unable to accomplish anything further in this matter while he lived. It is, therefore, not proper for the most wise council of Denmark to encumber their young lord and chosen king with such an alliance, filled as it is with the greatest danger; nor do they consider it to be in their power to do so. But, if the ranks and estates of the reformed religion jointly and with united counsel wish to treat for a general alliance, then, for the sake of the common welfare of the Christian church and in so far as it is possible and suitable, it [the council of Denmark] will neither refuse nor exclude itself from it. In the meantime, it will show all loyalty, love, neighbourly respect and affection which it is proper for confederates and close neighbours to show between themselves.

[Nicolaus] Kaas. Peder Munk. Jørgen Rozenkrantz.[8]
Christoffer Valkendorf. Henrik Ramel.

A short account of what the Danish ruling lords desire from the Scottish ambassadors on behalf of the noble princess, Lady Anne:

1. Since Denmark is to present a dowry of 75,000 daler, which is 100,000 guilders and commonly called a barrel of gold, with Lady Anne, and since it is customary to give a life-interest or morning gift of twice as much in return, it is the desire of the council of this esteemed kingdom on behalf of the esteemed Lady Anne that her grace be assigned and given as many castles, provinces and incomes by Scotland as exceed by double in valuation the dowry given with her grace by the kingdom here; that is to say, amount to a fortune of 150,000 daler. So that, when her grace so desires, she may use them according to her own free will and pleasure without anyone else's instruction; being in no doubt, of course, that her grace will behave

THE DANISH ACCOUNT

and conduct herself in a manner that may be justified to her lord and that he will be well pleased in all things.

2. That her grace may have the religion and divine worship of her choice, as may her servants; and, furthermore, she may keep her own preacher at the expense of his majesty of Scotland and may take the said preacher wherever her grace desires; and, when or as often as her priest dies, she may have the freedom to appoint another in the place of the deceased, selecting whichever priest she may wish irrespective of where he comes from.

3. In the case of the decease (which God forbid) of his royal majesty of Scotland before her grace, her grace is to be free to withdraw from Scotland within three years, or to remain there permanently, according to what seems most advisable and pleasing to her grace herself.

4. In the case of it pleasing her grace to withdraw permanently from the Scottish kingdom, the royal inheritors and successors are to recompense her royal highness for her morning gift and give 150,000 daler.

5. Should it happen that one of their majesties be carried off by death before the royal marriage has been entered into, everything that has heretofore been negotiated and decided with regard to the dowry and morning gift on both sides is to be completely discarded and nullified.

6. For important reasons, and so that all further delay and procrastination may be prevented, it has been decided that the royal ambassadors are to present a final decision in the matter before St Bartholomew's Day in the coming month [24 August], so that this highly important matter (which has long been delayed) may be brought to a conclusion; and if this does not occur (which God forbid), then neither our gracious and most mighty queen, nor our most gracious lord, prince and chosen king, Christian IV, nor his majesty's appointed ruling council, is under an obligation to pursue the matter further. May the gracious God guide all our counsel and actions to the honour of His Holy Name. Amen.

Nicolaus Kaas. Peder Munk. Jørgen Rozenkrantz.
Christoffer Valkendorf. Henrik Ramel.

King James's letter to Queen Sophia
Most mighty Princess Sophia, by the grace of God queen
and dowager of Denmark etc, our beloved lady mother.

Most mighty princess, dearest sister and cousin, your own majesty is sufficient witness to the profound love and particular longing and desire with which we await your noble and most dear daughter Princess Anne to be the companion of our life and of our kingdom; and to how we measure everything else against her person. To your will and pleasure we do not only subject that which may be considered peripheral and external in this matter, but also ourselves and all that is ours; and we desire that everything be performed in the manner that our mutual and only mother in the world arranges in accordance with her maternal desire and counsel. Since this relationship by marriage lies so close to our heart and mind, we have no higher desire than to behold in person this noble and lovable princess whose picture has fascinated our eyes and heart. We desire greatly from your royal grace that this may be permitted as soon as possible, and we anticipate it with joy. Everything else we leave to your grace's disposition and will. Whatever your royal grace — as the mother of both of us — wishes to do and arrange in the matter will not displease us. Our envoys will inform your grace further, and we await them with the desired answer, [hoping for] a happy outcome, and with our dear bride as soon as possible. May the most gracious God spare and preserve your royal grace in long and sound health. Aberdeen, 1 August 1589.[9]

Insertion i — The Marriage Treaty (summary)[10]

1. *A marriage has been arranged between Anne, second sister of King Christian, and King James, as agreed between the Danes and the Scottish envoys empowered to treat by James, according to his commission of 20 June 1589.*

2. *The envoys first contracted a betrothal 'per verba de futuro vice' through the Earl Marischal as proxy for James, and Anne, swearing there was no impediment to the marriage.*

3. *Christian gives Anne a dowry of 75,000 thalers [dalers] or 100,000 florins, which is known as a barrel of gold. This will be paid to the envoys on board ship, or on their arrival in Scotland.*

4. *The envoys grant to Anne as dower the palace of Linlithgow and castle of Falkland, and a third part of the property of the kingdom of Scotland, with all the revenues of these properties and their pertinents.*

5. *If James dies before Anne, she shall have freedom within three years to leave Scotland, or to remain there, as she chooses. If she leaves she is to have 150,000 thalers in compensation for her property in Scotland.*

6. *If either James or Anne dies before the marriage has been celebrated in Scotland, or has been consummated, the agreements concerning the dowry and morning gift will be void.*

THE DANISH ACCOUNT

7. *Anne and all her ministers are to have free profession and exercise of their religion, in meetings and in the administration of the sacraments in the vernacular and according to the custom of Denmark. To this end Anne is to have a Danish or German preacher, and if he dies or leaves Scotland she can choose another, at James's expense.*

8. *King Christian obliges himself and his heirs to fulfil the terms of the contract.*

9. *King James's envoys oblige themselves, James and his heirs to fulfil the terms of the contract.*

Insertion ii — The Civil Marriage[11]

A short specification of the solemnities to be made use of in the celebration of marriages.

In the first place, the illustrious and noble lords ambassadors will be led into the castle [Kronborg] next Tuesday [19 August] after lunch, and if they want to see the lady Anne, sister of the king [Christian IV] they will be admitted to her.

Then they will be led into a chamber prepared for them in which they will stay for as long as they choose.

In weddings of all princes and kings it is customary for an oath to be offered by ambassadors or their proctors (before anything else is done), to the effect that their lordships will ratify every one of the things included in the dowry agreements and contracts, and swear that they will safely and without deception perform all the things which were promised by themselves.

The illustrious [Scots] ambassadors will be briefed on this matter on the Wednesday following, and bind themselves by an oath of this kind, either before midday in their chamber, in the presence of the lords, or after midday in whatever place or manner may seem convenient to them.

On the same day they will consume a lunch in their chamber.

In the third hour after noon in the royal palace there will be a solemn promise of marriage. Then there will be an address in the German language, made on behalf of the most serene king of Scotland by the illustrious and noble lord earl [the Earl Marischal] as head of this delegation. This will be followed shortly by mounting the bed. Since it is the custom of kings and princes in these ceremonies that wedding torches are brought in, twelve nobles from one side and twelve from the other will be chosen to bear them before the bride. And because a particular colours are customarily assigned to the torches, the illustrious and noble lords ambassadors are to be asked which colours should be assigned to their torches, according to their pleasure.

These ceremonies having been completed, the illustrious and noble lords will again be led into their chamber and not long after to the royal table in order to take a meal.

After these things, it remains for the illustrious and noble lords ambassadors to determine at what time the departure to Scotland will be undertaken.

From the point of view of the celebrated lady bride, for many reasons, it will be more convenient [for her] to go aboard ship at Hafnia [Copenhagen]. It will be at the choice of the lords and ambassadors whether or not they choose to send their own ships thither, so that they [and the Danish ships] can more easily set sail together, so that there would be no reason to delay in this place any longer.

II — NORWAY AND DENMARK

As everything was now prepared in Denmark and the royal fleet which was to accompany her grace to Scotland was ready, her grace sailed from Copenhagen on 5 September and came in the evening to Kronborg where her grace remained until between three and four o'clock in the morning when they set sail again.[1] They sailed no more than about a nautical mile, for the wind had gone against them, and therefore they lay for two days. Afterwards they set sail again and travelled fast until they turned west below Norway where, because the wind had turned against them, they put into Flekkerøy where they stayed for six days.[2] The noble Peder Munk, admiral to his royal majesty, had however arranged a sumptuous banquet at that place.

They set out to sea again and were under sail for three days with a half wind, but the wind once again became contrary so that they were forced to turn back and seek a haven by the name of Rekefjord where they remained no more than three hours, partly because the haven was dangerous and the storm came straight in through the mouth [of the fjord], and partly because the wind turned a point or two more favourable for them than before. They therefore set sail again at once, and remained at sea for four days.

THE DANISH ACCOUNT

But towards midnight the admiral bore away from the other ships and lay into Merdøy. Three or four ships (one of which had the Scottish earl [the Earl Marischal] aboard) went astray at sea, and for two days and nights [the admiral] sought sorrowfully for her grace. And when they could not find her they made for a harbour about forty miles away from where she was. The next day, after they had received news of her, they set sail again and, even though the wind was still against them and a storm was raging, they kept on tacking for two days and nights until they reached her. When they arrived there they got an exceedingly good wind but they could not get out of the harbour. That wind lasted about eight days.

When the admiral perceived that everything was going against them and the ship had even sprung a leak, all present decided it best for her grace to go ashore and lodge with a farmer on Flekkerøy until the ship was ready again. Her grace did this, and slept in a small farmhouse for two nights. King James also slept there when he landed on Flekkerøy later, saying that he desired to sleep in the same place as she had slept earlier.

Eight days later they set sail from there and were under sail for two days and one night. But God's wind and weather forced them back again, and once again they had to seek shelter at Flekkerøy. Finally Peder Munk, the Danish ambassadors and the whole Danish nobility decided that the most advisable course was to return to Denmark as soon as possible. This proposal was however changed at the earnest request and special pleading of George Keith, noble baron of Altrie and Inverugie, Earl Marischal of the kingdom of Scotland and royal ambassador. Because of him it was decided that her grace should travel to Oslo and stay there over the winter. At once all the ships [except three] were ordered to sail to the Sound. From these ships they took certain supplies that were useful and with them they provisioned three ships — the Gedeon (on which the princess was), the Gabriel (on which the earl and his people were) and the Duen (on which there were some Danes) — and thus they parted at Flekkerøy, the Danish ships for Denmark and the three aforementioned ships remaining at sea for two days and nights.

Because of a contrary wind they put into Sandefjord and lay there for eight days before sailing to Langesund. They moored there for one day. From there they sailed to Jomfruland and remained three days. Here her ladyship went ashore, and the others travelled in cutters to Oslo fjord where they were forced to desert the boats and travel on to Tønsberg (that was 22 October). From there they took cutters to Oslo. The following day (which was 23 October) the earl reached Bastøy and her ladyship came to Borre, to the house of Herr Nils [Hansen],[3] where she stayed overnight. The next day (which was 24 October) her ladyship came to Store Brevik and the earl to Lille Brevik. On the third day she came to Oslo (that was 25 October) at about three o'clock in the afternoon. Her grace was received here with all respect and reverence, for the whole clergy was gathered on the quay, the citizenry lined the street fully armed, and the governor and the chief men of the country humbly wished her grace good fortune and happiness. After that, George Keith, the Earl Marischal and ambassador, accompanied her grace into the Old Bishops' Palace, following behind the noble Steen Brahe[4] and Axel Gyldenstierne (governor of the realm [of Norway] and commander of Akershus Castle), Henning Giøye,[5] Ove Juel,[6] Hans Pedersen of Sem[7] and Peder Iversen,[8] the noble Fru Karen Gyldenstierne,[9] Fru Anne Skinckel,[10] Fru Margrethe Brede,[11] Peder Iversen's wife, Fru Dorrete Juel[12] and Jomfru Ulffvild (Peder Iversen's sister)[13] — to all of whom her grace gave her hand when she stepped on to the quay. Behind these walked the bishop [of Oslo], Jens Nilssøn][14] and the clergy, then Mayor Oluf Glad with the councillors and some distinguished citizens, then the common people who kept in armed ranks and formed into new ranks at the [Old] Bishops' Palace until her grace and the earl had entered, when they all fired their muskets or matchlocks as a salute and humble salvo to the greatest honour of her grace.

As the clock was now at half past four, Earl George bade her grace good night and took his leave. Axel Gyldenstierne and another noble gentleman accompanied him to his lodgings at the house of Anders Skraedder (who became mayor immediately after Easter). The earl walked between them, after them came the nobility, then the bishop and the canons followed by Mayor Oluf Glad and the councillors, and lastly the citizenry who fired their muskets and matchlocks in honour of the earl.

On 1 November (which was All Saints' Day) her grace finally decided to travel overland home to Denmark. Consequently the noble Fru Dorthea Juel got ready to travel in advance in order to prepare lodgings at her house [in Ellinggaard] for her grace. Then, however, there came a letter bearing the most urgent news that

THE DANISH ACCOUNT

King James of Scotland — against all expectations — had come to Norway with five ships and was hastening here with all speed to reach her grace as soon as possible. Because of this a young Scottish gentleman together with Ove Juel and three or four Scottish noblemen set off without delay on 3 November to meet his majesty of Scotland.

On 5 November Steen Brahe sent one of his servants to Bishop Jens [Nilssøn] on behalf of her grace to invite him to dinner. And when he arrived, her grace left her chamber, came to the hall and with the most gracious respect invited him together with noble Steen Brahe and Henning Giøye to her own table. The other gentlemen sat down at a second table, and the noble ladies and maidens at a third table. When the meal was over (it lasted no more than one and a half hours), the bishop together with noble Steen Brahe and Henning Giøye were invited to the ladies's withdrawing room where the noble ladies spoke to him about various matters. Among other things, the well-born Fru Ide remarked that he should arrange something for the entertainment of her ladyship. She did not want to say at this time what it should be but he would learn that on another occasion.

On 9 November Bishop Jens Nilssøn preached (at the request of noble Steen Brahe) before her grace. Present at this sermon were noble Steen Brahe who was her grace's chamberlain, Axel Gyldenstierne, Henning Giøye, and Steen Bille who had come to Oslo from the king of Scotland the day before. The king was then at Flekkerøy. Present at the same time were the following noble ladies: Fru Ide, Fru Anne Henning Giøye, Fru Karen Gyldenstierne, as well as other noble ladies and maidens. The service began between nine and ten o'clock and the order of service was as follows: her grace's court preacher, Master Johan Sering, with two schoolchildren (or descant singers)[15] began the hymn 'God Alone in Heaven' etc. Then Bishop Jens [Nilssøn's] sermon began. The text was the gospel of the official of the synagogue and the woman sick from bleeding, which falls on the 24th Sunday after Trinity, and he discussed the text until a quarter past ten. When the sermon was over they sang the hymn 'We Thank You Jesus Christ' etc. and finally everything ended with particular devoutness.

Immediately after the sermon the following were called to table. Steen Brahe, Axel Gyldenstierne, Steen Bille, the Scottish king's lord-in-waiting Andrew Sinclair (a tall young man who had arrived

89

the day before with Steen Bille from the king) and Bishop Jens Nilssøn were placed at her grace's table. Henning Giøye and those other gentlemen who were not waiting at table were at a second table. Fru Ide and Fru Anne and the other well-born ladies and maidens were at a third table.

On 11 November (which was St Martin's Day) Steen Brahe called the bishop to him and announced that her grace wished to go to church the following day. Then he, together with the two chief ladies-in-waiting and the bishop, went to the church to prepare a place and space suitable for her grace and her court. The bishop was instructed to preach the Danish sermon. King James reached Tønsberg that same day.

On 12 November her grace was led into the church by the Scottish earl and taken to the assigned chair, which was covered in tapestries. That day her ladyship was wearing a red velvet kirtle, a gold cap with white pearl decorations below it, and a black velvet cape lined with sable. The earl stood directly opposite her ladyship — his chair was covered with red damask. It was forbidden for anyone to occupy the seats above her ladyship or in front of her. When her ladyship went into or out of the church all the gentlemen preceded her — that is to say, Steen Brahe, Henning Giøye, Peder Iversen and the others. Immediately behind her grace walked all of her maidens dressed alike in brightly coloured scarlet gowns and red velvet bodices with yellow damask sleeves. After them came the chief ladies-in-waiting and the other Danish ladies; also the Norwegian ladies. Bishop Jens [Nilssøn] then read a passage from the Epistle to the Ephesians, chapter 2, verse 8: 'For by grace are ye saved through faith; and that is not of yourselves; it is the gift of God.'

King James's Arrival in Norway

On 3 November the noble and mighty prince, King James VI, arrived on Flekkerøy from Scotland with five ships. He went ashore and stayed with a poor man at the same place as her ladyship had lodged earlier. He remained there until the Friday of the same week. His majesty left there on 7 November and stayed at sea that day and the following night. On 8 November he tacked past Jomfruland and in the evening ran into Langesund where he remained for two nights, lodging with Anulf Eeg.[16] He moved on 10 November to Herr Peder Vaemundsen[17] in Sanden and stayed

THE DANISH ACCOUNT

there overnight. On 11 November he travelled on to Tønsberg and lodged there at Jörgen Lauritsen's for six nights.

Before daybreak on 17 November his majesty travelled to Borre where he had intended to cross the fjord but was prevented by storm; he therefore continued to Vaale and stayed there with Herr Rasmus Sørensen[18] until the next day. On 18 November his majesty set off so early that he covered five miles before daybreak and reached Sande where he slept about two hours. He then ate and after the meal travelled on to Lierbyen where the lights were already lit. He left there on 19 November and did not eat until he reached Asker where he had a meal. He then continued to Oslo, arriving there towards four o'clock in the afternoon of the same day. His royal majesty's [Christian IV's] governor, Axel Gyldenstierne, and the Danish, Scottish and Norwegian nobility had that same day travelled out to meet his majesty in the parish of Asker and they accompanied him into the town. When his majesty arrived, he went at once to the Old Bishops' Palace to meet her ladyship. This was the order of procession: first walked two Scottish noblemen (who were his royal majesty's heralds) each bearing a white stick as a sign of peace; next came Steen Brahe, Henning Giøye, Axel Gyldenstierne, Hans Pedersen, Ove Juel, Captain Normand and Peder Iversen; then came his majesty between the Scottish earl and another Scottish lord; after them came the king's courtiers and the Scottish nobility, all with their hats in their hands. The bishop and the clergy remained at Anders Skraedder's and awaited his majesty.

His majesty lingered with her ladyship about half an hour and then went straight to the lodgings arranged for him at Anders Skraedder's house and, as before, all the Danish and Norwegian nobility preceded him. Axel Gyldenstierne told the bishop that the king would take him by the hand; and, when the king came immediately in front of the bishop, the earl pointed the bishop out to him. He stopped and the bishop stepped forward, proffered his hand in the most humble fashion and gave a short Latin oration in which he wished his majesty good fortune. His majesty took off his hat, immediately put it on again and paid close attention to what the bishop was saying; and when the oration was finished, his majesty once again took off his hat, gave his hand to the bishop and thanked him respectfully. His majesty was a tall, slim gentleman with lean cheeks,[19] wearing a red velvet coat appliqued with pieces of gold so that there was a row of golden stars and another row

SCOTLAND'S LAST ROYAL WEDDING

where the velvet could be seen. He also wore a black velvet cloak lined with sable. His majesty also gave his hand to the mayor, whereafter he went straight up to his chamber.

At nine o'clock in the morning of 20 November his majesty went to be her ladyship's guest, and all the Danish and Norwegian gentlemen preceded him with their hats in their hands. On this day his royal majesty's livery was blue velvet appliqued with pieces of gold. Two Scottish earls[20] walked behind his majesty, followed by all the Norwegian gentlemen. There was no one else at table with his majesty except her ladyship and Steen Brahe. But the Scottish chancellor [Maitland of Thirlestane] and the earl [Marischal] served at table. When it was four o'clock in the afternoon his majesty returned home to his own lodging, with all the Danish and Norwegian gentlemen preceding him, the two earls immediately after him, and then the Scottish gentlemen.

On 23 November their royal wedding took place in the great hall in Christen Mule's house[21] with all the splendour possible at that time and place. The hall was decorated in the most costly way with tapestries, the floor where the king and her ladyship would stand was covered with a piece of red cloth, and on it there were two royal chairs covered in red damask. Two red velvet cushions lay upon them. When it was two o'clock all the Danish and Norwegian gentlemen went to Anders Skraedder's house and accompanied his majesty from there to her ladyship. The trumpeters, meanwhile, stood at Christen Mule's gate and blew. When their majesties arrived, they went up to the hall and the king walked first on to the red cloth where he stood with his hands on his hips. Her ladyship came after him and stood at his majesty's side. The ceremony began with oral music — but only for a very short time. After that his majesty's court preacher David Lindsay stepped forward and preached a sermon in French concerning marriage. In the meantime they themselves joined hands.

An Exhortation which his royal majesty's preacher, Mr David Lindsay, made in French in Oslo when James VI, king of Scotland, and Lady Anne, daughter of the king of Denmark, entered into marriage, 23 November 1589[22]

May the Almighty God, for the sake of His goodness and mercy, be present in this marriage so that that which is begun may progress happily and end in blessedness, to the honour of His name, to the

THE DANISH ACCOUNT

solace of the king and queen, and to the eternal joy of the kingdoms of Scotland and Denmark. The reason for this worthy gathering is so that which his royal majesty's ambassadors began may now at last be completed in the presence of his grace; for which reason I humbly pray that the mighty king and queen will pay heed and recognise in their hearts that the fundament and basis of all Christian people is that they begin nothing unless it be lawful, honourable and in agreement with the word of God. That marriage is such a matter is proven by these following arguments.

The first is that God, whose will no one may violate, has ordered it and introduced it even in Paradise between Adam and Eve who are the parents of all mankind and who were created by God's almighty word. The second is that Adam and Eve were joined in marriage when they were in a state of perfection and we may thus easily understand that marriage is lawful. The third and definitive reason why marriage was introduced is that the human race may multiply; which is good and in complete agreement with God's wisdom. The fourth is that God has wished to bless the lawful joining together of man and woman as he has shown with many examples, such as Abraham and Sara, Isaac and Jacob and their wives. The fifth is that intercourse between man and woman, when it occurs outside marriage, is forbidden by God's word and, since the sin is great, chastisement and punishment are prescribed; and there are various kinds of unlawful intercourse, such as incest, whoredom and fornication. The sixth is that marriage is honourable among all people and that it is in agreement with God's word — as is proved by certain passages in Holy Scripture such as Genesis 2, 1 Corinthians 7, Ephesians 5, Christ with his first miracle at the wedding which he honoured with his presence, also St Paul. The strongest knot that binds man and woman together in marriage is the burning love that people feel for one another. Those who are bound together by this bond will leave their parents and remain together throughout their lifetimes.

There are three other reasons, in particular, why man shall live in marriage; the first is that man may have a helpmate who is like him, the second is that he may beget children, the third is for the avoidance of fornication and all other unlawful intercourse.

The role of married people lies particularly in these four following matters: 1. They shall join themselves together through fear of the Lord and call upon Him with all their heart to bless them in their marriage; 2. They should promise sincere love towards each other so that they can patiently suffer whatever God apportions them, whether good fortune or misfortune; 3. They shall unite their minds in all their deeds as though they were only one person, and the one should tell the other whatever he owns, whether it be riches, land or anything else; 4. The man owes the woman service just as she owes service to him to an equal extent. It should take this form: the man shall watch for his wife diligently, and, since he is her head, he shall see for her with his eyes, hear for her with his ears and answer for her with his tongue. But the wife, on the other hand, shall obey her husband in all things and always have in mind the maxim that God pronounced after the Fall, which is that she is commanded to be submissive for eternity. There is also a spiritual marriage between Christ and His church, which is made perfect in the hearts of all the chosen by means of the Holy Spirit, by means of Christ as bridegroom while also head of the Christian church, and by means of the mutual love between Him and His bride. Therefore I will humbly request his royal majesty and her grace the queen to call upon God's gracious help so that He may give this their marriage a blissful beginning and end, and that He will bless it in his ineffable mercy.

When this ended and they had given each other their troth and promise in the matter of marriage, the blessing took place in the form of a short prayer that Almighty God, in Whose name they were joined together, would include them in His spiritual and physical blessings, and that their marriage might have a blissful progress to the honour of His holy name, to their own consolation and to the advantage of both kingdoms. And when this act was finished the bishop stepped forward, delivered an oration to their majesties in Danish, and then everything ended with music. Her grace went out first with the well-born ladies and maidens. Then the king went out, and the bishop saluted his royal majesty in Latin, wishing him good fortune in his newly entered marriage and a blessed reign. To which his majesty replied: 'Hoc scio te ex corde precari', that is: 'I know that you wish it from your heart.' And his chancellor, who was standing by, said: 'Certe ex corde precatur', that is: 'certainly he wishes it from his heart.' His majesty then answered and said: 'Hoc lubens accipio,' that is: 'it is dear to me.' It was three o'clock when the king went out.

On 25 November Mr David Lindsay, the king's court preacher together with two Scottish noblemen and Mr Johan Sering, the princess's court preacher, were invited to be guests of the bishop along with a number of others. In the evening of the same day the king had all the Scottish noblemen as his guests.

On 27 November the chief ladies-in-waiting had the Scottish chancellor approach Bishop Jens [Nilssøn] regarding an intercession to his majesty on behalf of a Scottish nobleman [Cunningham of

THE DANISH ACCOUNT

Robertland] who had been involved when an earl [Eglinton] close to the king had been killed in Scotland. Therefore, the chancellor, the earl and the other nobles, together with the chamberlain, both chief ladies-in-waiting and ladies and maidens, went to the king in the [Old] Bishops' Palace. At their request they were given a gracious audience and the Scottish nobleman was pardoned.

On 30 November about fifty Scots left by boat.

On 3 December a Scottish nobleman by the name of Constable [Scrymgeour of Dudhope, constable of Dundee] left for Scotland. That same day his majesty went hunting on Hovedøya with Steen Brahe, Axel Gyldenstierne, Henning Giöye and the Scottish noblemen. They arrived back at two o'clock in the afternoon and the Danish signal was fired from the castle with three cannon.

On 10 December two members of the council of the kingdom of Denmark arrived here from Denmark together with a doctor by the name of Dr Povel Beck.

On 15 December noble Steen Brahe and Steen Bille left for Denmark.

On 16 December his majesty sent two gilded silver plates to the bishop by his servant, a very well-dressed man who could not speak Latin; nor did he speak Scots to the bishop but said through an interpreter: 'the king wishes you a good day, and here is something he is sending in your honour, requesting that you shall accept it as thanks.' For which the bishop most humbly thanked his majesty and the chancellor with devout good wishes for the journey his majesty had undertaken etc. At eleven o'clock in the morning of the same day the chancellor and all his people with him departed, and between one and two o'clock the earl and his followers also left.

On 19 December his majesty's court preacher Mr David Lindsay sent a piece of gold by his son Mr David Lindsay junior,[23] and on it was his majesty's effigy or portrait. He stated that the bishop should thank his majesty personally for the gift. That same day William Schaw[24] came and told the bishop to come to the king and, when the bishop was shown into the king's chamber, his majesty himself was not present as he was in the queen's apartment playing[25] with her — this was at two o'clock. But about three o'clock his majesty and some noblemen came into his own apartment and spoke to the bishop for about half an hour about his majesty's journey here from Scotland; they also had other general conversation.

SCOTLAND'S LAST ROYAL WEDDING

When the bishop thanked his majesty most humbly for his royal generosity towards him, his majesty answered that it was a meagre gift; after that his majesty drank a full goblet of wine to the bishop and, when he had had it re-filled, his majesty himself took the goblet and handed it to the bishop. William [Schaw] said that his majesty had never done that to anyone before.[26]

At eight o'clock in the morning of 22 December his majesty and his majesty's beloved wife Lady Anne departed for Denmark. And as his majesty was leaving he stood up in the sledge and bade all the people good night not only in Scots but also in Danish; he was accompanied by all his court, nobles and commoners alike, and also by the noble Governor Axel Gyldenstierne. And all of them travelled overland through Viken.

On 1 January (which was New Year's Day) his majesty, his wife and the other good gentlemen reached Bohus between twelve and one and were entertained regally. On Sunday 4 January three sermons were preached at the castle. First of all, her grace had a German sermon given for her in her room. The Danes had a Danish sermon given for themselves in the church — noble Henrik Gyldenstierne himself went to the altar and requested Mr Mickel [Basse] to give a short account of the text concerning Christ's exile in Egypt; which he did. When the service was over Henrik Gyldenstierne went back to the altar where they were preparing the king's chair and ordered that the candles should be taken from the altar. Mr Mickel objected, being of the opinion that our religious freedom would thereby be infringed, but it was done nevertheless. After that his majesty and the royal court entered the church, yet in an informal manner, without procession or regard for rank. The song was the 6th Psalm of David but with lively music. The text was Romans 8, v.34. His majesty sat in noble Henrik Gyldenstierne's chair and listened to the sermon with particular devotion and piety. In the church he did not take his own hat off or replace it, since one of his attendants did it for him. When the sermon was over they were called to table by a fanfare of eight trumpets. His majesty was royally feasted in the great hall. Noble Henrik Gyldenstierne drank a toast to him with suitable good wishes and welcomes; he also proposed toasts on behalf of the queen of Denmark, the young lord [Christian IV] and Princess Anne, the ladies, and the council of the kingdom of Denmark. After the drinking of each

THE DANISH ACCOUNT

toast six cannon were fired. Then the king and her ladyship danced. The king danced her to noble Henrik Gyldenstierne and then chose among the other noble ladies and maidens. The dancing continued late into the evening with much delight and joy.

On the 6 January (Three Kings' Day) [Epiphany, or Twelfth Night] there was a great storm and it was so unpleasant that her grace was very ill at ease.

On 7 January his majesty departed from Bohus in great disarray between eleven and twelve even though her majesty was quite weak — so much so that she had to lie in the sledge as in a bed. She lay in a cot (which her grace's lady mother had sent from Denmark) fitted on a sledge. It was covered with black velvet and the back was velvet embroidered with gilded roses and silver sprigs — all very elaborate and valuable. Two dark brown horses drew the sledge. The same cot had formerly belonged to the lady mother of our most gracious queen, the wife of the noble lord Duke Ulrich.[27] A sledge had also been sent up from Denmark for King James. It was covered in black velvet and had two velvet cushions. It was drawn by two young chestnut horses in velvet cloths very splendidly embroidered with roses, stars and silver sprigs. There was no lack of noise or powder put into firing volleys in their honour from the walls and round towers.

So they travelled in the name of the Lord on the ice along the Göta River to the ferry place. There the Swedish lords met the Danish envoys who had requested escort through the Swedish borders on behalf of the king of Scotland; and each side showed the other great respect. Straightaway the Danish noblemen rode back to the king and assured his grace of a safe and neighbourly escort. The Swedish cavalrymen held their ranks — 600 men, splendidly equipped — until the Swedish lords had visited the king and the princess and saluted and congratulated them with the greatest respect. Then they and the Danes accompanied his majesty [through Swedish territory] to the [Danish] border. When they reached the fortress at Götalejon ['Guldberg'] the Swedish signal was fired double — four shots; the same at Älvsborg and also Otterhälla in order to show great respect and good wishes. That night his majesty lay at the house of a man called Peder Skriver who lived right on the border.

On 8 January they travelled twenty-five miles to Varberg where his majesty remained for six days. On 14 January they travelled from Varberg to Falkenberg — that is fifteen miles.

SCOTLAND'S LAST ROYAL WEDDING

On the 15th the twenty miles to Halmstad, on the 16th the fifteen miles to Laholm.

On the 17th the fifteen miles to Ängelholm where they had a meal and immediately afterwards on the same day went the fifteen miles to Helsingborg where His majesty remained for three days.

Insertion iii — Letter from King John III of Sweden to the governor of Älvsborg Castle, 12 December 1589[28]

To Jören Erickson concerning the king of Scotland, and that he shall not allow Count Axel [Gyldenstierne] and Andrew Keith [Lord Dingwall] into to the fortresses. Stockholm, 12 December 1589.

Conveying our special favour and gracious will. Since you, Jören Erickson, have let Us know that the king of Scotland, who recently held his wedding in Norway, seems to intend as soon as possible to travel from there through our country to Denmark. And for that reason you ask how you should comport yourself in this matter. In case the worthy king undertakes the journey without our safe-conduct, then we give you this answer, that if the king of Scotland does not in advance seek a safe-conduct from us, then we will in no way allow him to move through our country. For that reason [we] have ordered our true man and captain of horse Jören Passe that he shall without delay take himself to Älvsborg, assembling both noblemen, court servants and soldiers, so many as have horses and can be gathered together beforehand, and with them prevent the same [James] from travelling. But if the worthy king of Scotland requests our safe-conduct, you may give as an answer that we must be consulted about it, and that until an answer comes back from us, there is nothing you can do. And for that reason the king of Scotland and his retinue can for that time remain in Norway, wherever it it is most convenient for him. But as soon as our safe conduct is sent from here, then you should so arrange things that the king of Scotland and his retinue may be received suitably, with respect and honour. Arrange things so (and if it is needful) that nothing is lacking for their entertainment — but against payment. As far as our fortresses are concerned, we want you to take very good care that no foreigner or suspect may be admitted to them. Also in the same way our earnest will and command is that neither Count Axel, who has recently departed from there, nor Andrew

THE DANISH ACCOUNT

Keith be admitted to the castle, Älvsborg or Götalejon ['Gulborg'], whatever pretext they may offer. Which we have caused to give you as an answer, and you are to see that you carry it out.

On 21 January a small boat covered in red Cambrai velvet came from Kronborg to fetch his majesty. He departed at precisely nine o'clock in it and reached Kronborg at twelve o'clock. Queen Sophia, the young Lord Christian [IV], Duke Ulrick and the four members of the ruling council [regents] of Denmark met them there. They remained there for eight days. They then travelled together from there to Copenhagen.

On 7 March his royal majesty went with a splendid accompaniment to the Royal Academy in Copenhagen and for two hours listened first to Dr Hans Slangerup, the theologian, and then to Dr Anders Christensen, the physician. At the end Dr Povel [Mathias], bishop of the diocese of Zealand, humbly congratulated his majesty and thanked him for his graciousness in visiting their academy etc. As his majesty was going out, he stood in the door until Dr Povel came and then he gave him his hand in the most gracious manner saying: 'Ego a teneris annis addictus sum litteris, quod etiam hodie volui declarare,' Which is: 'I have since childhood been given to the literary arts and have had joy in them — and I should like to declare that today.' To which Dr Povel replied: 'His grace has thereby left behind him here at the Royal Academy a name that will forever be highly praised.' He then took his leave. Later his majesty sent (by the hand of his court preacher) a gilded cup and seven volumes or large books to Dr Povel — they were valued at seventy-two daler.

After that his majesty travelled to Roskilde where his majesty had [Niels] Hemmingsen as his guest midday and evening and discussed, with acute perception, predestination. For in that respect he was completely a disciple of Calvin. Then his majesty presented Hemmingsen with a gilded cup valued at forty-eight daler.

Then his majesty travelled through Frederiksborg to Elsinore where he visited the widely famed and well born mathematician Tyge Brahe at Ven [Hven]. Meanwhile reports came announcing the arrival of Duke Henry of Brunswick who celebrated his royal marriage with the high-born Lady Elizabeth, other daughter of King Frederick and Queen Anne's sister, on 19 April, which was Easter Day.

SCOTLAND'S LAST ROYAL WEDDING

III — SCOTLAND: THE CORONATION

Immediately after that, on the third day of Easter [21 April], His Majesty King James of Scotland with his noble and dear wife Lady Anne set sail home for Scotland. They remained at sea continuously with various winds, both favourable and unfavourable, for nine days. On 1 May his majesty and the whole fleet arrived safely in Scotland[1]. They landed at a small town by the name of Leith. At one o'clock in the afternoon William Stewart and a number of other Scottish gentlemen came to his majesty and his charming wife with most humble and respectful greetings. At this the cannons of the fleet fired the Danish signal with great splendour. Nor did the Scottish ships spare noise and powder in expressing the joy of the country at the gracious arrival of their lord king and queen. At five o'clock in the evening his majesty and his charming wife went ashore[2] and then all the cannon on the ships were fired. The Scottish nobility, who were gathered at that time and place together with the common people, received his majesty and her grace with the most humble congratulations, delight and joy. The street, all the way from the quay to the house where their majesties were to sleep, was strewn with cloth.[3] When they went indoors each of them sat upon a regally decorated chair, after which James Elphinstone,[4] one of the king's council, delivered a long oration. As soon as it was finished his majesty and the queen went into the church,[5] and after that the queen was led to her royal chamber.

On 3 May the Danish royal envoys sent Dr Nicolaus Theophilus[6] to the Scottish chancellor [Maitland of Thirlestane] to discuss which day should be decided on for her grace's coronation; and to urge that, since that day had not yet been fixed, the chancellor would press that it should be settled as soon as possible so that they could set off home again. He was given the answer that 17 May had been decided on, and it could not be brought forward as that would exclude the estates of the realm from it. He [the chancellor], for his own part, would be glad to assist and please the royal lords and envoys in all other matters, great or small. When the Danish envoys heard this they sent a second message to the chancellor requesting that, since the day of the coronation was so far in advance, they desired in the meantime to achieve something. It was therefore their intention to go and examine the place which was to be the queen's life-interest or morning gift as stated in the

THE DANISH ACCOUNT

dowry contract, so that they could approve and accept it on her behalf. To which the chancellor replied that he would lay their request before the king and reach a decision by the next day. That same day the Danish envoys were guests of his majesty for the evening meal.

On 4 May the Danish lords once again applied to the chancellor for a decision. The chancellor made the excuse that there were all sorts of other matters to be settled which had prevented him arranging a time when the houses or the castles, fortresses and counties might be viewed; and furthermore, with regard to the viewing, the factors would need to take the oath of loyalty before the lands were taken possession of. That, he said, might easily be dealt with, but that they should be put to the inconvenience of having to take an oath so soon was not the custom of the country and had not been heard of before. Therefore it could not take place in such a short time etc., but he would approach his majesty about all this at the first opportunity and bring his majesty's explanation to the royal envoys and council.

On 5 May nothing was done except that his majesty went hunting with the Danish royal envoys.

On 6 May his majesty and his charming wife travelled to Edinburgh, which is the capital of Scotland. The order of procession was as follows: the king with his earls and lords left a little in advance; then her grace followed dressed in white bliant,[7] sitting in her own carriage (which she had brought from Denmark) drawn by eight brown horses.[8] Before her rode three earls who were temporarily attached to the Danish envoys. The citizens of Edinburgh stood on both sides in full ranks with flying banners. All the Danish and Scottish noblemen with their servants rode before her grace's carriage. Behind her grace rode her maidens. When they arrived outside the West Port twenty-four councillors and citizens were lined up, all in beautiful long clothes, and a doctor of laws who was standing among them delivered a short oration and speech congratulating her grace on behalf of the common estates of Scotland.[9]

On 8 May the queen's life interest was discussed in writing.

On the 10th Peter Young asked insistently whether the noble envoys had with them the marriage contract or documents between King James III and Queen Margaret as it would be so much the better to be able to appeal to them and act according to them in this act of dowry. For his majesty wished the royal envoys to have

101

good information. But, when he realised that the noble Danish envoys did not have the aforementioned documents, the situation remained as it was. Towards evening the same day the chancellor had Dr Nicolaus called to him and passed to him an extract of the oft-requested inventory and list of the annual income and duties from her grace's life-interest or morning gift.

The noble royal envoys, on the other hand, put before the chancellor the form of the oath which the aforementioned factor[s] as well as the subjects must immediately swear with regard to the said life-interest.[10]

Form of the Scottish Oath: That is,

You shall swear that you will be loyal and faithful to her grace in all respects, that you will demand and promote her majesty's benefit and prevent all injury to her with your utmost ability. And you shall deliver to her majesty all annual income from her majesty's life-interest etc. Item, you shall demand the customary oath from all those who live in your fief, irrespective of which rank or estate they may be. Furthermore, you shall behave in all ways as befits a loyal and diligent judge. May God and His holy gospel help you.

Inventory of the annual rent and income of her majesty's morning gift.[11]

That same day noble Peder Munk, admiral of the kingdom of Denmark, checked and estimated on behalf of her majesty the annual rent and income of her life-interest, and it amounted approximately in Danish currency to an income of 7,000 daler not including cheese, butter, capons, lime and such other things as are not specified in the valuation. And as a morning gift her grace was assigned Falkland, Linlithgow, Lithton[12] and Dunfermline with the places and farmers subject to them.

On 11 May[13] the Danish royal councillors and envoys travelled from Edinburgh to Leith, and at midday they were invited to be guests of Sir Robert Melville of Murdocarny,[14] the king's treasurer, by whom they were splendidly entertained.

On the 12th the aforementioned envoys travelled on to Falkland, where the queen's domain began, in order to view her grace's life-interest. Here the factor, James Beaton of Creich, came to meet them with sixty horses and led them into the royal house.[15] Mr John Skene had openly published here a printed and sealed royal

THE DANISH ACCOUNT

mandate in which the seneschal is commanded by his majesty of Scotland to surrender the fief and the castles of the whole sheriffdom of Fife together with all the places in Falkland and to hand them over to the royal envoys for the benefit of the queen in Scotland. Which the seneschal, as a loyal subject, also did, immediately handing Lord Admiral Peder Munk a stone and earth as is the custom among the Scots, thereby placing the possession of the aforementioned sheriffdom in the hands of the Danish envoys.[16] Whereupon the Danish lords and royal envoys requested that John Hay,[17] royal notary public, should record this in written documents.

Later the same day they travelled on to Newhouse where Lord William Douglas, earl of Morton,[18] received them particularly splendidly, having ridden to meet them at the boundaries of his lands with seventy riders and greeted them with all respect.

On the 13th the Danish envoys travelled to Dumfermline[19] which is also one of the places in her grace's morning gift. Here, Robert Dury[20] came to meet them with one hundred horses and received them with great magnificence. Dumfermline is a royal house, [and] lies in a pleasant place with beautiful hills. This fief was passed over to the Danish envoys in exactly the same manner as was described for the sheriffdom of Fife.

On 14 May the Danish lords travelled to Linlithgow where Lewis Bellenden,[21] knight, royal councillor and governor of the palace of Linlithgow, rode out with fifty horsemen, received them splendidly and delivered Linlithgow to them just as has been said with regard to Falkland in Fife. At the same time Lord Claud Hamilton[22] and Lewis Bellenden took their oaths in the manner prescribed. After that the Danish envoys travelled the twelve miles back to Edinburgh.

On 15 May, after this inspection had come to an end and the Danish lords had returned to Edinburgh, they at once sent a request to the chancellor that certain letters that they required from him should be ready as soon as possible in order that they [the Danes] would not be delayed once the coronation was over.

On 17 May the coronation took place,[23] and on that morning His Majesty King James VI of Scotland dubbed fifty of the most prominent nobles as knights, and made chancellor John Maitland knight commander and baron of Thirlestane, and also chose and honoured him as the leading gentleman of parliament.[24]

103

SCOTLAND'S LAST ROYAL WEDDING

A Description of the Coronation

The coronation took place in the church of the Holy Cross in Holyrood Abbey next to the king's palace. A high place had been prepared on the gallery in the church for the king and queen. Trumpeters and many servants, who kept the people to one side, walked in front of the king, who was the first to enter the church.[25] After them rode the royal chamberlain and the master of horse, then knights, barons, court officials and noblemen. After them, when they had all passed into the church in good order, came the heralds in their yellow livery (into which red lions were embroidered) with gold chains around their necks in which red lions were entwined. After them followed the lion [lyon king of arms], a baron and a military commander.[26] Next came Andrew, Lord Dingwall, the under-marshal; Alexander Lindsay, the vice-chamberlain; and William [Douglas], earl [of Angus] and lord of Douglas and Abernethy,[27] bearing the golden sword for the king. He was followed by John, Lord Hamilton[28] with the sceptre. Then came Lewis, duke of Lennox[29], the great chamberlain of Scotland, and he was bearing the crown.

After all these came the king in his livery, all of purple. Five earls bore the king's long, full coat behind his majesty. Then her grace followed, with [the following] order of procession. First went trumpeters, followed by the Danes of nobility and then some Scottish gentlemen. Behind them came two heralds with their officer, and next the chancellor bearing the queen's crown. Then came her grace herself. At her right hand walked Sir Robert Bowes,[30] the English ordinary envoy; at her left hand was noble Peder Munk, admiral of the Danish Kingdom and member of the ruling council of the kingdom.[31] Immediately after them walked the wife of the English envoy and the [dowager] countess of Mar,[32] who had brought up His Majesty King James of Scotland during his childhood. Next came Margaret Bothwell,[33] wife of the Scottish Admiral; and Joan, countess of Orkney.[34] These four countesses bore her grace's long train. They were followed by some other Scottish countesses and ladies, among whom were the wives of the chancellor and Lewis Bellenden.[35] Last came the queen's maidens, Cathrina Schinckel[36] and Anne Kaas,[37] together with many Scottish maidens as well. Thus everyone entered the church and went to their assigned places. The sermon began after the singing

THE DANISH ACCOUNT

of Psalms 40 and 48.[38] After this service Robert Bruce, the bishop,[39] stepped forward with a short oration prefacing the impending ceremony he had been commanded to perform.[40] Meanwhile, the countess of Mar went up to the queen and bared a little of the queen's right arm and shoulder. Robert Bruce immediately poured the queen's oil onto her bare arm and shoulder. The duke of Lennox, Lord Hamilton and the countess of Mar, followed by the aforementioned royal ladies-in-waiting, then led her grace into her tent,[41] where her grace donned queenly clothes and royal robes[42] and then came out of the tent and returned to her former place. Silence was called for. Then his majesty had the crown delivered to her. It was passed to Robert Bruce who, standing below the duke of Lennox, Lord Hamilton and the chancellor, placed the crown on her majesty's head.[43] Immediately afterwards his majesty delivered the sceptre to Robert Bruce that he might pass it to the queen;[44] which he did, making the following oration:

> By royal might and power, and on behalf of all the estates, we place this crown on your royal majesty's head and give into your majesty's hands this sceptre, whereby we acknowledge your majesty as our most gracious lady and queen of Scotland. We also pledge our most humble and dutiful obedience in all that concerns the honour of God, the comfort of His church and the welfare of your majesty.

These words were repeated by David Lindsay, the second minister of the parish, in the French language so that her majesty could understand them. She answered 'yes' to them, and, in order to confirm and reinforce them, her majesty placed her hand on the Bible and gave her oath as follows:

The Queen's Oath:

> We Anne, by the grace of God queen of Scotland, acknowledge and witness before God and His holy angels that we, as long as we live and as far as is possible, will love and honour this same eternal God according to the manifestation of His will as revealed in Holy Scripture; that we will advance and support religion with true and reliable ceremonies, will repudiate and work against all popish superstition and false teaching, which is against God's word, whatever name it may be called by; that we will love justice and equity, advance the Christian church in this kingdom and support peace and tranquillity as truly as we wish that Our Lord and Father will be gracious to us in all His mercy.

SCOTLAND'S LAST ROYAL WEDDING

After this Robert Bruce exhorted the people to pray that God, in His great mercy, would grant the queen the grace to complete and keep unflinchingly that which she had sworn. When this had happened the heralds called out with loud and clear voices 'May Our Lord and God protect and keep the queen.' All the common people similarly called out good wishes to the queen and the trumpeters blew immediately. Meanwhile, the queen went from her seat up to a higher seat and stood there on the right of the duke of Lennox and Lord Hamilton; and, when she sat down with the crown on her head and the sceptre in her right hand, Andrew Melville, professor of theology in the university of St Andrews, stepped forward and congratulated her majesty with two hundred verses.[45]

After this Robert Bruce gave the listeners a short explanation of the great and high benevolence that Almighty God had shown to them, in that He had firstly given the kingdom of Scotland such a learned lord who was so fully confirmed in his religion etc. and devoted to the kingdom; secondly, that he had granted as a companion to his royal majesty such a majestic and virtuous queen, gifted with the knowledge of God to the comfort of all Christians. Next he exhorted the nobles and the common people to be heartily joyful at this homage to, and coronation of, her majesty. Now they were to swear their oaths. After this admonition the duke of Lennox, Lord Hamilton, Robert Bruce, David Lindsay, the worthy provosts[46] of the towns of Edinburgh and Dundee, Colonel David Seton of Parbroth[47] and John Cockburn of Ormiston turned to the queen, kneeled and with raised hands gave their oath on behalf of the common Scottish people. It was as follows:

The oath of the Scottish estates to Queen Anne:

> In the name of and on behalf of all of the ranks and estates in this kingdom of Scotland, we swear to and assure your grace, who is our most gracious queen and the true and dear wife of our most gracious lord and king, that we shall be loyal, faithful and obedient; and, as the most humble subjects of our most gracious lord and king, we shall with all diligence and service be found to be respectful and favourably disposed towards your grace with regard to life and property; as truly as God is gracious to us and makes us partake in the splendour of His Heavenly Kingdom according to the Holy Scripture.

After this, the chancellor and the other nobility and also the common men similarly swore loyalty and faithfulness with raised

THE DANISH ACCOUNT

hands and with great joy and happiness. Then the trumpeters blew gaily.[48] After that the parish priest of that place, Patrick Galloway, stepped up to the pulpit and blessed both of their majesties with great devoutness. Thus the coronation ended. Then the king went to the queen and wished her majesty good fortune and blessings. They left the church as before, except that the queen kept the royal crown on her head and the chancellor walked before her with the sceptre.

IV — SCOTLAND: THE ENTRY INTO EDINBURGH

On 18 May it was once again suggested to the chancellor that everything should be completed at the first opportunity so that the Danish legates should not be delayed too long and could leave within a week.

On 19 May the queen was taken from Holyrood in her own coach and brought to Edinburgh shortly before two o'clock.[1] The following gentlemen rode before her majesty:[2]

Danish Gentlemen	*Scottish Gentlemen*
Peder Munk	Lord Hamilton
Steen Brahe	Earl of Angus
Breide Rantzau	Earl of Morton
Henrik Gyldenstierne	'Her van Meidt'
Henning Giøye	Lord Seton
Ove Liunge	'Her van Hiundt'
Gotzlef Bude	Lord Boyd
Hannibal Gyldenstierne	Lord Sinclair
Anders Thot	Lord Lindsay
Jørgen Brahe	Lord Livingston
Jacob Krabbe	Colonel William Stewart
Henning Reuentlou	Sir John Carmichael of that Ilk[3]
Kasten Dyring	Justice Clerk [Sir Lewis Bellenden]
Stein Madtzon	John Home of Coldenknowes
Erick Kaas	David Murray
Gaadske Rantzau	'Joen Aaffskar'
Jørgen von Espen	John Lindsay
Christen Høg	'Vellzan Hiren'[4]

Behind her coach[5] rode the master of horse with a spare horse in case the queen desired to ride. Then came four ladies and behind them Cathrine Schinckel, Sophia Kaas and six Scottish maidens. When they came under the West Port a number of cannon were fired from the castle that lies up on a high cliff. Immediately after that Robert Bruce gave her majesty a blessing.

SCOTLAND'S LAST ROYAL WEDDING

The gate was hung with rich tapestries and above them was a cleverly constructed arch on which musicians and instrumentalists stood and joyfully made themselves heard. A large globe was lowered from this arch; it was red, blue and green in colour with a skilfully constructed iron frame. In this globe there was the son of a councillor[6] — about eight years old and dressed in red velvet clothing; and over the red velvet clothes he wore a white taffeta cloak.[7] His globe was so cleverly made that when it was lowered by a pulley it opened up and the child could be seen standing in the globe on the same level as her majesty's carriage. On a shield the boy carried a book and two bunches of keys wrapped in gold cloth, with around twenty keys in each bunch.[8] Like an angel sent down from Heaven, he was to persuade her majesty to keep God's holy name in the greatest respect and honour it, above all else. Thereupon he kissed the book (which was the Bible)[9] and handed it to her majesty saying:

> O gracious queen, you are to understand
> that I am the angel of the town you are entering.
> I am sent by the one above
> to bring you the true understanding
> that you shall love and keep God's word above all things;
> that is why I am giving you this good Bible
> that I have brought from one on high.
> He promises to protect your country
> and to drive away everything that might harm it,
> so that everything may be turned to your advantage.

At this the boy passed a gilded key to her majesty and said as follows:

> Here is the key of the city, take care of it
> so that you may keep guard of us.
> You shall have the power to do to us
> whatever law and justice suggests to you
> and to bring justice to all men.
> We give you again the promise that we carry in our hearts.

Apart from this he gave her majesty a valuable piece of jewellery with a deep bow — it was a gift from the city to her majesty — and then he gave a blessing and wished her majesty much good fortune. In exchange, her majesty immediately gave him a gift. At that he was at once winched up again, so cleverly that before their very eyes his globe closed up so that nothing could be seen apart from a round, well-appointed and cleverly coloured globe.

THE DANISH ACCOUNT

Because of the numerous people who were pressing to see the queen, fifty people had been ordered to walk the whole time in front of her majesty's coach to make space and room. These people were masked with faces of lead, iron and copper which were made so cleverly that it was not easy to tell that they were made of these materials, so natural were they. Some had blackened their faces so that their heads were just like those of blackamoors, but an absolutely real and native blackamoor was their leader.[10] He had a drawn sword in his hand but the others only had long white staffs in order to make space.[11] On their bodies they only had the sort of tunics seamen wear, something like boatsmen's half smocks, and these were made of white bliant[12] with half-sleeves and no collar. Their necks, arms and hands were blackened, and around their necks they had beautiful gold chains.

A few of them had black silk sleeves and black gloves on, while all of them had their arms decorated with gold chains and bracelets and they had gold rings on almost every finger. In their noses and mouths they had gold chains of three or four links with precious stones in the links, and many of them had gold rings in their ears. Their trousers were quite short and tight, reaching no further than the middle of the thigh, and they were all made of white bliant. All other parts of their thighs were blackened so that they shone, and they were even decorated with gold chains. Each of them had been assigned a particular and special gait in imitation of various sorts of people. Some walked erect and defiant, some as if in a half dance, some like storks in the water with long, high steps, some as if they were drunk and staggering from side to side, some were bent low and hung their heads. By means of such strange gaits they made enough room and space without recourse to blows and pushes for, as they lumbered or staggered forward, the common people moved to the side. They also had black shoes which reached a little above the ankle; they were black, red or white, set with gold sprigs and some with gold chains in the shape of hearts, diamonds and crosses.

Meanwhile six worthy citizens were walking by her majesty's carriage bearing a brown or liver-coloured square velvet canopy over the coach.[13] This canopy was likewise decorated with costly and valuable gold fringes and various precious stones. The houses on both sides of the street were all bedecked and decorated with various tapestries. Then they entered a small narrow street[14] where there was a high wall on which a small boy was positioned, dressed in the garb of an astronomer. Pretending to be a mathematician, he stood by a brass sphere[15] and had various mathematical instruments with him. He greeted the queen with the very deepest bow and said:

> O gracious queen, you will discover
> what sort of holy woman I am;
> I am a goddess, as you can imagine,
> and I can prophesy your fortune.
> You are to remember that God has created you,
> and I am aware that Heaven has favoured you.
> I will tell you in all honour that your planet
> signifies that you would be daughter of a king
> and foretold that you would become a queen.
> I will say without lying
> — believe me in this and it will prove true —
> that you will bear royal children with honour,
> and also become a woman of intelligence
> whose virtues will shine both inwardly and outwardly.
> You will inspire your lord to good deeds
> and convert the people to the fear of God.
> As long as you are alive, Scotland may rejoice,
> and after your death, weep piteously.
> Therefore O queen and gracious woman,
> may the good fortune that is in your soul befall you,
> may God give you your heart's desire
> and may what your stars foretell come to pass.
> Do not take my speech and short prophecy
> as derision or as mockery.
> And as a sign sent from heaven
> so that you may perceive at this very time and place
> that all will be blissful,
> Nature will now send you rain and hail,
> white, hard and sweet —
> behold, here it is in your lap.
> It is a certain sign that my speech
> is true. With that, farewell.[16]

At this, finely ground sugar and various sweets were thrown from the windows on all sides. Then the air was filled with oral and instrumental music simultaneously.

Next, when they came to the Butter Tron,[17] there was a palace built of planks in which there were many singers and instrumentalists who gave full measure of their art. Above the palace nine[18] worthy

THE DANISH ACCOUNT

daughters of the citizenry were placed. They were most splendidly dressed and they had beautiful gilded books in their hands.[19] When her majesty arrived they curtsied deeply and a young person[20] addressed her majesty on their behalf in the following way, as though they were the nine muses, etc:

> O excellent queen, I say in truth
> that you must not believe this kingdom to be so lowly
> that it has neither possessions nor achievements.
> Behold here goddesses who curtsey to you!
> You shall not consider our people unintelligent
> even if our clothes make us appear so.
> I tell you in truth that our gracious king
> is a most learned man with regard to books.
> Let me tell you more about this:
> his wisdom encompasses both spiritual and temporal matters,
> we are his servants and he rules over us,
> therefore we follow in his footsteps.
> We are not mortal beings as you may think,
> for we are from the pure angelic choir,
> we are goddesses and we bear their names;
> you may dwell here with us with honour.
> We will serve you and show you honour,
> you shall be the first and best among us.
> We will treat you as our mother
> and you shall be our brave refuge.
> We promise you all the support
> the king may need upon this earth.

After this the queen was drawn further along the street[21] to the great church below the tolbooth where a large theatre or stage had been built, and on it stood Virtue or Piety among her four daughters, all in black silk clothes.[22] The mother, who was Virtus or Virtue herself, had a golden crown on her head but the daughters, who represented Prudence, Justice, Fortitude and Temperance, had wreaths and flowers on them. These daughters now stood up and faced her majesty with delicate curtseys, and the mother Virtue gave the queen the golden crown with her right hand, and a horn, filled with various fragrant things, with her left hand. Thereupon she began her speech to her majesty in the following manner:

> I am Virtue and people call me praiseworthy,
> I had four daughters in all.
> Gracious queen, if you take them to you,

111

SCOTLAND'S LAST ROYAL WEDDING

> you will achieve great fortune
> in your house and all your courts,
> for their eyes are always watchful
> and they bring benefit with their constant attention.
> If you believe in them you will be beyond danger.
> You will gain a sufficiency of personal and public benefits,
> for they are very virtuous women.
> You will receive great honour from them
> even when your hair has turned quite grey;
> even when you are laid to sleep in the grave
> every man will praise your name.
> But whoever does not obey my counsel
> will very soon regret it,
> for whoever does not attend to piety and virtue
> may expect a sorrowful career.
> Vice is a shameful woman
> who dazzles the eyes of many,
> she brings with her the sort of gifts
> that gods do not desire to have,
> and leads many a man into sin and blame
> so that his name is passed on in shame.

Prudence

Prudence had an astrolabe in her right hand and a book in the other.[23] She begins her speech to the queen thus:

> My mother has four daughters in all
> and I am the one called Prudence.
> I reckon the passing seasons well
> and pay attention to the future with good reason.
> I teach my servants what is right
> so that indolence does not harm them;
> I am sagacious and give good advice
> so that misfortune does not come to us.
> If you take me into your service then I will
> never bring any harm to the two of you.

Justice

Then Justice, the second daughter, stands up with a sword in one hand and a set of scales in the other. She begins her speech to the queen in this way:

> I am called Justice by everyone,
> I call the lords to judgement.
> There is no city, castle or fortress

THE DANISH ACCOUNT

in which I should not be guest;
I take nothing from anyone
without giving him value in exchange.
Anyone who offers something other than justice
will enjoy but little good fortune.
Great and strong castles are built on me
and no one can easily demolish them.
I would advise you to follow Justice
for without me both of you will lose so much.

Fortitude

The third daughter, that is Fortitude, stands up and has in one hand the club of Hercules and in the other a shield.[24] She speaks thus:

You may notice that I am called Fortitude,
a name I was given by learned clerks.
If your majesty knows the art that I can teach
you will find it very hard to do without me,
for in me you will find the art of overcoming success and failure.
In success you should be simple and pious,
in failure you should be patient and take your time.
So that you may best control sorrow
you should pay it no particular attention.
The wheel of fortune turns quickly
if only you keep a steadfast mind.

Temperance

The fourth daughter, Temperance, stands up and has a bridle in one hand and an hourglass in the other.[25] She speaks thus:

This is what I have seen and wish to conquer:
great lords let themselves be fettered —
for when sensual pleasure and great wealth
sing together with one voice
they soon bring harm and misfortune
unless they are bridled quickly.
If you wish to overcome this
then take me as your serving-woman.
I can teach you to do what is right
so that you can keep everything within bounds,
and so that your great wealth and queenly honour
may lead to honour of God and of the kingdom.
You should ever bear in mind
your lovely person and your royal attire.

SCOTLAND'S LAST ROYAL WEDDING

> If you will obey and follow me
> we will stand here as two beautiful women
> and the kingdom will become mighty
> just as my mother Virtue has said.

Virtue

Next Virtue, the old mother, stands up once again and speaks to the queen thus:

> You hear now, brave princess and queen,
> that this kingdom is praiseworthy in so many ways
> that it has few equals
> — I tell you that in truth.
> You should bear these words in mind:
> the fear of God brings honour and might,
> let the word of God be your greatest wealth,
> be virtuous and pious towards your subjects.
> If you do that then I, Virtue, and all my children
> will gladly follow your footsteps.

When this play came to an end the singers began to sing the 120th Psalm of David to a lively melody: 'In my distress I cried unto the Lord' etc.[26]

After that they came to the great church, called St Giles Church which stands in the middle of the town. Four councillors then stepped forward and bore a canopy of red velvet on four long red poles over her majesty as she went from the carriage to the church door. Meanwhile, the singers sang the 19th Psalm of David: 'The heavens declare the glory of God' etc. Her majesty was led into the church by Peder Munk and the Scottish Lord Hamilton. Mr Robert [Bruce] preached on some verses of the 107th Psalm, and after this sermon they sang the 23rd Psalm. Then her majesty was led out to the carriage again by the aforementioned gentlemen, and the red velvet canopy was born over her grace to Holyrood where the king was.

When they had come out of the church onto the square a palace had been erected on which there were the queen's ancestry and the arms of Denmark together with the freedoms and arms of all the Scottish queens. On one side stood instrumentalists with their various instruments. Among them stood a big fellow on a wine barrel.[27] He had a wreath on his head, was dressed in nothing but nightclothes and had a whole lot of glasses[28] full of wine, some of which he drank and some of which he threw among the people. On the other side, which was turned towards the church, they saw four young lads in maidens' clothing among whom two were supposed to represent Bacchus and Ceres. In front of them they had nuts, corn, straw, silver plates with sugar and silver dishes with grapes. They spoke to the queen as follows:

> We have come from Heaven with great honour and repute
> and with wine and bread in our charge
> for your benefit.
> Hear us, O gracious queen!
> As a morning gift from us you shall have
> as much of them as you desire.
> We have sufficient on this earth
> for your arrival and your great pleasure.
> If you but favour us
> then you shall have lively days.
> Every year you may expect
> wine and bread, and that with interest.
> To be joyful both winter and spring
> you shall have as much as you desire.
> We do not want to miss a good party
> so I will take this beaker
> and drink to your health —
> I shall not leave a drop in it.
> Thus I can forget both sorrow and need
> and live in joy as God bade me.
> My children! sing a new song
> so that it sounds over the whole town.

After that the singers began to sing, the instrumentalists to play and the old fellow to throw sugar, apples, nuts and sweets around among the common people. A little further down the main street[29] they had erected a high column or tree decorated with May leaves and green plants. The column had five small stages or steps on it and on each step there were two young lads sitting, one on the left side and one on the right. Scotland's coat-of-arms and genealogical table hung from each of those on the left hand side, and Denmark's coat-of-arms and her kings from Christian I hung from those on the right.[30] Each of these young children had a crown on his head, a shield before his chest and a royal sceptre in his hand. Below the lowest step, right under their feet and at the base of the tree, there lay a young man on a bed. He was in a full cuirass and armour. These people and coats-of-arms together were supposed to make manifest the blood relationship between Denmark and Scotland and to show how closely King James VI of Scotland and Queen Anne, daughter of the late King Frederick of Denmark, were related. The man who lay at the base of the tree represented King Christian I from whom both King James VI and Queen Anne were descended in the manner shown by the following table:[31]

Christian I, king of the Danes was the ancestor of —
Margaret   Frederick 1
James 4   Christian 3
James 5   Frederick 2
Mary
James 6   Anne

Above this tree or pillar there stood a lad who explained the meaning of the tree to her majesty in the following way. He had a gilded stick in his hand and with it he pointed to each coat-of-arms individually and said:[32]

O gracious queen, we would like
to give you truthfully that certain knowledge
that people strive for;
if you pay attention it will be enjoyable.
You will notice and discover
that Denmark and Scotland are not two
and that you are not the first shoot
that this friendship has born.
I shall show you this without much trouble
if you and your carriage remain here a while.
It is a hundred years and two and twenty more
— I do not lie — since there was
a pious man in Denmark
by the name of King Christian.   [Christian I]
He gave his daughter's hand to King James [III].
She was Margaret, queen in Scotland,   [Margaret]
who bore a son to her great bliss   [James IV]
and he became king of the Scots.
He was King James IV by name
and he brought the Scots great benefit.
He fathered a son of great beauty   [James V]
who received Scotland as his right.
He was called King James V
and he ruled over all the Scots.
The same King James I am speaking of

THE DANISH ACCOUNT

    had great happiness and joy.
    God gave him a daughter   [Mary]
    who was to be queen of France and Scotland;
    she left behind her a mighty man
    who is now King James of all Scotland.   [James VI]
    His name is King James
    — a name he bears with great honour —
    and he is the sixth of that name.
    May God give him good fortune and profit.
    That same King Christian I spoke of
    fathered a son, delightful and pious,
    who was King Frederick I,   [Frederick I]
    a king of the kingdom of Denmark and Norway.
    A son was born to this king: [Christian III]
    he was Christian, highly praised and handsome.
    He was as fine a king of Denmark
    as flesh and blood could be.
    He always loved God above all else
    and therefore good fortune was his lot.
    He had a son while he lived
    who was to be Danish king after him.
    This Christian man was called King Frederick.   [Frederick II]
    His name is famous in all lands
    and he never forgot his father's virtue
    — so that it had passed into very good hands.
    His dear wife Sophia was to
    bear him a virtuous daughter with honour.
    This high-born woman was called Anne   [Anne]
    and she is now binding herself to our king:
    thus the king and the queen are of royal blood
    and both arisen from one root.
    I am telling you truly that the king is
    the fifth man from the root, the queen the fourth.
    Imagine, then, that the fifth and the fourth
    are bound together by the links of marriage.
    May God give them peace and eternal grace
    to live long and to rule well.

After this the queen moved out to the edge of the town and came as far as the East Port[33] where a little play had been arranged about how the queen of Sheba visited King Solomon.[34] They spoke thus:

SCOTLAND'S LAST ROYAL WEDDING

The Queen of Sheba

O gracious lord and mighty prince!
I desired to come to you
not to bear precious gifts
but to study your wisdom by talking to you.
It is a wisdom that the whole world speaks of
and that is why I turn to you.
Now that I have seen it I must admit
that I may never find your equal
and, though I have heard much said of this place,
its splendour goes far beyond that.
Your temple and divine service are so great
that there cannot be any greater on the earth.
That is why I say to you that
your equal is not to be found anywhere.

Solomon

What I have here, as you may remark,
are riches, wisdom, and priests
and all the other things that you see here.
I must have received them from God
whom I can never fully thank,
I'll tell you that if you wish to hear.

The Queen

You have taught me many things
which I formerly did not know.
I cannot repay your royal grace
but I will recommend you into God's power.
I will not speak of money
— that is too lowly for your majesty —
but I will tell you truly
that I will praise your splendour to all men.
I am making you a gift of balsam
which cannot grow in this land:
this is not to pay you for your wisdom
but as a sign of love from my side.
O, how blissful you must be
and also the people you rule over.
And O, what wisdom those who daily
consort with you must gain.
There is great joy in being in your company,
just as for those who drink from Pallas's breast.

THE DANISH ACCOUNT

Solomon

O gracious queen, I cannot fully
praise the gift you give me.
You shall remain with me in respect and honour.
As long as I am here in the world
I shall do everything that is dear to you
for you seem to be worthy of that.
With that I bid you good-night.
May God quickly send you to your kingdom.

At this place it had also been arranged for a young person, richly dressed and on behalf of the town, to interpret the meaning of this play to the queen. The same person presented her majesty with a gold chain set with valuable stones and jewels and valued at 22,000 daler.[35] Then he spoke:[36]

O gracious queen, we intend
to show you that it is the great and widespread friendliness,
both here and in the whole country,
that will give you power.
The king's love is great, as you will see.
That is why he contemplated the cruel waves
and set to sea with winter approaching,
all so that you could be with him.
The queen of Sheba must have had a great desire
for King Solomon before she went to him
to learn from his great wisdom and wealth
even though she bore none of it home.
But you shall be the king's heart
and enjoy all royal honour with him.
He shall be to you next to your father and mother.
He shares with you the best he has.
The whole kingdom will serve you
whether you are on land or sea.
For your sake we will forego
our houses and goods, even our lives.
Now we present you with a humble gift,
and in return you may remain gracious to us.
Note well that it is a sign
that we love you with good cause.
Everything we have belongs to you,
and we grant it to you gladly.
May God permit us to live together here
so that later we may enjoy eternal peace.

SCOTLAND'S LAST ROYAL WEDDING

With this, all of the acts ended and her majesty moved on to the royal palace[37] and was led into her chamber. After supper some young and healthy men began a fine sword-dance in the courtyard and both their majesties stood in the window and watched.

V — THE DEPARTURE OF THE DANISH AMBASSADORS, AND LIST OF THE SCOTS NOBLES WHO WERE IN NORWAY

On 20 May the ratification of the marriage contract and wedding gifts was delivered to the Danish lords and envoys.[1] On 21 and 22 May nothing else occurred other than that the Scottish chancellor was requested to expedite the matter. The chancellor came to the Danish lords with the excuse that the charters were not yet ready but would be completed at the first opportunity. On 24 May[2] the noble envoys were his majesty's guests and, when they approached his majesty on the matter of expediting the business and their journey home, his majesty answered that he would like nothing better than that the envoys were in a position to remain with him the whole year round. But, since he could easily understand their circumstances, both from their own point-of-view and that of the kingdom of Denmark, he did not wish to delay them any longer; and to the best of his knowledge the letters they desired were ready.[3] They thanked him in a suitable manner.

On the 26th the Danish lords bade their farewells, thanked both of their majesties and commended them into the faithful power of God with enduring health and royal bliss.[4] After a meal they travelled to Leith with some Scottish gentlemen who were keeping them company. The Danish envoys invited them as guests and entertained them there as befitted their rank. And so they remained that night in harbour.[5]

On 27 May they set sail at four o'clock in the afternoon and on 30 May they arrived at Hitteröy in Norway, which is four nautical miles north of Lindesnes. They remained at sea with a north-west wind down the Norwegian coast and around Skagen. On 1 June they had to lay the rudder over and run into Kalvsund in Norway. Towards evening on 3 June they set sail with a west-north-west wind and crossed the sea until they arrived at Kronborg at twelve o'clock on 4 June. Early in the morning of 5 June they entered Copenhagen, and with that the whole journey was brought to a happy end.

THE DANISH ACCOUNT

The names of the lords who were sent [to Denmark] by the privy council, and of the principal nobles who went with [King James] to Norway, according to their ranks and offices:

    John Maitland, knight, great chancellor of the kingdom and secretary
    George Keith, Earl Marischal, the leader of the king's ambassadors in Denmark
    Lewis Bellenden, knight and justice clerk
    Mr Robert Douglas, provost of Lincluden and collector general
    Andrew Keith, Lord Dingwall
    Alexander Lindsay, vice-chamberlain of the kingdom
    James Scrymgeour of Dudhope, constable of Dundee
    Patrick Vaus of Barnbarroch, one of the senators of the college of justice
    John Carmichael, knight and one of the masters of horse
    William Keith, knight, master of the king's wardrobe
    William Stewart, colonel of the kingdom
    Peter Young, the king's tutor and eleemosynar

All these were sent by the privy council. Three of them (the vice-chamberlain, the colonel and the master of horse) went before the king, and the rest followed.[6]

The next in rank after them:

    Mr David Lindsay, the king's preacher
    Mr John Skene
    Mr George Young, vice-secretary

After these, the next [in rank] were the gentlemen of the king's chamber and the gentlemen who attended the lords of the privy council, in the following order:

    Mr George Douglas, second son of the earl of Angus
    Archibald Douglas, son of the earl of Morton
    Andrew Sinclair, master of the king's household
    Mr George Murray, captain, brother of Lord Tullibardine
    James Sandilands, son of the laird of Calder, first keeper of the king's chamber
    George Hume
    David Murray
    William Schaw [master of works]
    John Gib
    William Stuart
    Roger Aschetoun [? Eston]

All these performed their offices in the king's household

SCOTLAND'S LAST ROYAL WEDDING

The following were added:

    James Douglas, heir of the laird of Lochleven
    George Douglas of Langniddrie
    George Douglas, the heir of the earl of Morton's brother
    Mr George Kerr, brother of the commendator of Newbattle, heir of the laird of Lasswade.

NOTES

Chapter 1   The Quest for a Bride

1. *CSPS, 1574–81*, 354, 371, 377, 522; J Dow, 'Scottish relations with Sweden, 1500–1625' (typescript of unfinished thesis, held by John Simpson, Department of Scottish History, University of Edinburgh).
2. *CSPS, 1581–3*, 403, 437–8.
3. *James the Sext*, 211–12.
4. 1546–1625: *DBL*, xi, 161–3.
5. 1540–1606: *DBL*, i, 551.
6. 1541–1604. Theophilus was a doctor of laws: *DBL*, xiv, 436–7.
7. J Melville, *Memoirs* (Bannatyne Club, 1827), 336–46; *CSPS, 1584–5*, 659, 676, 678–80; *CSPS, 1585–6*, 20; *RPCS, 1578–85*, 749n; J Bain (ed.), *The Hamilton papers* (2 vols, 1890–2), ii, 645, 650–1, 652, 658; Moysie, *Memoirs*, 53; W Fraser, *Memorials of the earls of Haddington* (2 vols, Edinburgh, 1889), ii, xxi, 52.
8. *Calendar of State Papers, Foreign, 1585–6* (1921), 90.
9. Front cover, and The Weiss Gallery, *Tudor and Stuart Portraits, 1530–1660* (London, 1995), no. 12.
10. Riis, *Auld acquaintance*, i, 110–11, ii, 78–9; J Ferguson (ed.), *Papers illustrating the history of the Scots Brigade in the service of the United Netherlands* (3 vols, SHS, 1899–1901), i, 116–18n; NLS, Adv. 33. 1. 11, vol 28, no. 30 — translated in the manuscript Calendar, vol 4; Macray, 'Third Report,' 41; *RSS, 1581–4*, no. 1044.
11. *Warrender papers*, ii, 46–9; *CSPS, 1585–6*, 330, 336–7; Melville, *Memoirs*, 346, 353, 362; R. Bell (ed.), *Extract from the despatches of M Courcelles, French ambassador at the court of Scotland* (Bannatyne Club, 1828), 9. For Frederick's letter to Stewart see NLS, Denmylne Mss, vol 28, no. 35.
12. Melville, *Memoirs*, 362–3; Vaus, *Correspondence*, ii, 378–9, 381–5, 390–1; *RPCS, 1585–92*, 169–70.
13. *Warrender papers*, ii, 44–6.
14. Niels Kaas, 1534–94, had been brought up partly by Niels Hemmingsen (the noted theologian), having been orphaned at an early age. He studied widely abroad before becoming chancellor to Frederick II in 1573. He was a major patron of the church, education and science in Denmark: *DBL*, viii, 430–2.

123

SCOTLAND'S LAST ROYAL WEDDING

15 Henrik Ramel, 1550–1610. Born in Pomerania, Ramel travelled widely before joining the service of Frederick II in 1581. The king showed him much favour: Ramel was naturalised, ennobled, and frequently consulted on foreign affairs. He was appointed councillor of the realm and chamberlain. *DBL*, xi, 590–1.

16 This account of the 1587 mission is taken mainly from Young's narrative of proceedings: *Warrender papers*, ii, 35–42. An incomplete account by Barnbarroch differs in a number of details: Vaus, *Correspondence*, ii, 396–400. See also Ibid, ii, 374–5, 403–4; *Despatches of M Courcelles*, 59, 77; *CSPS, 1586–8*, 496. One report from Denmark optimistically reported that the king's daughter had sailed for Scotland, her marriage having been agreed: *Calendar of State Papers, Foreign, 1586–8* (1927), 349.

17 Melville, *Memoirs*, 364; *CSPS, 1586–8*, 475–6, 478, 496; *RPCS, 1585–92*, 218.

18 Melville, *Memoirs*, 363–4.

19 Lee, *Thirlestane* 194–6.

20 Melville, *Memoirs*, 368.

21 H G Stafford, *James VI of Scotland and the throne of England* (New York, 1940), 53.

22 *Calendar of State Papers, Foreign, 1586–8*, 369; Macray, 'Third Report,' p. 49.

23 *CSPS, 1586–8*, 540–1.

24 *CSPS, 1586–8*, 610, 616, 635, 638, 648, 681; Historical Manuscripts Commission, *Salisbury (Cecil) Mss*, iii (1889), 334–5; Melville, *Memoirs*, 364; Moysie, *Memoirs*, 70.

25 *CSPS, 1586–8*, 655.

26 *APS*, iii, 437, 523.

27 *CSPS, 1589–93*, 77.

28 *CSPS, 1689–93*, 86, 87; Stafford, *James VI*, 52–3; Lee, *Thirlestane* 193. Lee describes the incident as a riot in the streets of Edinburgh, but there does not seem to be evidence to justify this.

29 Melville, *Memoirs*, 368.

30 Lee, *Thirlestane*, 198; *CSPS, 1589–93*, 97.

31 *CSPS, 1589–93*, 94–5, 96–7; D H Willson, *King James VI and I* (London, 1966), 23.

NOTES

Chapter 2   Negotiations and Proxy Marriage

1   Melville, *Memoirs*, 367; *CSPS, 1589–93*, 96.
2   *Despatches of M Courcelles*, 79.
3   K Brown, 'Aristocratic finances and the origins of the Scottish Revolution,' *English Historical Review*, civ (1989), 49.
4   *CSPS, 1589–93*, 95, quoted in Lee, *Thirlestane*, 198; Riis, *Auld acquaintance*, ii, 64–5.
5   G P V Akrigg (ed.), *Letters of James VI and I* (Berkeley, 1984), 95.
6   Dow, 'Scottish relations with Sweden'; *CSPS, 1571–4*, 692.
7   SRO, PS.1/59, ff. 100r–v; Fraser, *Earls of Haddington*, ii, xxi–xxii, 52–3.
8   *Scots peerage*, iii, 115–16.
9   Dow, 'Scottish relations'; Riis, *Auld acquaintance*, ii, 64.
10 *CSPS, 1584–5*, 682; Riis, *Auld acquaintance*, ii, 74.
11 Melville, *Memoirs*, 366.
12 *Edin. recs., 1573–89*, 543–4.
13 H W Meikle (ed.), *The works of William Fowler* (3 vols, Scottish Text Society, 1914–40), iii, xxii–xxiii.
14 Calderwood, *History*, v, 59; Moysie, *Memoirs*, 78.
15 *CSPS, 1589–93*, 95, 110; Lee, *Thirlestane*, 198–9.
16 *CSPS, 1589–93*, 103–4; HMC, *Salisbury Mss*, iii, 420–39. See the notes to the Account for the main variations between the two sets of instructions.
17 *CSPS, 1589–93*, 115, 122.
18 *CSPS, 1589–93*, 123–32, 137; D. Laing (ed.), *Original letters of Mr John Colville* (Bannatyne Club, 1858), 247; Melville, *Memoirs*, 368–9. For the text of James's letter see the Account, below.
19 *James the Sext*, 78; *CSPS, 1589–93*, 150.
20 T C Smout, 'Scottish marriage, regular and irregular, 1500–1940,' *Marriage and society. Studies in the social history of marriage* (London, 1981), 210–13 for some of the problems (not least for historians) arising from the separate civil and religious laws regarding marriage.
21 Thirlestane's Accounts, f.8v.
22 O Kongsted, H Ilsøe, etc. (eds.), *Festmusik fra Renaissancen* (Copenhagen, 1990), 47. The only complete copy of Praetorius's music is at BL, K.3.f.2.

Chapter 3 Storm-tossed Lovers

1 Macray, 'Third Report,' 25.
2 1534–1623, *DBL*, x, 126–7.
3 Valckendorf, 1525–1601, had an outstandingly successful career as an administrator under Frederick II, but made many enemies. He was one of the members of the council of regency and took part in the negotiation of the marriage treaty with the Scots. His loss of office as treasurer in 1590 may indicate that his reputation was damaged by Munk's allegations. *DBL*, xv, 252–5.
4 1530–1602, *DBL*, viii, 236
5 *DBL*, viii, 235–8.
6 1556–1618, *DBL*, xi, 604–6. Rantzau gave John Skene books by himself and others in July 1590: NLS, Ms 2912.
7 Steen Bille, 1565–1629, was widely travelled, and was to serve on a number of diplomatic missions to Scotland: *DBL*, ii, 114. He travelled with James to Norway, and was present at the christening of James's and Anne's son, Prince Henry, at Stirling in 1594: T Jexlev, 'Scottish history in the light of records in the Danish National Archives,' *SHR*, xlviii (1969), 106.
8 Andrew Sinclair, 1555–1625 was the third son of Henry, 5th Lord Sinclair. Andrew had presumably accompanied the Earl Marischal to Denmark, and the contacts he made on the trip evidently determined his career. He became a member of Christian IV's court in 1591 and later served that king in a number of offices in government and the army, as well as on a number of diplomatic missions: Riis, *Auld acquaintance*, i, 111, ii, 74; *Scots peerage*, iv, 575.
9 *CSPS, 1589–93*, 155, 157, 159, 162, 164, 165, 166–7; Macray, 'Third Report' 25; W Murdin, *Collection of state papers…left by William Cecil, Lord Burghley* (London, 1759), 637; HMC, *Salisbury Mss*, iii, 438–9; Moysie, *Memoirs*, 79; Melville, *Memoirs*, 369–70; Akrigg, *Letters of James VI and I*, 95; *Warrender papers*, ii, 109–19; Riis, *Auld acquaintance*, i, 264–5; Macray, 'Third Report,' 25.
10 *CSPS, 1589–93*, 157, 164, 166.
11 J Craigie (ed.), *The poems of James VI* (2 vols, Scottish Text Society, 1955–8), II, xxiii, 68.
12 *CSPS, 1589–93*, 140, 144.
13 Laing, *Original letters of Mr John Colville*, 248; *CSPS, 1589–93*, 159, 160–2.
14 P Walker, *Documents relative to the reception at Edinburgh of the kings and queens of Scotland, AD 1561–1650* (Edinburgh, 1822), 34–48.

NOTES

15 J Stuart (ed.), *Miscellany of the Spalding Club*, ii (Spalding Club, 1842), 114; Vaus, *Correspondence*, ii, 439–40.

16 Lee, *Thirlestane*, 201–2; HMC, *Salisbury Mss*, iii, 438.

17 HMC, *Salisbury Mss*, iii, 438–9; *RPCS, 1585–92*, 420–1; *Marriage*, 4–6n; Lee, *Thirlestane*, 202.

18 *RPCS, 1585–92*, 422–3.

19 HMC, *Salisbury Mss*, iii, 438–9; Calderwood, *History*, v, 57; 'The diarey of Robert Birrel, burges of Edinburghe,' p. 25, in [J G Dalyell (ed.)], *Fragments of Scotish history* (Edinburgh, 1798).

20 *RPCS, 1585–92*, 427–9; *Marriage*, 12–16 Lee, *Thirlestane*, 202.

21 Lewis or Ludovic Stuart duke of Lennox.

22 *RPCS, 1585–92*, 423–7, 429–30; *Warrender papers*, ii, 110–113; *Marriage*, 3–11.

23 *RPCS, 1585–92*, 421.

24 Bellenden returned home before James, by way of England: *DNB*; Riis, *Auld acquaintance*, ii, 55.

25 For a letter from him from Elsinore on 3 April 1590 see Vaus, *Correspondence*, ii, 455–6. Riis, *Auld acquaintance*, ii, 59.

26 The warden of the West Marches: *DNB*, ixx, 130.

Chapter 4   Marriage in Norway

1   Craigie, *Poems of James VI*, ii, 69.

2   *Kancelliets Brevbøger*, 284; *CSPS, 1589–93*, 187.

3   *CSPS, 1589–93*, 187; *CSPS, 1593*, 62.

4   J Melville, *Autobiography and diary* (Wodrow Society, 1842), 277.

5   Lindsay was minister of South Leith from 1560 to 1613. He attended no fewer than fifty-one meetings of the General Assembly, and was moderator six times. He was to baptise three of the children of the royal marriage that had brought him to Norway, Henry (1594), Margaret (1599) and Charles (1600). In 1600 he became bishop of Ross and a privy councillor. *Fasti*, i, 160–1.

6   Millar, 'Wedding-Tour,' 151–2; G Stephens, 'James VI in Tønsberg. With photograph of an oaken tablet erected in the church of St Mary, in commemoration of his visit,' *Proceedings of the Society of Antiquaries of Scotland*, xi (1874–6), 462–4.

7   *DBL*, v, 411–12; Riis, *Auld acquaintance*, ii, 62.75.

8   The palace was rebuilt as a private residence in about 1720 and was further altered in the nineteenth century. It is now known as the

Ladegarden and houses a local history museum. Millar, 'Wedding-Tour,' 147–51.

9 Moysie, *Memoirs*, 80–1. Moysie's spelling has been modernised, and I've assumed the 'quietly' of the text to be an error for 'quickly,' which fits the sense much better.

10 *CSPD, 1589–93*, 188.

11 Macray, 'Third Report,' 25.

12 A later tale recounts that when the wedding party left after the ceremony James had four negro boys he had brought with him dance in the snow before him, as a result of which they subsequently died of pneumonia: [J A Gade, *The life and times of Tycho Brahe* (Princeton, 1947), 119; J A Gade, *Christian IV* (London, 1927, 39–40; Williams, *Anne*, 21] This rather unlikely tale may have arisen from some confused report of the 'moors' who danced before Anne's carriage at her entry to Edinburgh, acting as 'whifflers' to clear the way.

13 *Norske Rigs-registranter*, 93–5.

14 *CSPS, 1589–93*, 188.

15 O Kingsted etc, *Festmusik fra Renaissancen* (exhibition catalogue, Copenhagen, 1990), 49. A ms copy of the poem is at NLS, Adv Ms 19. 3. 29. Other Latin poems in honour of the wedding were published by Hercules Rollock (Edinburgh 1589); Hadrian Damman (Edinburgh, 1590) and Andrew Robertson (Copenhagen, 1590). L Nielsen, *Dansk Bibliografi, 1551–1600* (Copenhagen, 1931–3), nos. 1358, 1405, 1666.

16 Macray, 'Third Report, 250; SRO, SP.8/8; *Marriage*, 17–18; *RMS, 1580–93*, nos. 1731, 1732; *APS*, iii, 565.

17 HMC, *Salisbury Mss*, iii, 420–39.

18 *Norske Rigs-registranter*, 93–5.

19 *RPCS, 1585–92*, 438–40; *APS*, iii, 566–7.

20 H W Meikle (ed.), *The works of William Fowler* (3 vols, Scottish Text Society, 1914–40). Schein had been promised silken clothing befitting his office, but had had to sail with Anne in 1589 without it. The return to Denmark gave him the opportunity to ensure he got it in the end, *Kancelliets Brevbøger*, 330–1.

21 SRO, SP 13/117; Macray, 'Second Report,' 32; *James the Sext*, 239–40; K M Brown, *Bloodfeud in Scotland, 1573–1625* (Edinburgh, 1986), 88, 93–4; *Marriage*, 28; Riis, *Auld acquaintance*, i, 139–40, ii, 58.

22 *Norske Rigs-registranter*, 99–103.

23 *Norske Rigs-registranter*, 102–3.

24 *Norske Rigs-registranter*, 96.

25 Macray, 'Second Report,' 32; *Norske Rigs-registranter*, 96–7.

NOTES

26 *CSPS, 1589–93*, 188; NLS, Ms Adv. 33.1.11, Denmylne Mss, vol xxviii, no. 11, calendared in NLS, Catalogue of Manuscripts. State Papers. Denmylne Mss (5 volumes), iv.

27 *RMS, 1580–93*, no. 1717. Later Vaus was also granted a pension for his services: *APS*, iii, 568.

38 HMC *Hamilton Mss*, 65–6.

29 HMC *Salisbury Mss*, iii, 455.

30 *RPCS, 1585–92*, 444–5.

31 NLS, Ms Adv. 33.1.11, Denmylne Mss, vol xxviii, no. 31, calendared in NLS, Catalogue of Manuscripts. State Papers: Denmylne Mss (5 volumes), iv. Gert Rantzau (1558–1627) was a brother of Breide Rantzau. Gert had spent much of his youth in Holland and subsequently travelled widely. He served as governor of a number of counties and castles: *DBL*, xi 618–21.

Chapter 5   Winter Journey

1 As governor of Bohus he had been instructed to prepare for James's journey through the region. James presented Henrik with a chain, his wife with a ring: Thirlestane's Accounts, f. 8v. This Henrik is probably to be identified with the man of the same name who was in Scotland with Queen Anne in 1590 and was then vice-admiral and commander of the *Josaphad*: *CSPS, 1589–93*, 289.

2 Michael Jensson Basse or Bartze, priest in Konghelle between 1596 and 1608, *Norske Samingler*, 476n.

3 *List and analysis of State Papers, Foreign, Elizabeth I, 1589–1590*, 421.

4 Millar, 'Wedding-Tour,' 159–60. Millar also recounts a few other details of James's journey not mentioned in the Account. James stayed at the mansion house at Holme of Peder Bragge, where there was insufficient accommodation for the royal party. Korfit Wiffert (commander of Malmöhus Castle in Malmö), Jørgen Brahe (governor of Landskrona) and Steen Bille slept in the room called the 'Earth-parlour' while in the great hall twenty-six beds were prepared for the Scottish gentlemen. At Holde James had been met by Henrik Gyldenstierne, who had escorted him by way of Uddevalla to Bohus.

5 W Berg, *Elfsborgs Slott. I, Slottets Historia* (Göteborg, 1909), 208.

6 *Norske Rigs-registranter*, 98–101.

7 The text of King Johan's letter is inserted in the Account.

8 Spottiswoode, *History*, ii, 405.

9 Ibid, 405.

129

10 *Kancelliets Brevbøger*, 312, 314–15.
11 C F Bricka and S M Gjellerup, *Den Danske Adel i det 16de og 17de Aarhundrede*, 1st collection (Copenhagen, 1874–5), 197–8, with transcript of the epitaph at p. 200. I owe this reference to Harald Ilsøe.
12 *Norske Rigs-registranter*, 103–5.
13 Spottiswoode, *History*, ii, 405.

Chapter 6   Danish Diversions

1 *Kancelliets Brevbøger*, 323.
2 Melville, *Diary*, 277.
3 D Kirby, *Northern Europe in the Early Modern Period. The Baltic world, 1492–1772* (London, 1990), 41; P Envoldsen, 'Lensreformerne i Danmark, 1557–96,' *Historisk Tidsskrift*, 81 (1981–2), 398–9; J R Christianson, 'The reconstruction of the Scandinavian aristocracy,' *Scandinavian Studies*, 53, pt. 3 (1981), 292–7.
4 Kirby, *Northern Europe*, 39.
5 Ibid, 80, 95.
6 W Shakespeare, *Hamlet*, ed. H Jenkins (London, 1981), 190–1, 447–8.
7 P Yapp (ed.), *The travellers dictionary of quotations* (London, 1983), 103.
8 F Moryson, *An itinerary containing his ten yeeres travell* (4 vols, Glasgow, 1907–8), iv, 34–44, 67, 185.
9 Moryson, i, 123–5. Elsewhere (iii, 491) Moryson says Elsinore was very stately built: probably he meant the castle, not the town itself.
10 Eg, Calderwood, *History*, v, 83; Spottiswoode, *History*, ii, 405.
11 Moryson, *Itinerary*, i, 122, iii, 491.
12 Slangerup (Slangendorphius), who died in 1596, had received a doctorate of theology in Basle in 1583. He was *summus theologus* in Copenhagen in 1589 and *rector magnificus* in 1593. He was well known as a theologian through his many publications. *DBL*, xiii, 507.
13 Christensen died in 1606, *DBL*, iii, 232.
14 The university gave the carrier of the gifts, David Lindsay, 4 dalers as a present on 19 March: H F Rørdam, *Kjøbenhavns Universitets Historie fra 1537 til 1621*, part 4 (Copenhagen, 1868–74), 312 (though the year is given as 1589). The university in its list of benefactions states that the gift was made in February: *Universitetsbibliotekets Liber Daticus fra XVII Aarhundrede* (Copenhagen, 1935), 5. I owe both these references to Harald Ilsøe. The books had cost James 42 dalers, the cup 25 dalers (Thirlestane's Accounts, f.11r). Thus the Danish Account's

NOTES

estimate that together they were worth 72 daler is not far out. All that survives of these gifts is the damaged cup and sceptres. These had been recovered, an English visitor was told, after a fire in 1728: Horace Marryat, *A residence in Jutland, the Danish Isles and Copenhagen* (2 vols, London, 1860), i, 154. Perhaps this was Danish tact, for a Danish source says the gifts were destroyed during the British navy's bombardment of Copenhaven in 1807: *Universitets og Sole Annaler* (1811), 167n.

15 Moryson, *Itinerary*, i, 122.

16 Marryat, *Residence in Jutland*, i, 120.

17 *DBL*, vi, 247–9; *CSPS, 1589–93*, 281.

18 *Samlinger til Fyens Historie og Topographie*, 7 (Odense, 1878), 299. What purports to be an account of the discussion between James and Hemmingsen, in the form of questions and answers translated from Latin into Danish, survives in the Royal Library in Copenhagen, Ms NKS 20 g 8⁰. I owe both these references to Harald Ilsøe. Four books by Hemmingsen had been acquired for James's library in 1575, so he had had plenty of opportunities to become acquainted with his work: G F Warner (ed.), 'The library of James VI,' *Miscellany*, i (Scottish History Society, 1893), xlviii.

19 T L Christensen, 'Scoto-Danish relations in the sixteenth century: the historiography and some questions,' *SHR*, xlviii (1969), 96.

20 Thirlestane's Accounts, f. 11r.

21 Ibid, f.11r.

22 1546–1601 *DBL*, ii, 429–36.

23 Thirlestane's Accounts, f. 11r.

24 I D McFarlane, *Buchanan* (London, 1981), 463–4, 466, 533.

25 J Christianson, 'The celestial palace of Tycho Brahe,' *Scientific American*, 204, pt. 2 (1961), 118–28; J A Gade, *The life and times of Tycho Brahe* (Princeton, 1947), 120, 128. Marryat, *Residence in Jutland*, i, 307; I L E Dreyer, *Tycho Brahe. A picture of scientific life and work in the 16th century* (Edinburgh, 1890), 202–4.

26 'Coxe's travels in Denmark,' in J Pinkerton (ed.), *A general collection of the best and most interesting voyages and travels*, vi (London, 1809), 331; I L E Dreyer, *Tychonis Brahe Dani Opera Omnia* (15 vols, Copenhagen, 1913–29; reprinted Amsterdam, 1972), ii, 11–12.

27 HMC *Salisbury Mss*, iii, 403 (letter incorrectly dated 1589).

28 A W C Lindsay, earl of Crawford, *Lives of the Lindsays* (3 vols, London, 1849), i, 319, 321–3. The second letter has been reprinted a number of times, and there is a facsimile in *Marriage. Scots peerage*, i, 196. Lindsay was made Lord Spynie as soon as James returned to Scotland

in May 1590: *RMS, 1580–93)*, no. 1727. In 1593 Spynie duly married Jean Lyon, Riis, *Auld acquaintance*, ii, 67.

29. Vaus, *Correspondence*, 447; Spottiswoode, *History*, ii, 406.
30. Thirestane's Accounts, esp. ff. 6v, 8r, 12r.
31. *CSPS, 1589–93*, 277.
32. Ibid, ff. 9r, 10r, 11v, 12r, 25. Fraser, *Earls of Haddington*, ii, xxii–xxiii, 57–8.
33. R B Wernam (ed.), *List and analysis of State Papers, Foreign Series,... 1589–90*, 421.
34. Kongsted, *Festmusik fra Renaissancen* (Copenhagen, 1990), 37, 38, 48–9. Facsimilies of the signatures appear in L. Benedicht, *Bogtrykker og xylograf i København i Sidste Halvdel af det XVI aarhundrede* (Copenhagen, 1920), XXI. Christen Holck, though a councillor of the realm, evidently felt he could not aspire to royal autographs, but he collected those of Lewis Bellenden (Copenhagen, 15 March), the Earl Marischal (Kronborg, 21 April) and Maitland of Thirlestane (Elsinore, 23 April), all with Latin inscriptions: G L Grove, *Personalhistorisk Tidsskrift*, 5th series, 2 (Copenhagen, 1905), 9–10.
35. Thirlestane's Accounts, f. 13r.
36. Ibid, f. 13r. At first James acted responsibly: £100,000 of the money was lent to eleven of the royal burghs at 10% *per annum* interest. The king thus treated the burghs as banks in which to invest his capital — a role they only played with obvious reluctance. However, by 1594 James had withdrawn all these deposits, squandering the capital on paying off debts and paying expenses of government. See A Montgomerie, 'King James VI's tocher gude and a local authorities loan of 1590,' *SHR*, xxxvii (1958), 11–16; Riis, *Auld acquaintance*, i, 270–1.
37. Melville, *Memoirs*, 372–3; *CSPS, 1589–93*, 221–2, 257, 276, 281, 285; Spottiswoode, *History*, ii, 406. The position of Thirlestane and the others who had been appointed ambassadors to Denmark when they and the king sailed from Scotland is not clear. It may be that when Marischal's commission was declared void, Thirlestane and his colleagues took over as ambassadors — which would of course have intensified Marischal's fury.
38. *Calendar of State Papers, Foreign, 1588* (London, 1936), 77–8.

NOTES

Chapter 7   Scottish Celebrations

1 [P Walker (ed.)], *Documents relative to the reception at Edinburgh of the kings and queens of Scotland, AD 1561 — 1650* (Edinburgh, 1822), 36.
2 Walker, *Documents*, 46.
3 *RPCS, 1585–92*, 478–80.
4 *CSPS, 1589–93*, 863; Moysie, *Memoirs*, 83.
5 Calderwood, *History*, v, 94.
6 Moysie, *Memoirs*, 83.
7 *CSPS, 1589–93*, 295–6.
8 *Marriage*, 54.
9 Spottiswoode, *History*, ii, 407.
10 *CSPS, 1589–93*, 295; Walker, *Documents*, 46–7.
11 See Bergeron, *English civic pageantry*, chapter I; A J Mill, *Medieval plays in Scotland* (Oxford, 1927), 78–85, 89–90, 177–218.
12 Bergeron, *English civic pageantry*, 69.
13 Ibid, 67–9; Mill, *Mediaeval plays*, 80. For a rather more innovative Scottish entry see M Lynch, 'Queen Mary's triumph: the baptismal celebrations at Stirling in December 1566,' *SHR*, lxix (1990), 1–21. For Mary's 1561 entry see A A MacDonald, 'Mary Stewart's entry to Edinburgh: an ambiguous triumph,' *Innes Review*, xlii (1991), 101–10. The 1590 entry is among those discussed in M M Bartley, A preliminary study of the Scottish royal entries of Mary Stuart, James VI and Anne of Denmark (PhD thesis, university of Michigan, 1981; microfilm Ann Arbour, 1981), 130–83.
14 *Edin. recs., 1589–1603*, 329.
15 Moysie, *Memoirs*, 83.
16 Eg, Vaus, *Correspondence*, ii, 458–9.
17 R Chambers, *Domestic annals of Scotland* (3 vols, Edinburgh, 1859–61), i, 199; *Edin. Recs., 1589–1603*, 19–20; P Walker, *Documents*, 48.
18 *CSPS, 1589–93*, 304–5.
19 Melville, *Memoirs*, 413.
20 J Bain (ed.), *Hamilton papers* (London, 1890–2), ii, 710.

Chapter 8   And they did not live Happily Ever After

1   E Lodge (ed.), *Illustrations of British history* (3 vols, London, 1791), iii, 2.
2   Melville, *Memoirs*, 413.
3   Melville, *Memoirs*, 413–14; *CSPS, 1593–5*, 94, 101, 109–19, 119–20; W Fraser, *Memorials of the earls of Haddington* (2 vols, Edinburgh, 1889), ii, xxiv, 63–4; *RMS, 1580–93*, no. 2352; *RMS, 1593–1608*, nos. 73, 75; L Barroll, 'The court of the first Stuart queen,' in L L Peck (ed.), *The mental world of the Jacobean court* (Cambridge, 1991), 192–6.
4   Melville, *Memoirs*, 414–17.
5   Macray, 'Second Report,' 35.
6   *CSPS, 1593–5*, 363, 377, 385.
7   W Forbes-Leith (ed.), *Narratives of Scottish Catholics under Mary Stuart and James VI* (Edinburgh, 1885), 263–5, 272; A Bellesheim, *History of the Catholic Church in Scotland* (4 vols, Edinburgh, 1887–90), iii, 346–9, 450–5; *CSPD, 1603–10*, 74.
8   *CSPS, 1589–93*, 751–3, 755.
9   *The poems and songs of Robert Burns*, ed. J Kinsley (3 vols, Oxford, 1968), i, 484–5; I O J Gladstone, *The Lauries of Maxwelton and other Laurie families* (London, [1972]), 120–2.
10 J Nicols, *The progresses, processions, and magnificent festivities of King James the First* (4 vols, 1828), ii, 72–3.
11 Melville, *Memoirs*, 373.
12 *CSPS, 1589–93*, 297, 298–9.
13 E Lodge (ed.), *Illustrations of British history* (3 vols, London, 1791), iii, 1; *CSPS, 1589–93*, 306.
14 *CSPS, 1589–93*, 661.
15 E J Cowan, 'The darker vision of the Scottish Renaissance: the Devil and Francis Stewart,' *The Renaissance and Reformation in Scotland*, ed. I B Cowan & D Shaw (Edinburgh 1983), 125–4.
16 Cowan, 'Darker vision,' 127–8.
17 Riis, *Auld acquaintance*, i, 266–9. E W Monter, 'Scandinavian Witchcraft in Anglo-American Perspective,' in B Ankarloo and G Henningsen, *Early Modern European Witchcraft. Centres and Peripheries* (Oxford, 1990), 428, 431; J C Johansen, 'Denmark: The Sociology of Accusations,' in the same volume, 340.
18 Cowan, 'Darker Vision,' 131.
19 Williams, *Anne*, 35.

NOTES

20 Ibid, 52–6.

21 Ibid, 114–20.

22 Riis, *Auld acquaintance*, i, 121–30.

NOTES TO THE DANISH ACCOUNT

Danish Account I   The Making of the Treaty

1 The copy of the demands given to the Danes (at Kronborg) is in the Rigsarkivet. Copenhagen, Macray, 'Third Report,' 24. The demands were based on instructions James had given to his ambassadors in June 1589. The copy sent to England and annotated by Lord Burghley was evidently of a draft rather than the final version, as the demands to be made of the Danes are even more exorbitant than those listed in the Danish account: *CSPS, 1589–93*, 103–5; HMC, *Salisbury Mss, 1583–9*, 420–39.

2 The exchange rate being 1 daler = £2 Scots, the Scots were seeking a dowry of £500,000 Scots. The draft of the ambassadors' instructions had ordered them to ask for twice this sum, £1,000,000 Scots. Lord Burghley noted that, taking £1 Scots to be worth five shillings sterling, this amounted to £250,000 sterling.

3 'A large demand,' Lord Burghley commented.

4 The draft instructions had demanded 8,000 footmen and 2,000 horse.

5 The draft instructions had referred simply to the grant of ten warships.

6 The draft instructions had asked for an outright surrender of all Danish claims to the Orkneys.

7 The copy in the Rigsarkivet is dated 11 July: Macray, 'Third Report,' 24.

8 Jørgen Rozenkrantz, 1523–96. An orphan, Rozenkrantz had been brought up in Brandenburg. On returning to Denmark he served as constable of a number of royal castles and was frequently involved with diplomatic affairs. Appointed a member of the councillor of regents in 1588, and its most powerful member after the death of Niels Kaas in 1594: *DBL*, xii, 356–8.

9 The Account gives the letter in both Latin and Danish. This translation is taken from the latter version. The original is in the Rigsarkivet: Macray, 'Third Report,' 24. The Latin text is printed in *RPCS, 1585–92*, 822–3.

10 The summary of the treaty is taken from the Latin text in L Laursen, (ed.), *Traités du Danemark et de la Norvège. Danmark-Norges Traktater*, iii, *1523–1750* (Copenhagen, 1916), 14–21. The contract was ratified by King James in 'parliament' in a brief meeting on 17 May 1590, the

135

day of the queen's coronation, and again by parliament in 1592: Macray, 'Third Report,' 27; Laursen, *Traités*, iii, 14; *RMS, 1580–93*, no. 1733; *APS*, iii, 565. On the day of the marriage contract, 20 August, the Scottish envoys signed an agreement that the question of the Orkneys should not be discussed during the minority of King Christian: Macray, 'Third Report,' 24; Laursen, *Traités*, iii, 21–4; *RPCS, 1585–92*, 823–4; SRO, SP 8/7.

11 This 'insertion' relating to the proxy marriage is not a description of what happened, but of what it was planned should happen. There is, however, no reason to think that events diverged from intentions in this instance. For the translation I am most grateful to Dr Wendy B Stevenson and to Professor R P H Green, Professor of Humanity at the University of Glasgow.

Danish Account II Norway and Denmark

1 A much more detailed narrative than that in the Account of the voyage of Princess Anne to Oslo and the subsequent return of part of the Danish fleet to Copenhagen is contained in a journal of the voyage evidently kept by Niels Krag, in TKUA. The journal indicates that the fleet originally sailed from Copenhagen to Elsinore on 1 September. That evening a gun on board one of the ships exploded on firing a salute, killing two gunners. Next day two 'Scottish noblemen came on board to pay their respects to Anne: when they left another gun exploded on the firing of a salute, wounding eight or nine men. Obviously the date of leaving Copenhagen is incompatible with that given in the Account: perhaps it took several days for the fleet to assemble. Riis, *Auld acquaintance*, i, 264.

2 The fleet took refuge in Norway because of more than contrary winds. The flagship, *Gedeon*, sprung a leak in the gales and had to seek shelter on 10 September at Gamel Sellohe in Norway while repairs were carried out. Meanwhile other ships sheltered at Flekkerøy. There the *Samson* was also found to be damaged so she could not sail, having in the storms struck the *Josaphad* so hard that a ship's boat was crushed and two sailors killed. On 23 September a Scots ship ventured out from Gammel Sellohe, but returned two days later: she had got within twenty miles of Scotland but been driven back by gales. In the days that followed it is impossible to reconcile the Account with the journal and other sources in detail, though the overall story is much the same. According to the journal the fleet sailed again of 28 September, but was soon forced back by contrary gales — and by the fact that the *Gedeon* was leaking badly again. Most of the fleet reached refuge at Flekkerøy on 1 October, though the *Raphael*

NOTES

did not arrive until the next day. Most of the larger ships were now damaged, and seamen's weather lore predicted that the weather prevailing at Michaelmas — 29 September — would continue until Christmas. The demoralised Danes resolved to write home for instructions as to whether to continue to try to get Anne to Denmark in such circumstances. Meanwhile Steen Bille would be sent to Scotland, if a small ship could get through where the pride of the Danish fleet had failed humiliatingly, to explain the situation. But before he left William Stewart arrived from Scotland. He urged a new attempt to reach Scotland. But the *Gedeon's* leak was worsening, so the next day the decision was taken to retreat to Oslo to await instructions, Stewart and Bille journeying to Scotland with a letter (7 October) explaining this decision. Riis, *Auld acquaintance*, i, 264–5.

3 Nils Hansen, priest, died in 1603, *Norske Samlinger*, i, 464n.
4 Steen Brahe, 1547–1620, was a brother of the astronomer Tyge Brahe, and had become a councillor of the realm in 1578. He was sent on many diplomatic missions abroad, appointed chamberlain to Princess Anne in 1589 and accompanied her to Scotland. He became a member of the council of regents in 1593, *DBL*, ii, 428–9.
5 Henning Giøye was a member of a well-known family of the Danish *uradel* or 'original aristocracy.' Henning and his wife had originally agreed to go to Scotland with Anne, but then changed their minds. A letter from the Danish council hinting at withdrawal of royal favour had persuaded him to agree to go after all, *Kancelliets Brevbøger*, 160, 209. Several ladies showed similar reluctance to accompany Anne: ibid, 159–60,
6 Ove Juel of Kieldgaard, Commander of Bratsberg Len, and earlier of Akershus, *Norske Samlinger*, i, 465n. A member of a Danish *uradel* family.
7 Hans Pedersen of Sem, later of Foss, *c.* 1540–1602. Governor of the county of Bergenhus and chancellor of Norway, regarded as a very wealthy man.
8 Peder Iversen of Fridsø and Brynla. Referred to as a nobleman at Ellinggård who died in 1616, *Norske Samlinger*, i, 465n.
9 Fru Karen Gyldenstierne. The wife of Axel Gyldenstierne, *DBL*, v, 411.
10 Fru Anne Skinckel was the second wife (1587) of Peder Iversen.
11 Fru Margrethe Brede was the wife of Hans Pedersen, *Norske Samlinger*, i, 465n.
12 Fru Dorrete Juel was the widow of Henrik Brockenhuus of Ellinggaard, sheriff of the county of Onsøy and later of Bratsberg. He had died in 1588, *Norske Samlinger*, i, 465n.
13 Jomfru Ulffvild was Peder Iversen's sister.

SCOTLAND'S LAST ROYAL WEDDING

14 Bishop (or Superintendent) of Norway, Jens Nilssøn, 1539–1600, is best known for his manuscripts and as a copiest of Snorri Sturluson's codex Jofraskinna. This Icelandic codex, dating from *c.* 1325, contained much of Snorri's *Heimskringla* but was destroyed by fire in 1728. Nilssøn became bishop of Oslo and Hamar in 1580. He was a learned humanist and fervent Lutheran, *Norske Samlinger*, i, 465n.

15 A list of Anne's household in Scotland in 1591 includes the preacher's boys: *Marriage*, 28. It seems likely that they are identical with the trained choirboys who, with Sering, began the singing of the hymn in Oslo.

16 Anulf Eeg. Probably lived at, or named after, the farm of Ek in Bramle, *Norske Samlinger*, i, 468n.

17 Peder Vaemundsen was priest in the district of Sande from 1567 to 1626. His wife was Ragnhild Holk from Tønsberg. It is said that on King James asking Vaemundsen to name a reward for the hospitality he had shown the king, he suggested that James arrange that the deanery of Laurvig (of which he was dean) be enlarged by the addition of two parishes. This was done, Rollag and Flesberg being added to the deanery, *Norske Samlinger*, i, 468n.

18 Rasmus Sørensen is known to have been the priest in Vaale as early as 1564, *Norske Samlinger*, i, 468n.

19 The literal translation is 'thin under the eyes': Millar, 'Wedding-Tour,' 156, translates this as 'deep-set eyes.'

20 There was in fact only one Scottish earl present, the Earl Marischal. 'Earls' is presumably a mistake for 'nobles,' the second noble being Lord Dingwall.

21 Christen Mule's house: in other words, the Old Bishops' Palace.

22 The text gives both Latin and Danish translations of Lindsay's French sermon.

23 David Lindsay younger, *c.* 1566–1627, was minister of a number of parishes from 1590, he became minister of the second charge at South Leith in 1609, thus acting as assistant to his ageing father, whom he succeeded in 1613: *Fasti*, i, 161. Lindsay had written home about how he had arrived in Oslo after divers perils and troublesome journeys by both sea and land. He had evidently wished to return with the Scots James had sent home, but James refused him permission: Calderwood, *History*, v, 69.

24 William Schaw, King James's master of works since 1583, played a key role he played in the founding of modern freemasonry: D. Stevenson, *The origins of freemasonry. Scotland's century, 1590–1710* (Cambridge, 1988), chapter 3. He rebuild Dunfermline Palace for Anne of Denmark.

NOTES

25 'Playing' in the sense of gambling.

26 Millar, 'Wedding-Tour,' 159, indicates that the meaning is that James had never been so generous before. But it is more likely to mean that James had never himself handed anyone a cup of wine before.

27 Duke Ulrick of Mecklenburg was the father of Queen Sophia.

28 Swedish Archives: James Dow drew attention to the letter, and discussed the episode, in his 'Scottish Relations with Sweden, 1500–1625' (unfinished thesis, held by John Simpson, Department of Scottish History, University of Edinburgh).

Danish Account III   Scotland: The Coronation

1   The official diary (in German) of the Danish ambassadors to Scotland of their mission, 21 April — 5 June 1590 is at TKUA Skotland, A II 4 (on microfilm TKUA Skotland, 1–7, III). The Danish Account's narrative of events in Scotland from the landing in Scotland to the departure of the Danish ambassadors is closely related to the ambassadors' diary. At some point the Danish Account compresses the diary's narrative, at others — notably the coronation and the queen's entry — the Account is much more expansive, giving more detail and the texts of speeches, etc.

2   At 7 pm, according to an English agent: *CSPS, 1589–93*, 863, 'at night' according to Moysie, *Memoirs*, 83, who records that the reception committee was led by the duke of Lennox, Lord Hamilton and the earl of Bothwell.

3   Calderwood, *History*, v, 94, explains that the queen was led through a 'trance' or covered way, all (including the floor) lined with tapestry and cloth of gold so that her feet never touched the ground.

4   James Elphinstone. P A Munch's identification of 'Sistonius' as probably Sir John Seyton of Barns is thus incorrect. Elphinstone's oration was in Latin. For a Scots account of 'The receiving of King James the Sixt and his Queene at Lyeth,' published in 1590, see *Marriage*, 37–45.

5   In the church Patrick Galloway preached a sermon in English. Galloway, *c*. 1551–1626, had become a minister in 1576. He was appointed minister to the king's household on 11 February 1590, but had evidently been already attached to the household before the king left for Denmark, being left behind to attend the privy council. Galloway was moderator of the general assembly in 1590 and 1602, and became a minister of Edinburgh in 1607: *Fasti*, i, 53–4; *DNB*, xx, 356–7. Early in 1590 he had been sent by the privy council with William Stewart and the ships which were to bring the king home, arriving at Elsinore

in April: Spottiswoode, *History*, ii, 405; Riis, *Auld acquaintance*, ii, 61. Before going into the kirk James shook hands with all the chief ladies present, and talked for a long time with Robert Bruce.

6 Nicolaus Theophilus, 1541–1604. had received a doctorate of Law at Rostock in 1569, and became professor of laws at Copenhagen in 1580. He served as rector several times, and was employed in a number of diplomatic missions, especially to Saxony and Scotland: *DBL*, xiv, 436–7. He had been appointed royal librarian on 21 December 1589: *Kancelliets Brevbøger*, 312.

7 Bliant. See n. 12 in notes to Chapter IV, below.

8 The horses, according to the Scots account, were 'capparisoned in velvet, imbrodred with silver and gold, very rich': *Marriage*, 38. Calderwood, *History*, v, 94–5, says they were apparelled in cloth of gold and purple velvet.

9 The Account omits to say where the queen was taken — Holyrood. There James took her by the hand and led her to her chambers, richly hung with cloth of gold and silver: Calderwood, *History*, v, 94–5.

10 The text of the Danish Account gives a Latin as well as a Danish version of the oath.

11 A brief summary of the basis for this calculation is given in the Danish ambassadors' diary.

12 'Lithton' is an obvious error for 'Lithgow,' a common contraction of Linlithgow, the two here being taken to be separate places.

13 On the same day James issued confirmations of the grants of property he had made to Anne: Macray, 'Third Report,' 25.

14 Sir Robert Melville of Murdocarny did not hold the office of treasurer but that of treasurer depute, from 1582 to 1597, *James the Sext*, ix–x. On the night of 11 May the Danes stayed at the House of Wemyss, James having written to David Wemyss of Wemyss instructing him to receive them: W. Fraser, *Memorials of the family of Wemyss of Wemyss* (3 vols, Edinburgh, 1888), iii, 28–9; Moysie, *Memoirs*, 158.

15 On 12 May the Danes were received and banqueted by the laird of Creich, before moving on to Newhouse: Moysie, *Memoirs*, 158.

16 The symbolic handing over of earth and stones when granting sasine or possession of land in Scotland.

17 The three notorial instruments of sasine giving Anne possession of the county of Fife and the palace of Falkland; the domain and house of Dunfermline; and the palace of Linlithgow are in the Rigsarkivet. The notary was John Hay. Macray, 'Third Report,' 25). The name 'Cajus' given to the notary in the Danish Account is presumably a corruption of a Latinised form of his name such as 'Haius' — a

NOTES

suggestion I owe to Peter Graves. The Danish ambassadors' diary gives the name as 'Laijus.' A Mr John Hay was mentioned as a clerk of session in 1592, and a clerk of the same name resigned as one of the clerks of the privy council in 1596: *RPCS, 1585–92*, 741; *RPCS, 1592–9*, 279.

18 See Moysie, *Memoirs*, 158. William Douglas, 7th earl of Morton, *c.* 1539–1606, had succeeded to the title in 1588. *DNB*, xv, 365–6.

19 The Danes spent the night of 13 May at Niddrie: Moysie, *Memoirs*, 158.

20 Robert Dury, commendator of Dunfermline.

21 Sir Lewis Bellenden of Auchinoul and Broughton, justice clerk and governor of Linlithgow Palace. He had been in Denmark with James, but returned home before James by way of England: *DNB*, iv, 168–9; Riis, *Auld acquaintance*, ii, 55.

22 Lord Claud Hamilton, Lord Paisley.

23 The Danish Account's narrative of the coronation is closely based on a Scottish account, of which a copy was preserved in the archives of the earls of Mar, and published in *Marriage*, 49–56. The Danish writer must have had a version of this to hand when he wrote, though he leaves out some details and introduces some errors. On the same day as the coronation the king ratified the marriage contract: *RMS, 1580–93*, no. 1733. A copy of this confirmation on parchment, signed and sealed by thirty nobles and representatives of seven burghs and with the great seal of Scotland attached in an engraved box, is in the Rigsarkivet in Copenhagen: Macray, 'Third Report,' 26.

24 The Scottish account of the coronation says James only created fifteen knights, *Marriage*, 49, while Moysie, *Memoirs*, 159 gives the figure as seventeen or eighteen. Thirlestane being the 'leading gentleman' in parliament means that as chancellor he had precedence and acted as president of of the meeting.

25 James was first to enter the church in the sense that he entered before the queen: but as the the Account itself goes on to narrate, the king was preceded by heralds, trumpeters, the bearers of the honours, etc: Moysie, *Memoirs*, 159.

26 Sir David Lindsay of Rathillet, born *c.* 1507, was lord lyon king of arms (in command of Scotland's heralds) from 1568 to 1591.

27 Earl of Angus, *DNB*, xv, 366.

28 John, Lord Hamilton. He took the place of his brother, the earl of Arran, in the coronation as the latter was ill: *Marriage*, 52.

29 Lewis or Ludovic Stuart, duke of Lennox, 1574–1624, had succeeded to the title in 1583. He was created earl of Richmond in 1613 and earl of Newcastle and duke of Richmond in 1623. *DNB*, iv, 107–8.

141

30 Sir Robert Bowes, the English envoy.

31 According to the Scots account of the coronation, at Anne's left hand was not just Peder Munk but also the two other Danish ambassadors, Steen Brahe and Breide Rantzau: *Marriage*, 51.

32 Annabella, countess of Mar.

33 Margaret, countess of Bothwell, was the wife of Francis Stewart, earl of Bothwell. His title was forfeited in 1593. *DNB*, xxvi. 140–5.

34 Joan, countess of Orkney.

35 To Jean Fleming, Lady Thirlestane and Margaret Livingston, Lady Auchinoul the Scots account adds Isobel, Lady Seton at this point: *Marriage*, 52.

36 Cathrina Schinkel attended the coronation as one of the queen's maidens.

37 Anne Kaas, probably related to Sophia Kaas, listed as one of the queen's household in 1591: *Marriage*, appendix, 27. Sophia had been with Breide Rantzau's wife in April 1589 when the Danish council had been urging her to agree to go to Scotland: *Kancelliets Brevbøger*, 160.

38 This first part of the service is described by the Scots account as being taken by Patrick Galloway. The Scots account says he began the coronation service with prayers, and then preached on a text from the 45th Psalm: *Marriage*, 52. Calderwood, *History*, vi, 96 says there were three sermons, in Latin, French and English. The first was presumably that by Galloway the second that mentioned in the Account. Perhaps the third was a repeat of one of these two in a different language.

39 Robert Bruce, c. 1554–1631, was not a bishop: he was indeed a leading presbyterian minister. He had become one of the ministers of Edinburgh in 1587, and he was given a seat on the privy council during James's absence in 1589–90. But he was to be banished in 1596 for his activities and deposed in 1600. *Fasti*, i, 54–5.

40 Bruce, accompanied by Lennox, Lord Hamilton, and David Lindsay, stood before the king when he delivered this oration, *Marriage*, 52–3. Calderwood, *History*, v, 96 says John Craig (a chaplain to James VI since 1579, *Fasti*, vi, 35–6) also made a short oration to the queen at this point, perhaps repeating one of the other two in a different language.

41 The queen 'reteires hir selff to ane secret pairt prepared for that effect, to remaine ane certaine space': *Marriage*, 53. Calderwood, *History*, v, 96, says she went into a 'cabinet.'

42 Accounts survive for the robe made for his majesty's dearest bedfellow for the day of her coronation. Materials include thirty ells of purple

NOTES

velvet and sixteen ells of white Spanish taffeta. Cloth was also supplied for dressing six pages and four lackeys, SRO, E.21/67, Accounts of the Treasurer, 1588–90, ff. 199r–201v

43 The crown was first passed to the king (presumably by the chancellor, Lord Thirlestane, who had carried it into the church). James then passed it to Bruce, who passed it to Lennox, Hamilton and Thirlestane, who placed it on the queen's head: *Marriage*, 53.

44 Calderwood, *History*, v, 96 says Hamilton gave her the sceptre, Angus the sword.

45 Andrew Melville, 1545–1622, was leader of the presbyterian faction in the Scottish church. At this time James was attempting to reach a compromise with the presbyterians over matters of church-state relations and church government. The attempt failed, and James ultimately destroyed his opponents, imprisoning Melville in the Tower of London in 1607–11. The rest of his life was spent in exile in France. His 200 Latin verses at the coronation were published as *Stephaniskion. Ad Scotiae regem, habitum in Coronatione Reginae*, and are reprinted in *Marriage*. Calderwood, *History*, v, 97–8 mistakenly recorded Melville making his 'oration' at the queen's entry to Edinburgh.

46 The Danish Account is confused, referring to these two men as pastors instead of provosts. The men who swore homage thus consisted of two representatives of the nobility, two of the lairds or lesser barons, two of the royal burghs, and two of the ministers of the church.

47 David Seton of Parbroath, who held the office of comptroller from 1588 to 1596.

48 According to Calderwood, *History*, v, 96, the trumpets and drums sounded for a long time and the cannon in the castle thundered.

Danish Account IV Scotland: The Entry to Edinburgh

1 John Burel produced a verse 'Discription of the Queenis Maiesties maist honorable entry into the toun of Edinburgh.' It was first printed in 1712, and reprinted in *Marriage*. It does not attempt to reproduce the allegorical speeches like the Danish account, but contains much detail of the visual imagery in mythological and allegorical paintings, tapestries, etc. The Scots prose account of the receiving of James and Anne at Leith (see n. 4 in the notes to *Danish Account III* above) also describes the queen's entry to Edinburgh, and another account of it was published in London: *The joyful receiving of Iames the Sixt of that name king of Scotland...*(London, 1590).

2 The Scottish prose account of the entry of the queen to Edinburgh states that thirty-six Danes rode before the queen's carriage, each

accompanied by a Scottish lord or knight: *Marriage*, 39. But the Danish account lists eighteen Danes and eighteen Scots, a total of thirty-six horsemen, and as their names are all given this seems more likely to be correct. On leaving Holyrood Palace the queen's party had circled round to the south of Edinburgh, so she could make her formal entry through the West Port: Moysie, *Memoirs*, 159.

3   Lee, *Thirlestane*, 207, 208; *DNB*, ixx, 130; Riis, *Auld acquaintance*, ii, 56.

4   Thirteen of the eighteen Danes are among those names in a list of Danish nobles and gentlemen in Scotland: *CSPS, 1589–93*, 289. Stephen Madzon is listed as lieutenant to the admiral, Peder Munk, on the *Gedeon*; Henrik Gyldenstierne, vice-admiral, commanded the *Josaphad*. Some of the Scottish names are so corrupt that they defy identification.

5   The coach was drawn by eight horses: Calderwood, *History*, v, 97.

6   The boy was a son of Mr John Russell: *The joyful receiving*, 4–5; *Marriage*, 39. Russell was an Edinburgh lawyer, who became a member of the faculty of advocates in 1575 and died in 1612 (Grant, 184). His Latin oration (a facsimile of the Edinburgh, 1590 edition is printed in *Marriage*) was commissioned by the burgh as a welcome to the queen. Both *Marriage*, 39–40 and Calderwood, *History*, v, 97 can be read as indicating that the elder Russell delivered the oration, but *The joyful receiving* suggests the boy delivered it, and the Danish Account is unclear. Perhaps the father actually spoke the words, the son acting the part of the angel with appropriate gestures. Globes descending and then opening and revealing boys had featured in the 1566 Stirling and the 1579 Edinburgh entries: *James the Sext*, 178. A boy had been sent in September 1589 to bring a globe for the entry from Dundee, and was paid 16/- for his labours. The globe was then covered in 'hardin' — a type of coarse cloth — after a blacksmith had repaired it: *Edin. recs., 1589–1603*, 328, 331. Thus it seems likely that this was the same globe that had been used in the earlier entries.

7   The taffeta for the cloak cost £4 12/-: *Edin. recs., 1589–1603*, 332.

8   Payment is recorded of 18/- for two silver keys given to the queen: *Edin. recs., 1589–1603*, 332.

9   A Bible and psalm book, presumably bound together: Calderwood, *History*, v, 96.

10 The Scots account says that sixty young townsmen, all dressed like Moors, went before the carriage, not fifty, and it adds that the provost and baillies of Edinburgh rode with them: *Marriage*, 40. The burgh accounts refer to seventeen masks 'to the moiris' hanging in the council house which had cost 33/-, and records expenditure of 42/- 'for painting the young men': *Edin. recs., 1589–1603*, 332. *The joyful*

NOTES

receiving, 5, also says there were sixty moors, but Moysie, *Memoirs*, 83, 159, says there were forty-two young men 'clad in white taffeta, and visors of black colour on their faces like moors, all full of gold chains' (spelling modernised). Calderwood, *History*, v, 97 adds to the confusion by saying there were twenty-four 'moors,' some in cloth of silver, others in white taffeta.

11 Payment is recorded for painting seven staffs: *Edin. recs., 1589–1603*, 332.

12 The Scottish account of the entry says they were dressed in 'cloth of silver' with chains about their necks and braclets on their arms set with diamonds, very gorgeous to the eye: *Marriage*, 40. 'Bliant' may therefore be a kind of silver brocade. On the other hand, it may refer to the white taffeta mentioned by Moysie. *Norske Samlinger*, i, 481n.

13 The Scots account says the canopy was green, while Calderwood, *History*, v, 97 records it as purple!

14 The West Bow.

15 *The joyful receiving*, 5, says the 'sphere' was a globe of the whole world on a table, which is plausible, but in saying the boy represented a king it is clearly confused.

16 Calderwood, *History*, v, 97 says Hercules Rollock, master of the Grammar School made the oration in the West Bow. Probably he was in fact author of the oration the boy delivered. Rollock had published Latin verses on the marriage the previous year.

17 The text reads 'Butter Square,' meaning (as the Scots account makes clear) the Butter Tron — that is, a building containing the public steelyard for weighing butter and other produce for sale. The Butter Tron (or Over Tron) stood at the junction of the West Bow and Castle Hill. It was replaced by the Weigh House in 1614.

18 The text reads eight, but presumably there were nine as they were supposed to represent the nine muses.

19 The Scots account says they were dressed in cloth of silver and gold, and that they 'sung verie sweete musicke' while a 'brave youth played upon the organs.' That *The joyful receiving*, 5 uses almost exactly the same words indicates the close relationship of the two accounts. See also Calderwood, *History*, v, 97.

20 A son of John Craig: Calderwood, *History*, v, 97.

21 *The joyful receiving*, 5 indicates that the street was decked with tapestries from top to bottom. Bartley, 236–7 lists these tapestries as described in Burel's poetic description of the entry. The subjects depicted on the tapestries all concerned classical mythology, and seem to have consisted simply of what was available rather than any themes.

SCOTLAND'S LAST ROYAL WEDDING

22 *The joyful receiving*, describes the stage as a high tower by the tolbooth. Calderwood, *History*, v, 97 calls the actors five youths dressed as gentlewomen, and is confused as to what they represented.

23 The Scots account and *The joyful receiving* state that Prudence held a serpent and a dove in her hands.

24 The Scots account and *The joyful receiving* state that Fortitude held a broken pillar in her hand.

25 The Scots account and *The joyful receiving* state that Temperance had a cup of wine in one hand, a cup of water in the other. The simplest explanation of the conflicts of the two accounts over the symbolic attributes held by three of the four cardinal virtues is that they at some point put down some items and picked up others to symbolise different points, both accounts being incomplete. The Danish Account's list of the attributes is the same as that in the Danish ambassadors' diary, and it receives some support from Calderwood, *History*, v, 97, in that though the latter is confused he mentions a book and a shield among the attributes displayed.

26 The Scots account says she moved on from the stage carrying the virtues to the town cross, where the psalm was sung.

27 This 'palace' was evidently at the Mercat Cross, and the 'old fellow' was, according to the Scots account, Bacchus. The wine barrel suggests that this is correct. Bacchus had presided at the Mercat Cross during James's entry in 1579, representing liberality and plenty: *James the Sext*, 179.

28 Gold and silver cups, according to the Scots account, set on a table at the cross — and the cross itself 'ranne claret wine upon the caulsway.' But Calderwood, *History*, v, 97 says Bacchus was casting glasses while violers played and musicians sang.

29 To the Salt Tron, says the Scots account. See also Calderwood, *History*, v, 97.

30 At King James's entry to the town in 1579 there was a painted genealogy of the kings of Scotland at the Salt Tron: *James the Sext*, 179. John Workman was paid for painting 'four stoupes of ane bed at the salt trone with painting of Bachus': *Edin. recs., 1589–1603*, 332. The 'stoupes' are presumably the posts of a four-poster bed for the man representing Christian I to lie on. But what was a painting of Bacchus doing here? It may be that two separate items in the account have been lumped together, and Bacchus appeared elsewhere in the pageantry. Or could the painting have accompanied the sleeping Christian I as a cheeky allusion to the notorious drinking habits of Danes?

31 The Scots account says the man lay at the base of the tree as if sick, and was awakened by soldiers when the queen arrived, whereupon

NOTES

he made a Latin oration. Thus the Scots author seems not to realise he depicted Christian I, representing the root of the family tree, connecting James and Anne, which was displayed in the tableau. James Workman was paid for painting fourteen arms, fourteen crowns and fourteen sceptres, with certain coats of armour, as well as for much other work in preparation for the queen's entry: *Edin. recs., 1589–1603,* 328. Presumably most of them were used in this genealogical tableau.

32 In Latin, according to Calderwood, *History*, v, 97.

33 The Netherbow Port, dividing the High Street of Edinburgh from the Canongate leading down to Holyrood House. Calderwood, *History*, v, 97 says the seven planets were represented here.

34 Again the Scots account — and *The joyful receiving* — do not to understand the symbolism — that the king and queen were Solomon and the queen of Sheba.

35 The Scots account says a box was lowered from the top of the port on a silk string. The box was covered with purple velvet with A for Anne embroidered on it, and it was set with diamonds and precious stones valued at 20,000 crowns. The Scots description of Edinburgh's gift to the queen is the more accurate. The jewel in question had originally belonged to James VI himself, but in 1584 he had handed it over to the burgh of Edinburgh as a pledge or security for repayment of a loan of £4,000 made to the king. Then it was described as 'a tablet of gold in a case, and on the said tablet a diamond stone and an emerald stone' (spelling modernised): *Edin. recs., 1573–89,* 336. In September 1589, when the landing of Anne of Denmark was expected, the town council considered the honour of the town required that it give her a 'propine' or present. It was decided that this should be the king's jewel, and that the town should rely on the king's good will for repayment of his loan. Thus the thrifty burgesses contrived to give a suitable gift without digging into their own pockets directly! In June 1590 a goldsmith was paid 140 merks for his labours and workmanship on the jewel made for the queen, indicating that it was remodelled before its presentation, which formed the culmination of Edinburgh's formal welcome to the new queen. Calderwood, *History*, v, 97 calls it a fair jewel of great price, 'called the A.' *Edin. recs., 1589–1603,* 4, 20; *RPCS, 1585–92,* 420, 421.

36 Calderwood, *History*, v, 97 calls this the 'weird' — a prophesy or fortune-telling.

37 The Scots account says that before the queen left the Netherbow Port some psalms were sung with 'verie good musicke.'

SCOTLAND'S LAST ROYAL WEDDING

Danish Account V   The Departure of the Danish Ambassadors

1   These had been confirmed by James in parliament on 17 May, the same day as the coronation: Macray, 'Third Report,' 26.

2   On 23 May the Danes were given a banquet by the burgh of Edinburgh, in the lodging of Thomas Aitchison, master of the cunziehoue (mint) in Todrik's Wynd: *Edin. recs, 1589–1603*, 19–20; Calderwood, *History*, v, 98.

3   On 25 May James wrote to the Danish regents thanking them for his reception in Denmark. He also wrote commending the Danish ambassadors about to return home, singling out Admiral Peder Munk for his good offices: Macray, 'Third Report,' 26.

4   Calderwood, *History*, v, 98–9 says the Danes had received gifts of chains, plate and jewels worth thirteen or fourteen thousand crowns, plus seven or eight tuns of wine and ale, beef, mutton and bread in abundance to provision their ships. Sir James Melville, *Memoirs*, 373 says James gave them twelve gold chains and many gold medals with the king's picture on them. The treasury accounts also note the supply of gold chains for the Danish admiral and the nobles with him, while the account of the dowry shows payment of £1,356: 13: 4 for a gold chain for one of the Danish ambassadors: SRO, E.21/67, f. 202r; Thirlestane's Accounts. It is surprising that the Danish Account makes no mention of these gifts.

5   The earl of Mar and Lord Hamilton were among those who went on board with the Danes and had supper with them. When they went ashore the ships discharged a volley, which was answered by cannons from Edinburgh castle: Calderwood, *History*, v, 98.

6   This is confused: obviously Marischal and his fellow ambassadors had also gone before the king.

SELECT BIBLIOGRAPHY

Manuscript Sources

Bodleian Library, Oxford

Smith MS. 77, Copies of letters and papers relating to marriage of James VI, etc. Latin. Late C17th. (see esp. 429–32)

British Library, London

Add. Ms. 22958 Audited Accounts of Sir John Maitland of Thirlestane of money expended in 1589–90 on the occasion of James VI's marriage and visit to Norway and Denmark.

National Library of Scotland, Edinburgh

Adv. Ms. 19.3.29 Jacob Jacobsen Wolf, Poem in honour of the marriage of James VI and Anne of Denmark, 1589. Latin.

Adv. Ms. 33.1.11 (Demmylne Mss. 28) Negotiations with Denmark and Norway. Miscellaneous papers, including a number of letters of Frederick II and Christian IV. (See the NLS Catalogue of Manuscripts: State Papers. Denmylne MSS — 5 volumes. Vol 4 includes coverage of vol 28 of the original.)

MS. 2912 John Skene, Ane account of ane Embassie performed by William Steuart, Commendator of Pittenween, and by Mr John Skene to England, Denmark, and the Princess of Germanie in anno 1590. Late C17th copy.

Wodrow Folio Ms. LXI Papers relating to James VI's relations with Denmark.

Rigsarkivet, Copenhagen

TKUA Skotland 1–7 Seven volumes of materials relating to Scotland. Microfilms of these volumes are kept in the Department of Scottish History, University of Glasgow. They include:
    two volumes of correspondence between the ruling houses of Demmark and Scotland,
    two volumes concerning political relations, 1491–1640,
    one volume concerning the marriage, partly originals and partly copies, and two bundles concerning the Orkneys, 1266–1661.
A few specific items from TKUA Skotland are listed below:

In TKUA Scotland A I 2, Breve fra skotske Regeringsmyndigheder, Kong Jacob og Dronning Anna til Frederik II og Christian IV samt til det danske Rigsraad, 1567–1603, 1619.

SCOTLAND'S LAST ROYAL WEDDING

In TKUA Skotland AI 2, til Frederik II og Christian IV samt til det danske Rigsraad, 1567–1603, 1619.

In TKUA Skotland A II, Collections of parchments in oak chests.

These include: Frederik II's datter Anna, four boxes, 1589, 1590, 1593, 1603 (thirty parchments, and rental books of Linlithgow).

In TKUA Skotland A II, 3–5, 2 May 1590. Leith. Letter in German from the three Danish envoys to regency in Denmark. 30 June — 16 September 1594 and report of Christian Barnekow and Steen Bille on their mission to Scotland and participation in the royal christening at Stirling.

TKUA Skotland AA II 4, Akter og Dokumenter vedr. det politiske Forhold til Skotland, 1572–1640.

TKUA Skotland A II 5, Akter og Dokumenter vedr. Aegteskabet mellum Jacob VI af Skotland og Frederik II's Datter, Prinsesse Anna, 1589–93.

Scottish Record Office, Edinburgh

GD. 125/10/61, The Coronation of Queen Anne, 17 May 1590. 2 copies. Also printed in *Marriage*.

SP. 1/1, Epistola Regum Scotorum, 1505–1607.

SP. 7/7, Marriage Treaty of James VI and Princess Anna.

SP. 8/8, Morning Gift of Dunfermline to Queen Anne

SP. 13/117, Intercession by Christian IV on behalf of David Konningham, 1 September 1589.

SP. 13/118, Letter, James VI to Queen Sophia, 1 September 1589

Printed Works

Akrigg, G P V, *Letters of King James VI and I* (Berkeley, 1984).

APS, Acts of the Parliament of Scotland, ed. T Thomson and C Innes (12 vols, Edinburgh, 1844–75.

Bain, J (ed.), *The Hamilton papers. Letters and papers illustrating the political relations of England and Scotland in the XVIth Century. Formerly in the possession of the dukes of Hamilton, now in the British Museum* (2 vols, London, 1894–6).

Balfour, Sir James, *Historical works* (4 vols, Edinburgh, 1828–30).

Bering Liisberg, H C, Christian IV (Copenhagen, 1891).

Bliss, W, 'The religious belief of Anne of Denmark,' *English Historical Review*, iv (1889), 110.

Brahe, Tycho, *Tychonis Brahe Dani Opera Omnia*, ed. I L E Dreyer (15 vols, Copenhagen, 1913–29, reprinted Amsterdam, 1972).

BIBLIOGRAPHY

Calderwood, D, *The history of the kirk of Scotland* (8 vols, Wodrow Society, 1842–9).

Cameron, A I (ed.), *The Warrender papers* (2 vols, SHS, 1931).

Christensen, T L, 'Scoto-Danish relations in the sixteenth century: the historiography and some questions' *SHR*, xlviii (1969), 80–97.

Christiansen, J R, 'The reconstruction of the Scandinavian aristocracy, 1350–1600,' *Scandanavian Studies*, 53, no. 3 (1981), 289–301.

Christianson, J, 'The celestial palace of Tycho Brahe,' *Scientific American*, 204 (1961), pt. 2, 118–28.

Clarke, S, 'Protestant Demonology: Sin, superstition and society (c. 1520– c. 1630),' B Ankarloo and G Henningsen (eds.), *Early modern European witchcraft. Centres and peripheries* (Oxford, 1990), 45–81.

Colville, John, *Original letters*, ed. D Laing (Bannatyne Club, 1856).

Craig, J T G, *Papers relative to the marriage of King James the Sixth of Scotland, with the Princess Anna of Denmark* (Bannatyne Club, 1828).

CSPS, *Calendar of State Papers relating to Scotland and Mary, Queen of Scots, 1547–1603, preserved in the Public Record Office, the British Museum, and elsewhere in England* (13 vols, London, 1898–1969).

DBL, *Dansk Biografisk Leksikon* (16 vols, Copenhagen 1979–84).

DNB, *Dictionary of National Biography* (63 vols, 1880–1900).

Dreyer, I L E, *Tycho Brahe. A picture of scientific life and work in the 16th Century* (Edinburgh, 1894).

Edin. recs., 1573–89. Extracts from the records of the burgh of Edinburgh, AD 1573–1589, ed. J D Marwick (Scottish Burgh Record Society, 1882).

Edin. recs., 1589–1603, Extracts from the records of the burgh of Edinburgh, AD 1589–1603, ed. M Wood and R K Hannay (Edinburgh, 1927).

Enevoldsen, Peder, 'Lensreformerne i Danmark 1557–96,' *Historisk Tidsskrift* (Copenhagen), vol 81 (14th series, vol 2) (1981–2), English summary at 398–9.

Erichsen B, and Krarup, A, *Dansk historisk bibliografi* (3 vols, Copenhagen, 1929).

Exchequer Rolls, Rotuli Scaccarii Regum Scottorum. The Exchequer Rolls of Scotland, Vols xii and xiii, *1589–94* and *1595–1600* (1903–1908).

Fasti, Fasti Ecclesiae Scoticanae (10 vols, Edinburgh, 1915–81).

Glarbo, Henny, 'Om den dansk-engelske Forbindelse i Christian IV's og Jacob I's Tid,' *Fra Arkiv og Museum*, series 2, ii (1927–43), 49–80.

Harthan, J P, 'James VI of Scotland and Anne of Denmark: a Scandinavian honeymoon of the sixteenth century,' *Norseman*, 6, pt. 3 (1948), 158–64.

Ilsøe, H, 'Gesandtskaber som kulturformidlende faktor: Forbindelser mellum Danmark og England-Skotland,' *Historisk Tidsskrift*, raekke 11, bind 6 (Copenhagen, 1960–2), 574–98.

James VI, *The poems of James VI of Scotland*, ed. J Craigie (2 vols, Scottish Text Society, 1955–8).

James VI, *Minor prose works of King James VI and I*, ed. A Law (Scottish Text Society, 1982).

Jexlev, T, 'Scottish history in the light of records in the Danish National Archives,' *SHR*, xlviii (1969), 98–106.

Johansen, J C, 'Denmark: The sociology of accusations,' B Ankarloo and G Henningsen (eds.), *Early modern European witchcraft. Centres and peripheries* (Oxford, 1990), 339–65.

Johnsen, D A, *Tønsbergs Historie* (1934).

Larner, C, *Enemies of God. The witch-hunt in Scotland* (London, 1978).

Larner, C, 'James VI and Witchcraft,' A G R Smith (ed.), *The reign of James VI and I* (London, 1973), 74–90.

Laursen, L (ed.), *Traités du Danemark et de la Norvège. Danmark-Norges Traktater, 1523–1750*, iii (Copenhagen, 1916).

Lee, M, *John Maitland of Thirlestane and the foundation of Stewart Despotism in Scotland* (Princeton, NJ, 1959).

Leith, W Forbes- (ed.), *Narratives of Scottish Catholics under Mary Stuart and James VI* (Edinburgh, 1885).

Lindsay, A W C, Earl of Crawford, *Lives of the Lindsays: or a memoir of the houses of Crawford and Balcarres* (3 vols, London 1849).

Lundh, O G, and Sars, I (eds.), *Norske Rigs-Registranter...* tredie bind [vol 3], *1588–1602* (Christiania, 1865).

Lynch, M, 'Queen Mary's triumph: the baptismal celebrations at Stirling in December 1566,' *SHR*, lxix (1990), 1–21.

Macray, W D, 'Report on the Archives of Denmark,' *45th Report of the Deputy Keeper of the Public Records* (London, 1885), app. 2, no. 1, 1–56.

Macray, W D, 'Second report on the Royal Archives of Denmark, and Report on the Royal Library at Copenhagen,' *46th Report of the Deputy Keeper of the Public Records* (London, 1886), app. II, no. 1, 1–75.

Macray, W D , 'Third report on the Royal Archives of Denmark and Report on the Royal Library at Copenhagen,' *47th Report of the Deputy Keeper of the Public Records* (London, 1886), app. 5, 9–77.

Majoribanks, George, *Annals of Scotland*, ed. E Dalyell and John Graham (1814).

McFarlane, I D, *Buchanan* (London, 1981).

BIBLIOGRAPHY

Meldrum, R M (ed.), *Translations and facsimilies of the original latin letters of King James I of England (VI of Scotland), to his royal brother-in-law, King Christian IV of Denmark, 1603–1625* (Microfiche, Harvester Press, 1977).

Melvill, James, *Autobiography* (Wodrow Society, 1842).

Melville, Sir James, of Halhill, *Memoirs of his own life*, ed. T Thomson (Bannatyne Club, 1827).

Millar, A H, 'The Wedding Tour of James VI in Norway,' *Scottish Review*, xxi (1893), 142–61.

Monter, E W, 'Scandinavian Witchcraft in Anglo-American Perspective,' ed. B Ankarloo and G Henningsen, *Early modern European witchcraft. Centres and peripheries* (Oxford, 1990), 425–34.

Montgomerie, A., 'King James VI's tocher gude and a local authorities loan of 1590,' *SHR*, xxxvii (1958), 11–16.

Moysie, David, *Memoirs of the Affairs of Scotland* (Bannatyne Club, 1830).

Munch, P A (ed.), 'Samtidig Beretning om Prindsesse Annas, Christian den 4des Systers, Giftermaal med Kong Jacob d. 6te af Skotland og hendes paafolgende Kroning,' *Norske Samlinger*, i (1852), 450–512.

Nilssøn, Jens, *Biskop Jens Nilssøns Visitatsbøger og Reiscoptegnelser, 1574–1597* (Kristiania, 1885).

Nilssøn, Jens, *To og Tredive Praedikener holdt i aareme 1578–1586* (1917).

Norsk Biografisk Leksikon (19 vols, Oslo, 1923 — unfinished).

Overland, O A, *Illustretet Norges Historie* (5 vols, Christiania, 1885–95).

Old European Cities. 16th century city maps and texts from Ciuitates Orbis Terrarum (London, 1955 — 24 maps; London, 1965 — 32 maps).

Patrick, R W Cochran, *Catalogue of medals of Scotland* (Edinburgh, 1884).

Plenkers, W, 'Er Frederik II's Datter Anna, Dronning af Stor Britannien gaaet over til Katholicismen'. *Historik Tidsskrift*, vi (1887–8), 403–25. (Reprinted as a pamphlet, Copenhagen, 1888).

Riis, T, 'Scottish-Danish relations in the sixteenth century,' T C Smout (ed.), *Scotland and Europe, 1200–1850* (Edinburgh, 1986), 82–96.

Riis, Thomas, *Should auld acquaintaince be forgot...Scottish-Danish relations, c. 1450–1707.* (2 vols, Odense University Press, 1989).

RMS, Register of the Great Seal of Scotland. Magni Sigilli Regum Scotorum (11 vols, 1882–1914).

RPCS, Register of the Privy Council of Scotland, [First Series], *1545–1625* (14 vols, London, 1877–98).

RSS, Register of the Privy Seal of Scotland. Registrum Secreti Sigilli Regum Scotorum 8 vols, 1908–83).

Rørdam, H F, *Kjøbenhavns Universitets Historie fra 1537 til 1621*, part 4 (Copenhagen, 1868–74).

Shakespeare, W, *Hamlet*, ed. H Jenkins (London, 1981).

Skovgaard, J A, *A King's architecture. Christian IV and his buildings* (London, 1973).

Slange, N P, *Den Stormaegtigste Konges Christian den Fierdes...Historie*, ed. Hans Gram (Copenhagen, 1749).

Slange, N P, *Geschichte Christian des Vierten, Königs in Dannemark...* ed. J H Schlegel (3 pts., Copenhagen & Leipzig, 1757–71), i, 111–13.

Spottiswoode, John, *History of the Church of Scotland*, ed. M Napier and M Russell, (3 vols, Spottiswoode Society, 1847–51).

Stephens, George, 'James VI in Tønsberg, 1589. With Photograph of an Oaken Tablet erected in the Church of St Mary, in Commemoration of his Visit,' *Proceedings of the Society of Antiquaries of Scotland*, xi (1874–6), 462–4.

Strickland, Agnes, *Lives of the queens of Scotland* (8 vols, Edinburgh, 1850–9).

Svenskt Biografiskt Lexikon (24 vols, Stockholm, 1918 — unfinished.).

Thomson, T, ed., *The historie and life of King James the Sext: being an account of the affairs of Scotland from the year 1566, to the year 1596* (Bannatyne Club, 1825).

Vaus (Waus), Sir Patrick, of Barnbarroch, *Correspondence*, ed. Robert Agnew (2 vols, Edinburgh, 1886).

Walker, Patrick, *Documents relative to the reception at Edinburgh of the Kings and Queens of Scotland, AD 1561–1650* (Edinburgh, 1822).

Ward, A W, review of Plenkers' 'Er Frederik II's Datter Anna...,' *English Historical Review*, iii (1888), 795–8.

Wernham, R B (ed.), *List and analysis of State Papers, Foreign Series, Elizabeth I (1589–90)* (London, 1964).

Westergaard, P B C, *Danske portraetter i Kobberstik, Litografi og Traesnit. En Beskrivende Fortegnelse* (2 vols, 1930–4).

Williams, Ethel C, *Anne of Denmark. Wife of James VI of Scotland: James I of England* (London, 1970).

Willson, D H, *King James VI and I* (London, 1956).

INDEX

Aberdeen, 19, 20, 84
Affaskar, Joen, 107
Aitchison, Thomas, 148
Akershus Castle, 35, 88
Älvsborg (Elfsborg), 42, 97–9
Angus, earl of, see Douglas, William
Anne of Denmark, queen of Scots;
  Catholicism, 67–9; coronation, 56, 58–9, 100, 103–7; dowry, 20, 39, 53, 54–5, 62, 79–84, 132; entry to Edinburgh, 60–1, 107–20; morning gift (property on Scotland), 24, 36–7, 58, 62, 63–4, 74, 82–4, 100–3; preparations for arrival, 22, 27–8, 36, 57, 58; reception in Scotland, 57–8, 100–1; religious guarantees to, 59, 67, 83, 85
Antvorskov, 9
Arran, earl of, see Stewart, James
Aschetoun (Eston?), Roger, 121
Asker, 91

Bacchus, 61, 115, 146
Baltic Sea, 41
Bartas, Guillaume de Salluste du, 11
Basse (Bartz), Mickel, 40
Bastøy, 88
Beaton, James, of Creich, 102, 140
Beck, Povel, 95
Bellenden, Sir Lewis, of Auchinoul and Broughton, 33, 103, 104, 107, 121, 141
Below, Henrik, 5, 9
Bille, Steen, 26, 34, 89, 95, 126, 137
Bing, Anders, 43–4
bishops, in Scotland, 59
Bohus Castle, 40–3, 96–7, 129
Borre, 88, 91
Bothwell, earls of, see Hepburn, James, and Stewart, Francis
Bothwell, Margaret, countess of, see Douglas, Margaret
Bowes, Sir Robert, 104
Boyd, Thomas, Lord, 107
Boyne, laird of, 21
Bragge, Peder, 129
Brahe, Jørgen, governor of Landskrona, 38, 42, 43, 107, 129
Brahe, Steen, 39, 57, 88–92, 107, 137, 142
Brahe, Tyge (Tycho), 50–1, 54, 99
Brandenburg, 135
Bruce, Robert, 58–9, 105–7, 114, 142–3
Brun, Christern Nielsen, 49
Buchanan, George, 24, 51
Bude, Gotzlef, 107
Burel, John, 143
Burghley, Lord, see Cecil, William
Burns, Robert, 69–70
Burntisland, 25

Calvinism, 3, 11, 40–1, 49–50, 59, 67, 99
Canongate, 61
Carmichael, John, of that Ilk, 33, 56, 71, 107, 121
Catherine de Bourbon (Catherine of Navarre), 11, 13, 15, 16, 62
Cecil, William, Lord Burghly, 135
Charles, prince, later King Charles I, 75, 76
Christensen, Anders, 49, 99
Christian I, king of Denmark, 115–16, 146–7
Christian II, king of Denmark, 116
Christian III, king of Denmark, 116, 117
Christian IV, king of Denmark, 14, 24, 37, 38, 45, 47, 54, 56, 66, 70, 76, 79–80, 83–5, 99
Cockburn, John, of Ormiston, 106
Copenhahen (Köbenhavn; Hafnia), 20, 26, 38, 48–9, 86, 99, 120, 130–1
Counter-Reformation, 2, 68
Craig, John, 145
Cunningham, David, of Robertland, 37, 94–5

Dalkeith, 69
Damman, Hadrian, 128
Danish Account of the marriage, ms and authorship, ix–x, 139
Danzig, 7
Darnley, Lord, see Stuart, Henry
Denmark, Danes; drinking in, 10, 16, 40, 45, 51–2, 55, 69–70, 96–7, 146; government and society, 45–7; missions to Scotland, (1585), 4–6, (1590), 57–63, 100–4, 107, 142, (1592), 64, (1593), 64–5, (1594), 66
Dingwall, Lord, see Keith, Andrew
Douglas, Archibald, son of the earl of Morton, 121
Douglas, George, heir of Morton's brother, 122
Douglas, George, of Langniddrie, 122
Douglas, Mr George, son of the earl of Angus, 121
Douglas, James, heir of Lochleven, 122
Douglas, Margaret, countess of Bothwell, 104, 142
Douglas, Robert, 33, 121
Douglas, William, earl of Angus, 104, 107
Douglas, William, earl of Morton, 103, 107, 141
Duen, 87
Dundee, 106, 144
Dunfermline, 36–7, 58, 63–4, 65, 68–9, 74, 102, 103, 140
Dury, Robert, 103, 141
Dyring, Kasten, 107

155

SCOTLAND'S LAST ROYAL WEDDING

Edinburgh, 22, 27–8, 29, 103, 106; and missions to Denmark, 8, 15–16, 19; Anne in, 57–61, 103–20
Edward VI, king of England, 1, 2
Eeg, Arnulf, 98, 138
Eglinton, earl of, *see* Montgomery, Hugh
Elizabeth I, queen of England; 1–2, 13, 32, 53, 56; attitudes to James's marriage, 2–4, 8, 17, 21, 27; payments to James, 16, 20, 27, 62
Elizabeth, Princess, sister of Christian IV, 6, 9, 10, 11, 53, 99
Elizabeth, princess, daughter of James VI, 75
Ellingaard, 88
Elphinstone, James, 58, 100, 139
Elsinore (Helsingør), 6, 9 39, 44–5, 47, 48, 99
Erskine, John, earl of Mar, 74, 148
Espen, Jørgen von, 107

Falkenberg, 97
Falkland, 36, 58, 84, 102, 103, 140
Fife, 37, 38, 103, 140
Flekkerøy, 25, 86, 87, 89, 90, 136
Fleming, Jean, Lady Thirlestane, 104, 142
Fowler, Thomas, 16, 29
Fowler, William, 19, 20, 37
France, French, 1, 2, 3, 11–12; language, 20, 25, 54, 59, 92, 105, 138, 142
Francis II, dauphin, king of France, 1
Frederick I, king of Denmark,
Frederick II, king of Denmark, 3, 4, 8–11, 50, 66, 79–81, 116, 117; death of, 14, 49
Frederiksborg, 50

Gabriel, 87
Gedeon, 87, 136, 137, 144
Germany, Germans, 21, 45, 47, 53, 70; language, 7, 20, 54, 85, 95
Giøye, Fru Anne Henning, 89, 90
Giøye, Henning, 88–91, 95, 107, 137
Gib, John, 121
Gjedda (Gaedda), 41
Glad, Oluf, 88
Göta, River, 38, 97
Götalejon (Gulberg), 97, 99
Gotheburg, 42
Gyldenstierne, Axel, 35, 38, 88–9, 91, 95–6, 98
Gyldenstierne, Fru Karen, 88, 89, 137
Gyldenstierne, Hannibal, 107
Gyldenstierne, Henrik, 40, 54, 96–7, 107, 129, 144

Høg, Christen, 107
Halmstead, 98
Hamilton, Lord Claud (Lord Paisley), 141
Hamilton, Isobel, dowager Lady Seton, 141
Hamilton, Lord John (later marquis of Hamilton), 32, 39
Hamilton, John, Lord, brother of earl of Arran, 103–7, 114, 139, 141–3, 148

Hamlet, 47
Hansen, Herr Neils, 88
Harrington, Sir John, 70
Hay, John, notary, 103, 140–1
Heimskringla, 138
Helsingborg, 44, 98
Hemmingsen, Niels, 49, 99, 123, 131
Henry III, king of France, 62
Henry III, king of Navarre (Henry IV, king of France), 11, 62
Henry of Brunswick (Henrik Julius of Braunschweig-Wulfenbuttel), 53, 99
Henry VIII, king of England, 2, 66
Henry Frederick, prince, later prince of Wales, 66, 74, 75, 76
Hepburn, James, earl of Bothwell, 1, 12
Hiren, Vellzan, 107
Hitteröy, 120
Hiundt, Her van, 107
Holck, Christen, 132
Holme, 129
Holstein, duke of, 53
Holyrood (Abbey, House, Palace), 22, 36, 61, 114, 140
Home, John, of Coldenknowes, 107
Hovedøya, 95
Hume, George, 55, 121
Huntly, countess of, *see* Stuart, Henrietta

Ide, Fru, 89, 90
Iversen, Peder, of Fridsø, 89–91, 137

James III, king of Scots, 3, 101
James IV, king of Scots, 116
James V, king of Scots, 30, 116
James VI, king of Scots; attitudes to marriage, 1, 2, 6, 8–9, 12–14, 20–2, 27, 29, 31–2; fears of influence of 'the example of Denmark' on, 45–7, 54–6, 70–2; ; gambling, 53, 95, 139; hunting, 51, 95, 101; marriages (Kronborg), 22–3, 24, 85–6 (Oslo), 36, 92–4; and religion in Denmark, 40–1, 49–50, 96; and throne of England, 2–3, 5, 8, 62, 66, 68
Jarlsberg Hovegaard, 34
Johan III, king of Sweden, 18, 42–3, 98–9
Johnson, Ben, 47
Jomfruland, 87, 90
Josaphad, 136, 144
Juel, Fru Dorothea (Dorrete), 88, 137
Juel, Ove, of Kieldgaard, 88–9, 91, 137

Kaas, Anne, 104, 142
Kaas, Erick, 107
Kaas, Neils (Nicholas), 9–10, 82–3, 123
Kaas, Sophia, 107, 142
Kalvsund, 120
Keith, Andrew, Lord Dingwall, Baron Forsholm, 17–18, 20–1, 25, 80, 98, 121
Keith, George, Earl Marischal, 15–17, 121; in Denmark and Norway, 19, 21–3, 25–6,

INDEX

37, 55–6, 71, 80, 84, 87–8, 90–2, 95, 132, 148
Keith, Sir William, of Delny, 18, 33, 55
Kennedy, Janet, 25
Kennedy, Joan, countess of Orkney, 104
Kerr, Mr George, brother of commendator of Newbattle, heir of laird of Lasswade, 122
Kniblo, Dr Paul, 24, 42
Krabbe, Jacob, 107
Krag, Neils, 24
Kronborg Castle, 22, 39, 45, 47, 48, 51, 85, 86, 99, 120

Laholm, 98
Langesund, 87
Laurie, 'Sir Robert, of Maxwellton,' 70
Lauritsen, Jørgen, 34, 91
Leith, 15, 22, 25, 30, 58 100, 102, 120, 143
Lennox, duke of, see, Stuart, Ludovic
Lierbyen, 91
Lille Brevik, 88
Lindesnes, 120
Lindsay, Alexander, Lord Spynie, 52, 104, 121
Lindsay, Sir David, lord lyon king of arms, 104, 141
Lindsay, David, 34, 41, 59, 94–5, 105–6, 121, 127, 142
Lindsay, David, jnr., 95, 138
Lindsay, James, Lord, 107
Lindsay, John, of Menmuir, 64, 107?
Linlithgow, 33, 36, 37, 58, 84, 102–3, 140, 141
Liunge, Ove, 107
Livingston, Alexander, Lord, 107
Livingston, Margaret, Lady Auchinoul, 104, 142
Logie, laird of, 69
Lorraine, duke of, 3
Lothians, 58
Lutheranism, 3, 11, 16, 49–50, 59, 67, 69
Lyon, Jean, dowager countess of Angus, 52
lyon king of arms, see Lindsay, Sir David

Madtzon, Steen, 107, 144
Mair, George, 53
Maitland, Sir John, of Thirlestane (Lord Thirlestane), 39, 64, 71, 74, 100–1, 103, 121, 143; in Denmark and Norway, 51, 53, 55–6, 92, 132; and royal marriage (opposes), 14–17 (supports), 28–9, 31, 33
Malmö, 42, 129
Mar, countess of, see Murray, Annabella
Mar, earls of, see Erskine, John
Margaret, 'Maid of Norway,' 26
Margaret, princess, daughter of James VI, 75
Margaret of Denmark, wife of James III, 3, 4, 101, 116
Marischal, Earl, see Keith, George
Mary, queen of Scots, 1, 2, 3, 12–13, 60, 74, 117; execution of, 8, 9, 11
Mathias, Povel, bishop of Zealand, 49, 99

Mecklenburg, dukes of, see Ulrich
Meidt, Her van, 107
Melville, Andrew, 106, 142
Melville, Sir Andrew, 25
Melville, Sir James, 5, 15
Melville, Sir Robert, of Murdocarny, 102, 140
Merdøy, 87
Millar, H.H., ix
Montgomery, Hugh, earl of Eglinton, 37, 95
Morton, earl of, see Douglas, William
Moryson, Fynes, 47–9
Mule, Christen, 92, 138
Munch, P.A., ix–x
Munk, Peder, 24–5, 57–8, 72, 82–3, 86–7, 103–4, 114, 142
Murray, Annabella, dowager countess of Mar, 74, 104, 105, 107
Murray, David, 107, 121
Murray, Mr George, brother of Lord Tullibardine, 121
Murray, Captain William, 42

Nashe, Thomas, 47
Navarre, 11, 13, 15
Netherlands, 7
Newhouse, 103
Niddrie, 141
Nilssøn, Jens, bishop of Oslo, 39, 88–91, 94–6, 138
Normand, Captain, 91
North Berwick, 72, 73
Norway, 25, 26, 28, 33, 34–40, 42, 45

Öresund, see Sound, The
Orkney, countess of, see Kennedy, Joan
Orkney and Shetland Islands, 4, 8, 9, 10, 26, 80–2
Oslo, 26, 34–40, 44, 88–9, 91
Otterhälla (Ade), 97

Parsberg, Manderup, 5, 9
Passe, Jörgen, 98
Pederson, Hans, of Sem, 88, 91, 137
Philip II, duke of Pomerania, 53
Poland, Poles, 7, 66, 70
Praetorius, Abraham, 23
Presbyterianism, 7, 41, 50, 59, 67, 68
privy council, 15, 30, 32

Quille, 41

Ramel, Henrik, 10, 11, 82, 83, 124
Rantzau, Breide, 24, 57 107, 142
Rantzau, Gaadske, 107
Rantzau, Gert, 39, 54
Raphael, 136–7
Reformation, 2, 45
Rekefjord, 86
Reuentlou, Henning, 107
Robertson, Andrew, 128
Rollock, Hercules, 128, 145

157

Røsencrantz, Jörgen, 82, 83, 135
Roskilde, 49–50, 99
Russel, Mr John, 144
Russia, 70

Samson, 136
Sande, 91
Sandefjord, 87
Sanden, 90–1
Sandilands, James, son of the laird of Calder, 121
Saxons, 48
Schaw, William, master of works, 95, 96, 121, 138
Schein, Calixtus, x, 37, 128
Schinkel, Catherina, 104, 107
Scotland; missions to Denmark, (1586), 6–8, (1587), 8–11, 13, (1588), 14, (1589), 17–24, 26, 33, 55
Scrymgeour, James, of Dudhope, 17–19, 80, 95, 121
Sering, Johan, x, 67, 69, 89, 94, 138
Seton, Colonel David, of Parbroath, 106, 143
Seton, George, Lord, 107
Seton, Lady, *see* Hamilton, Isobel
Sheba, queen of, 118–19
Shetland Islands, *see* Orkney and Shetland Islands
Sigismund, king of Sweden and Poland, 18
Sinclair, Andrew, 26, 89–90, 121, 126
Sinclair, Henry, Lord, 107
Skagen, 120
Skaw, The, 25
Skene, John, 17, 19, 20, 80, 102, 121
Skinkel, Fru Anne, 88, 137
Skraedder, Anders, 88, 91
Skriver, Peder, 97
Slangerup (Slangendorphius), Hans Olufsen, 49, 99, 130
Snorri Sturluson, 138
Solomon, King, 118–19
Sophia (Sophie), queen of Denmark, 11, 25, 37, 38, 45, 53, 54, 80, 99
Sørensen, Ramus, 91, 138
Sound, The (Öresund), 41, 45; tolls, 15, 45, 48, 80, 81
Spain, 3, 12, 27
Stanbuk, Erick Gustavsen, 42
Stewart, Francis, earl of Bothwell, 28, 31, 65, 69, 72, 73, 139
Stewart, James, earl of Arran, 5, 6, 8, 18
Stewart, Sir William, of Pittenweem, 6–8, 14, 16, 21–2, 25, 32, 39, 100, 107, 121, 137, 139

Stirling, 22, 66
Stockholm, 42
Store Brevik, 88
Stuart, Henrietta, countess of Huntly, 64
Stuart, Henry, Lord Darnley, 1, 12, 66
Stuart, Lewis or Ludovic, duke of Lennox, 32, 104–6, 139, 142, 143
Stuart, William, 121
Sweden, 3, 5, 18, 37, 41, 46; passage of James through, 38, 41–3, 70, 87–9

Theophilus, Dr Nicholaus, x, 5, 100, 102
Thirlestane, Lord, *see* Maitland, Sir John
Thot, Anders, 107
Thuringia, 67
Tönsberg, 34–5, 88, 90, 91

Uddevalla, 129
Ulffvild, Jomfru, 88, 137
Ulfsparre, Jörgen Erickson, 98
Ulrich, duke of Mecklenburg (father of Queen Sophia), 97
Ulrich, duke of Mecklenburg (brother of Queen Sophia), 53, 54
Ulrick, Duke (brother of Christian IV), 45, 99
Uranienborg, 50–1

Vaale, 91
Vaemundsen, Peder, 90, 138
Valkendorf, Christoffer, 24, 73, 82, 83, 126
Vanson, Adrian, 6
Varberg, 37, 43–4, 97
Vaus (Waus), Sir Patrick, of Barnbarroch, 8, 9, 11, 13, 17, 33, 38
Ven (Hven), 50–1, 99
Vestland, 42
Viken, 96
Vinstarr, Margaret, 69

Wemyss, 140
Wemyss, David, of Wemyss, 140
Whitehall, 70
Wiffert, Korfit, 38, 42, 129
William, Prince of Orange, 7
witchcraft, 72–3
Wolf, Jacob Jacobsen, 36
Workman, James, 146, 147
Wotton, Edward, 4, 5

Young, Mr George, 17, 19, 80, 121
Young, Mr Peter, 6, 8–11, 13, 15, 16, 17, 51, 101, 121